Creeping Shadows

Creeping Shadows

Swede Hastings

ARPress
ILLUMINATING IDEAS.
EMPOWERING VOICES

ARPress
45 Dan Road Suite 5
Canton MA 02021

Hotline: 1(888) 821-0229
Fax: 1(508) 545-7580

Ordering Information:

Quantity sales. Special discounts are available on quantity purchases by corporations, associations, and others. For details, contact the publisher at the address above.

Printed in the United States of America.

ISBN-13:   Softcover   979-8-89330-308-7
                eBook   979-8-89330-309-4
                Hardcover   979-8-89389-514-8

Library of Congress Control Number: 2024900496

T o my dear late Brother,
Mom and Dad

My dear brother, who was always the special person in my youth, when any saw one of us, they would usually see the other. We had a special bond that was cut off way too short, yet so many memories linger on. He was "My Buddy", even to this day. I believe he knows how sorry I am and how dearly I have always loved him and miss him.

And to my sweet, fragile Mom, who cared for everyone more than herself. She was content even with nothing, but richer than any I've known with love and compassion, touching the hearts of many in her path. The smiles and warmth she projected were unequalled. The enthusiasm of her desire "to live while I'm alive", truly was the inspiration for my life.

Then, finally, to my dad, a unique person who under any circumstances, worried not about the stresses in life. His laughter was always from the heart. Nothing was a "put on". He spoke his mind calling a spade a spade. He was a tough and simple man but sensitive and caring. Without respect of persons, he saw everyone in a positive way and was a true good friend to the few who earned it. He was always himself, not attempting to impress anyone, without question, my best friend and my hero.

TABLE OF CONTENTS

INTRODUCTION

With a very special appreciation for the simpler things in this life come these poems. Great values were gained from the most wonderful parents any human could have. My Dad and Mom gave me a precious, memorable and unequalled childhood filled with love and sensitivity, which is a rare find. They were truly the example givers. Any and all shortcomings throughout my life were because of my own foolishness.

My folks were simple, honest, hard working people. They not only gave of themselves but none around them would ever have a reason to go hungry or without. They were always helping the less fortunate. In my earlier years, whether living in a fruit picker's shed or sharing a tent together, there was always much laughter or music around the campfire after working in the cotton, potato or onion fields. The folks followed the fruit to its harvest in their seasons. Dad drove truck, skid logs and took whatever jobs available. Mom, as well, cooked in the logging camps, picked harvest, and did laundry with a scrub brush on the rocks in a shallow creek. She labored as no woman I have ever known. At the close of the day, there was happiness in the accomplishment of hard labor with the sound of crickets, or echo of the owls against the still of the nights. I can still smell the evergreen, mixed with campfire smoke where Mom cooked dinner. Likewise, I still hear the music, whether alongside the highways or in the orchards. I can also see my Dad getting out his guitar and Mom, her violin. Often, when the occasion arose, others joined in with their instruments playing long into the night. Together they sang old time tunes that cheered our hearts with happy dancing and sharing stories of old.

Then, for the next 25 years, Dad drove trucks and was well known by other truckers simply as "Red" and did many long hauls across the United States. I, occasionally, during summer vacation, had the privilege of going on a few trips with him. He was an inspiration and a unique person in my life.

At age 18, I lost a very close brother and found myself confused concerning the nature of life and death. Being unable to discuss the matter with anyone, I spent much of my time jotting down rhythmic letters to myself as to what I felt inside. Thereafter, each loss of a special friend or loved one caused an emotional or spontaneous reason to write these poetic letters to myself. It was my personal way of dealing with each situation and I had no intent to ever share these with anyone.

These poems are collected from dreams dreamt, stories told, my experiences, trials, and my own personal perception of life, nature, or family matters; be it heartbreak from the loss of a loved one, songs of a bird, smell of the fir, pine or the juniper. Then, as the years passed, the collection of poems grew. From 1959 to date, more have been burned then saved. As circumstances changed in my life, I found no reason to keep certain poems.

Deep inside I am very grateful and humble before God. It's all because of Him that I can exist or reveal. I thank my middle son who prepared it for book form, and the artistry of **Jim Rozewski of Bend, Oregon,** who expressed so much in each drawing.

I am thankful for this opportunity to be able to express myself within these poems; without seeking anyone's approval or audience. Neither am I concerned by criticism, but I delight in expressing memories that still live within my heart that I have not yet forgotten. The rest, only the Lord knows.

~Swede

1946

Mom with kids *(left to right)*
Jonnie Mae *(sister)* ~ Jerry *(Swede)*
Billy *(brother)* ~ Reggie *(brother)*

1952

Portland, Oregon (left to right)
Jonnie Mae (sister) ~ Jerry *(Swede)* ~ Billy *(brother)*

1947

Outside Bedroom ~ Sister, Jonnie Mae,
and Jerry *(Swede)* a battle with the bees

1957

At home *(left to right)*
Reggie *(brother)* ~ Jerry *(Swede)*
Billy *(brother)* ~ Jonnie Mae *(sister)*

1947

Sutherlin, Oregon *(left to right)*
Jerry *(Swede)* ~ Aunt Bea ~ Aunt Peggy
Jonnie Mae *(sister)* ~ Billy *(brother)* ~ Reggie *(brother)*

YOUR HAPPY TIMES

YOUR HAPPY TIMES

IN ALL OF OUR DAYS, IN ALL YOUR WAYS,
    THE THINGS THAT I MOST RECALL,
ARE HAPPY TIMES OF SMILES AN' SHINES,
    SO JOYFUL TIMES WERE THEY ALL.

I SAW YOUR SMILES IN DIFFERENT STYLES,
    AND ONLY I COULD RECOGNIZE,
WHAT THEY MEAN, WHEN THEY ARE SEEN,
    HIDDEN SECRETS TO EMPHASIZE

THE SADDER THINGS HEARTACHE BRINGS
    WERE FORGOTTEN SO LONG AGO,
ONLY WARMEST THOUGHTS, COME IN LOTS,
    AND GIVES MY HEART A GLOW.

YOU LAUGH IN CHEER, OR SHED A TEAR,
    GIGGLE AT THINGS WE DO OR SAY,
MAY FROWN A WHILE BEFORE YOU SMILE
    HAPPY TIMES COME YOUR WAY

A TIME TO EMPLOY AND SHARE THE JOY,
    DELIGHT OF CHEER THAT SHINES,
BECAUSE THE GOAL IS DEEP IN MY SOUL
    IS TO SHARE YOUR HAPPY TIMES.

~

WHAT IS WRONG WITH ME

WHAT IS WRONG WITH ME

LO! WHAT IS WRONG WITH ME LORD?
    DO I NEED TWINE OF HEAVY CORD,
        TO TIE AND BIND AND HOLD ME DOWN?
THY RIGHTEOUSNESS IS HARD TO FOLLOW,
    MY JAWS GET TIGHT AND I SWALLOW
        THUS, OH MY LORD...I DO FEEL BOUN'

LO! WHAT IS WRONG WITH ME LORD?
    DO I NEED CHAINLINKS RESTORED
        TO HOLD ME PLACED WITHIN YOUR WILL?
I'LL CONTINUE SEEKING TRUTH WITH FEAR,
    FOR IN YOUR WORD I FIND IT CLEAR,
        ALTHOUGH YOUR VOICE REMAINS STILL.

LO! WHAT IS WRONG WITH ME LORD?
    DO I NEED TO BE CUT BY A SWORD,
        WHEN MY OTHER SELF WANTS TO STRAY?
FOR WHEN SHACKLES DO BREAK OR BEND,
    I'M REMINDED OF WHO IS MY FRIEND.
        AND WHY IS IT SO OFTEN I GO HALFWAY?

LO! WHAT IS WRONG WITH ME LORD?
    DO I NEED MY PRAYERS IGNORED,
        ALAS! WHERE IN THIS LIFE DO I BELONG?
THROUGH HOLLOW EYES I REALLY DO CARE,
    FOR WHAT IS RIGHT OR WHAT IS FAIR,
        WHY, I ASK, DO I CONTINUE IN WRONG?

LO! WHAT IS WRONG WITH ME LORD?
    DO I NEED CAUSE FOR MY DISCORD?
        ANOTHER TRIAL BY FIRE TO BE SET FREE?
ALTHOUGH I'LL STRIVE TO STRAY NO MORE,
    WITH ATTEMPTS TO DAILY RESTORE?
        I ASK, "LORD, WHAT IS WRONG WITH ME?"

~

LIFE'S BEAUTY

LIFE'S BEAUTY

PASSING SCARLET CLOUDS,
      AN' LATE SUMMER SPRAY,
FLOATING SHADOWS BREATH,
      A FULFILLMENT OF DISPLAY.

FROM THE AUTUMNAL SKY,
      WEBS OF A GLARING SUN,
GREETS THE LILY SO FAIR,
      WHERE EARTHLY JOY SPUN.

BENDING A SMOOTH PATH,
      SUDDEN TRACKLESS BLOW,
OH, HOW SWEETLY TO HEAR,
      SOFTEST WINDS WIFFLE LOW.

ON ROCKY BOTTOM WATERS
      A BABBLING TO ENTHRALL,
A CLEAR FLOWING MURMUR,
      OF MOUNTAIN WATERFALL...

SO IMMENSE, SO BEAUTIFUL,
      THE GRANITE STONE CLIFF,
LICHEN COVERED ROCKS,
      WHICH SUN-HEATED STIFF.

A NATURAL TEMPEST STONE,
      A TINGE OF GRAY BROWN,
FLINTY EMERALD BOULDER,
      DEEPLY ENTERS GROUND.

AN UNFOLDING MOIST BUD,
      RADIANT, EXTENDED ROSE,
BLANKET IN SWEET SMELLING,
      UNRESTFUL BLOOM GROWS.

AGAIN THE GENTLE BREEZE,
      IN EARLY SILENT FALL SWELL
LEAVES SWAYED A MISSION,
      MOVED ABOUT THEN FELL...

VARIOUS UNSHAPELY TREES,
      TALL, STURDY AND STOUT,
MIXED SWOLLEN OR BRITTLE,
      THEN PLACED ALL ABOUT...

AN AMPLE KNOTTED BOUGH,
      HANGING TO THE GROUND,
SPRAWLING FORTH FRIENDLY,
      UNTRIMMED AND BOUND

BRIGHT SUN WALKS THE SKY,
      GREETING A SWEPT GLARE,
BIRDS TWITTER WIDE OPEN,
      MERRY WHISTLE A PRAYER

UNTOLD FEATHERED BEAUTY,
      FREELY SING AS THEY FLEW,
BREATH TAKING GREAT EAGLE,
      THE KING OF AZURE BLUE...

LIFE HAS A MYSTIC BEAUTY,
      IT'S A SECRET FEW CAN SEE,
IT'S SECLUDED AND HIDDEN,
      'CAUSE WE ALLOW IT TO BE...

SO FROM AGE OF THE DUST,
      SECRETS OF NATURE AVAIL...
LIFE'S BEAUTY IS THE MOOD,
      THAT'S SHARED ON ITS TRAIL

~

THE GIFT

I HEAR SOME ARE OFFENDED 'CAUSE I DIDN'T
                    KEEP THE GIFT THEY GAVE
IF FINDING NO USE, OR NEED FOR THAT ITEM
                    WHY THEN SHOULD I SAVE?
WHEN EVEN FOR MYSELF, MAKING A CHOICE,
                    I'LL REALLY HAVE TO HUNT,
SO, OCCASIONALLY, I WILL EXCHANGE A GIFT,
                    FOR EXACTLY WHAT I WANT

I WOULD, FRIEND, THAT YOU'LL UNDERSTAND
                    BEING PERSONAL, IT'S NOT
AND ALTHOUGH I MIGHT NOT KEEP THE GIFT,
                    I APPRECIATE THE THOUGHT
IF STILL PERHAPS YOU'RE HURT OR OFFENDED,
                    ADVICE TO YOU WOULD BE
KINDLY GIVE THE GIFT TO A "SOMEONE ELSE",
                    WANTING IT MORE THAN ME

NEITHER WILL I KEEP A GIFT JUST BECAUSE
                    FOR ME YOU'D SELECTED IT
IF I CAN'T JUSTIFY ITS USEFULNESS MYSELF
                    I'LL CHOOSE TO NOT INHERIT
IT'S TRUE I MAY GET RID OF CERTAIN THINGS,
                    IF I FIND NO CURRENT NEED,
THEREFORE NOT KEEP YOUR GIFT OR CARD,
                    LEST I HAVE WANT INDEED

BE IT YOUR GIFT OR BE IT YOUR THOUGHTS
                    YOU NEED WEAR MY SHOE
I PREFER YOUR THOUGHTS ABOVE THE GIFT,
                    AND FOR THAT I THANK YOU
SO, FORGIVE ME IF I DON'T KEEP THE GIFT
                    YOU HAD BOUGHT OR MADE
LIKEWISE THE GIFT I SOUGHT OUT FOR YOU,
                    ENJOY IT OR SELL OR TRADE!!

~

I REMEMBER MY DREAMS

I REMEMBER MY DREAMS

~My First Poem to Carole Moore~
(1960)

I REMEMBER

OUR LOVELY TIMES WE SPENT TOGETHER
THEY SEEMED LIKE SUCH A LITTLE WHILE

WITH BROWN TWINKLING ANGEL EYES,
AND SWEET, SPARKISH, CHEERFUL SMILE.

YOUR PROTRUDED AN TURNED UP NOSE
TO THE GLOSSY SOFTNESS IN YOUR HAIR.

WITH BENEVOLENCE LIKE THAT OF WINE,
A FRIENDSHIP ANYONE COULD SHARE....

MY DREAMS

ARE TO EMBRACE YOU DEAR ONCE MORE,
A MEMORY PATH TO OLD TIME PLEASURE.

BUT THE PATH IS NOW ODOR OF THE SEA,
AND THE SEA FAR BEYOND ALL MEASURE...

~

SEEK AND SEARCH

SEEK AND SEARCH

I'M THINKING OF YOU DEAR
    THIS SPECIAL DAY,
  TOGETHER UPON A CLOUD
    WANDERING AWAY
    ON A STRAYED BREEZE NEARBY.

OH, MINUTE MEMORIES
    OF A CHILDISH TALK,
  HOW TOGETHER WE DREAM
    TOGETHER WE WALK
    ATOP SOME CLOUD, YOU AND I.

YOUR FUNNY LITTLE WORDS,
    IN THOUGHT BRINGS,
  LIKE QUESTIONS YOU ASK,
    OF DIFFERENT THINGS,
    TOGETHER WE SEEK AN SEARCH

DOES A WINDING CREEK
    COUNT ALL ITS FISH,
  OR THE FISH GO UPSTREAM
    FOR WANT OR WISH,
    CAN GOLDFISH TALK TO PERCH?

WHAT KEEPS THE CLOUDS
    FROM FALLING DOWN
  THEY GRACEFULLY FLOAT, AS
    A MODIFIED CROWN,
    IS IT GOD'S EYE WATCHING YE?

AND WHEN WINDS BLOW,
    ISN'T THIS THEIR TALK
  OR WHEN A TREE WHISTLES
    IS IT GIVING MOCK,
    DO THE WINDS TALK UNTO THEE?

LET'S COUNT THE STARS,
　　　　IN ONES AND TWOS
AND WE'LL ASK THE SKIES
　　　　TO CHANGE ITS BLUES
　　　　YES, CHILDISH SIMPLE THINGS.

NOW, WHAT CAN WE NAME
　　　　GONE AND FADED
WHICH MANS DESTROYED,
　　　　THAT GOD CREATED,
　　　　GONE WITH THE ANGEL'S WINGS.

OH, SWEET SMELLING FLOWER,
　　　　SNOWFLAKE SNOW,
IS NOT SOMEONE TRYING
　　　　TO TELL OR SHOW,
　　　　THOSE BEAUTIES IN LIFE FOR US.

FROM THE SKIES ABOVE
　　　　TO THE LIFE BELOW,
ITS FREE, WONDERFUL GIFT,
　　　　I'D LIKE TO KNOW
　　　　WHY DO PEOPLE HAVE TO FUSS.

OH, HOW MIGHT A CHILD,
　　　　FEEL DEEP INSIDE
WILL THEIR GLADS AND SADS
　　　　OR WONDERS HIDE?
　　　　WHAT MAKES IMAGINATION BE.

OR DEGREE OF DISCOMFORT.
　　　　OLDER PEOPLE FEEL,
THAT WE JUST CAN'T SEEM
　　　　TO KNOW HOW REAL
　　　　IF ONLY A PAIN WE COULD SEE.

Who can know the heart
       Its love in measure
But so many will claim to
       Discern its treasure
       Never having an observation.

Let us try to understand
       Of unfilled dreams
Or the cries from a desire
       For what redeems
       The cost of man's hesitation.

Oh, awaken fantasies,
       As mysteries apply,
Somewhere another time
       Another by and by
       'Til our dreams come aware.

We'll seek and search
       From tos and fros
Then together discover
       In midst of echoes
       Hidden pleasures to declare.

~

OL' PAL

OL' PAL

Ol' pal, I'm so sorry,
    That I hurt your feelings this way,
An' really didn't mean
    To say the things that I had to say.

Ol' pal, stop looking,
    As if you are forever mad at me,
An try to understand,
    A correction sometimes must be.

Ol' pal, don't frown so,
    You are still greatest in my book,
But make me feel so hurt,
    As ya look at me the way ya look.

Ol' pal, what's happened,
    Did I use wrong words with you?
Won't you now forgive?
    An smile the way ya normally do.

Ol' pal, now once again,
    Let me share in your laughing fun.
Don't forget, I'm your dad
    And you, my son, just barely one...

~

FADING HOURS

YEA BEAMS OF CRIMSON,
    HORIZON'S SUNSET VIEW,
A TWILIGHT DRAWN CLEAR,
    GREETS IMMORTAL DEW.

DARK CURTAINS UNFURL,
    A MOST GRATEFUL SHADE,
DENSER GREEN OF TREES,
    WHERE SHADOWS FADE.

A BULK OF THE DARK,
    AT THE BASE OF THE HILL,
A STREAM OF MUSIC,
    ALLOWS TO FLOW AT WILL.

AT SHADOWED SLOPE,
    OF THE MOUNTAIN SIDE,
STAND BLADES OF GRASS,
    IN THE MEADOW'S WIDE.

AND THROUGH THE NIGHT,
    REFLECTIONS FROM AFAR,
A MESSENGER OF GOD,
    IS IN EACH WAKEN STAR.

BIRDS HAVE ALIGHTED,
    AND ARE SOFT TO SLEEP.
FROGS CROAKING SOUND,
    UTTER ECHO'S IN DEEP.

LIGHTS FROM HEAVEN
    ENGULF SWEET FLOWERS,
WALK THIS LONELY NIGHT,
    INTO ITS FADING HOURS.

~

THINGS TO CONSIDER

IT'S A BETTER CHOICE TO SAY NOTHING
    THEN NO ONE WILL HAVE ANYTHING TO REPEAT
AND GOOD TO REMEMBER TO FORGET
    TO FOCUS ON THE THINGS THAT CAUSE DEFEAT
DON'T EVER UNDERESTIMATE YOURSELF
    OR GIVE IN TO CRITICISM FROM THOSE NEARBY
YOU'LL NEVER KNOW ALL YOU CAN DO
    UNTIL YOU AT LEAST MAKE GOOD EFFORT TO TRY
A PERSON'S HEART SIZE IS MEASURED
    BY THE LITTLE IT TAKES TO DISCOURAGE THEM
A GREATEST VICTORY IS NOT SUCCESS
    BUT DEFYING FAILURE IN SPITE THE PROBLEM
SOME WELL-TO-DOS LACK THE PEACE
    IN SPITE OF ALL THEY MIGHT OWN, WHEREAS,
A CONTENT HEART IS ALWAYS CONTENT
    IN WHATEVER SMALL AMOUNT THAT ONE HAS
FOOLS SPEND WHAT THEY DON'T HAVE
    THEY OVEREXTEND THEIR CREDIT THEREABOUT
BUYING THE THINGS THEY DON'T NEED
    TO IMPRESS MANY THEY DON'T CARE ABOUT.

~

THE DITCH

I DIDN'T KNOW FOR SURE WHAT IT COULD BE,
THOUGH IT FELT UNUSUALLY STRANGE TO ME.
WAS IT NOT JUST FEELINGS THAT I ASSUMED,
SPINNING FROM IMAGINATION, I GROOMED?

THEN QUESTION AGAIN ANOTHER THOUGHT,
COULD IT BE CERTAIN EMOTIONS I SOUGHT?
IN SEARCHING THE MATTER AN' THE CAUSE,
THEN WHAT I BELIEVED, CAME TO A PAUSE.

WAS I OBSESSED, AN' GAVE UP THE FIGHT?
THEN IT DAWNED ON ME THAT VERY NIGHT,
I MYSELF MADE CHOICE AND CONCLUDED.
WITH SIGNS, FAIR JUDGEMENT I EXCLUDED.

THE POEM TOLD OF A DITCH ON A PATHWAY,
THIS FOOL FELL IN THE DITCH DAY AFTER DAY.
AFTER FALLING IN SEVERAL TIMES, HE FOUND,
A BETTER PATH IS TO TURN AND GO AROUND.

I GRASP FAMILIAR WAYS, BUT ONLY TO FAIL.
SOUGHT FOR CHANCE TO CHANGE MY TRAIL,
AROUND THE DITCH TO PATTERN MY WAYS.
TO BLEND-IN WITH LIFE, FOR HAPPIER DAYS.

IT'S THROUGH OUR TRIBULATIONS OR TRIALS.
COMBINED WITH UPS, DOWNS AND SMILES.
THAT BRINGS A PEACE, OF BEING SATISFIED,
OF LOVE, CHARITY AND WISDOM AT OUR SIDE.

It took many stumbles, before a switch.
To exit that old pathway, into the ditch.
Behold, other ways were strange to me,
But then I saw a new path to my jubilee.

A world of empty hopes, in discontent.
Nor could I perceive, what a life meant.
Grasping for less, inside wanted more.
Oh, but now I have, my foot in the door.

Trials of faith are directly settled here,
So now to walk in Spirit and not in fear.
Of courage, our faith must remain true,
Lord today, I'm content to be with you!

Indeed, what did I learn in this affair?
Whatever the world offers you, beware.
An' let not your heart be troubled again.
Avoid the ditch you once before, fell in.

~

VOICE FROM THE GLOW

WAS MID OF NIGHT, NINETEEN SEVENTY ONE.
AS THE LORD'S MYSTERY IN MY LIFE BEGUN.
    I FELT FINAL BEATS FALL HEAVY UPON MY HEART
    IT STOPPED... PAUSED... AND AGAIN TO START.

ONCE MORE IT STOPPED, NOR COULD I FEEL IT.
UNCLEAR IF ALIVE, OR IF DEAD IN THE SPIRIT.
    THEN SAW MYSELF STANDING, ATOP OF THE BED.
    CRYING WITH A JOY, YEARNING TO DIE INSTEAD.

WEEPING TEARS, WITH HANDS LIFTED UP HIGH.
WITHOUT ANY DOUBT, IT WAS MY TIME TO DIE.
    THEN A MYSTERIOUS BRIGHT GLOW APPEARED.
    FROM IN THE GLOW CAME THE VOICE I FEARED.

SPOKE "NOT YET, I'M NOT FINISHED WITH YOU".
SUDDENLY, MY HEART BEGAN TO BEAT ANEW.
    EVEN TO THIS DAY, IT IS ALL A MYSTERY TO ME.
    HAVING NAUGHT TO GIVE, THAT I CAN FORESEE.

TWO QUESTIONS I ASKED MYSELF TO EXPLAIN,
THE FIRST ONE SIMPLE, THE SECOND REMAIN.
    FIRST, FOR WHAT COULD I POSSIBLY BE USED?
    THE VOICE FROM THE GLOW LEFT ME CONFUSED.

IN ANSWER TO THE FIRST, I CAN NOW DISCLOSE,
TO LOVE MY FAMILY, WHICH THE LORD CHOSE.
    BUT THE SECOND QUESTION, WHY AM I HERE?
    WILL NEED FURTHER EXPLAINING, TO BE CLEAR.

MANY OF LIFE'S PLEASURES, THAT WERE MINE,
ABOVE ALL I HAVE ENJOYED, IN MY LIFETIME.
    ONLY ONE STANDS OUT, FROM ALL OF THE REST,
    IT IS A JOY OF GIVING, THAT FULFILLS MY QUEST.

Ive been amongst, tribulations and trials,
Often concealed heartaches, with smiles.
    I've been through more, than many claim,
    Yes, I know being down, is not all shame.

Oh' foolish man, as I have become today,
Avoiding the trends, how man leads way.
    With popular views, in a world of choice.
    I follow the path of the mysterious voice.

To modify this fray world, I've no desire,
I'd rather see a smile, of triumph inspire,
    Or observe change, worry puts on a face,
    When held by the Spirit's sweet embrace.

The comfort, from that voice in the glow,
Follows even today, wherever I might go.
    I see bad decisions made over and again,
    From my foolish heart when I look within.

I cannot find fit words, that reveal regret.
Of things I have done and cannot forget.
    To justify guilt, I then turn my insides out,
    I will find ways to give, somehow no doubt.

Laws of the flesh do not make us whole.
But lifting of the Spirit, revives the soul.
    Life's greatest bounty, is the satisfied grin,
    A sigh of relief, a glimpse as love fades-in.

In hearts glance, I've no need, or desires,
For I have much more, than life requires.
    Very content, no needs for such and such,
    Yet victory, giving another's heart a touch.

BE IT FINANCIAL, LABOR TO HARVEST OR MORE,
I'D ROLL UP MY SLEEVE TO PURSUE THE CHORE.
    TO ASSIST, IN HOPE, CONTRIBUTE WHEN I CAN,
    HOWEVER, TO HELP, IS A PLEASURE, MY PLAN.

BY LOOKING IN CERTAIN PEOPLE'S EYES, I KNEW,
I FELT THEIR HURT INSIDE, FOR IT HURT ME TOO.
    SO, I QUESTION THIS OPPORTUNITY OF CHOICE,
    FROM WORDS I ONCE HEARD FROM THAT VOICE.

IN WAYS HOW LIFE REALLY IS, I JUST DIDN'T SEE.
VIEWING IT ONLY, HOW I THINK IT SHOULD BE.
    OCCASIONALLY I AM FOOLED, NOW AND THEN.
    FOR REASONS UN-KNOWN, I JUST DO IT AGAIN.

COULD THE VOICE FROM THE GLOW BE THE CLUE?
TO HELP OTHERS WITH WAYS, I SHOULD PURSUE.
    FAMILY AND GOOD FRIENDS, HELP ME SURVIVE,
    THEY ARE THE CAUSE, MY PURPOSE TO BE ALIVE.

YES, I HELPED CERTAIN PEOPLE THAT I CHOOSE,
OTHERS BY WAYSIDE, I JUST COULD NOT REFUSE.
    WHAT BETTER REASON TO LIVE, COULD I FIND.
    FOR, TO GIVE IS MY JOY, WITH PEACE OF MIND.

~

IMAGINARY LINE

To question a matter is our safety
    Consider what the spirit may tell.
So better to stand with God alone
    Then follow a crowd into Hell.

Man takes salvation for granted
    He can pray, claim but not define.
Justify, convinced, be sure in heart
    But only God can draw that line.

Many doctrines, so many wrong
    As sowed tares among the wheat
Mingled with Truth in the Word
    Are thistles to distract, to defeat.

If man thinks he knows anything
    Knowing not as he ought to know.
Of seeking not the imaginary line
    For to live above and not below.

Imaginary lines are for the Elect
    The Lord will judge what will be.
The Book of Life will then unfold
    Separating the lost from the free.

Unto whomsoever much is given
    From him shall be much required.
And to finding the edge of much
    Are a people spiritually inspired

WHAT DOTH THE LORD REQUIRE OF THEE?
 IS JUST DO JUSTLY, AND TO LOVE MERCY,
AND TO WALK HUMBLY WITH THY GOD.
 WITH A FAIR MEASURE OF THESE THREE.

SO HERE A LITTLE AND THERE A LITTLE,
 PRECEPT ON PRECEPT, LINE UPON LINE.
BEHOLD, HE LAY DOWN A FOUNDATION,
 FOR HIS CHOSEN PEOPLE TO BE A SIGN.

YET WITH OPENED EYES, I DID NOT SEE,
 SHADOWED VISIONS WITHIN MY TALK.
I SOUGHT A PATH TO SHOW THE WAY
 TO VARY CHANGE, TO WALK THE WALK.

TO JUDGE MYSELF. IT SO DISGUSTED ME
 FROM CHOICES MADE UPON MY OWN.
THOUGH HE WALKED ALONG MY SIDE
 I OFTEN TURNED, AN WALKED ALONE.

WE KNOW NOT ABOUT THE MORROW
 AFTER ALL, WHAT IS OUR LIFE TODAY
IT IS, BUT A VAPOR THAT APPEARETH
 FOR LITTLE TIME, AN VANISHES AWAY

WHY BEHOLDEST A MOTE IN THE EYE
 OF A BROTHER FOR SOME SELF ESTEEM
OH HYPOCRITE, CONSIDER THE FLAWS
 BUT FIRST CAST OUT OUR OWN BEAM

So cried, Wretched man that I am,
 Who shall deliver me from death?
Knowing flesh cannot please God
 Below a line that gave me breath.

Yea, Lord, my God, forget me not,
 As your mercy changes by design
Open to me Lord, my heart, my eyes
 To detect my own, Imaginary Line

For inside that Line, it will define
 Judge not what you think of me
The line of yours, differs than mine
 So judge the better you could be.

~

TO RECOGNIZE

Often, Man does not identify
    How all blessings in a life relates
    God's guideline for a joyous path
We pursue our own direction
    Into a way the world illustrates
    A source and root of God's wrath

Forgive my iniquities and sin
    Help me Lord to better recognize
    Of things I don't consider, reveal
Your ways I marvel in wonder
    Go before me Lord, remove surprise
    So I'm not confused what is real

What signs am I unaware of?
    Make it clear this once metaphor
    That all doubt can be made clear
Expose intent I can recognize.
    Which were signs, wonders before
    O' Lord, give heed, incline Thy ear

Should man not be punished
    For foolish, unwise choices done?
    Of course he should, being a fool
Knowing the options for life
    And course of death are not one
    The blessings in life are God's rule

Lord give me a whole heart
    That won't depart from Your way
    And to receive Your instruction
To cherish every move more
    Ever follow You, and not stray
    Into enemy's path of destruction.

Cursed be a man trusting man
    He goes forth in God's whirlwind
    Provoking You, Lord into anger
A fool says, "There is no God."
    Recognizing joy in a false pretend
    Substituting all of hope with fear

So much You have given to us
    Even when tribulations hardened
    Realizing You Lord, try the reins
My heart smiles in a wonder
    How much your mercy pardoned
    By recognizing all of these things

The mystery of types, shadows
    Come satisfied to hear and behold
    These symbols, gestures in our days
To clear questions of dispute
    Be aware daily as blessings unfold
    Expressing much gratitude in praise

Cease all thoughts of doubt
    By clue or hint in your experience
    Knowledge of wisdom once hidden
For change in life's adventure
    Yea, remove a little of the suspense
    To better recognize the forbidden

Unmindful of our blessings
    Usually we take much for granted
    Every move made to every thought
From the last breath taken.
    To recognize every move preceded
    Then to appreciate all we ought.

~

FLOWER OF DAWN

Alas! Now it is,
  She's on a different path
Abandon this life
  And all that it's required
  Leaving each little dream made
She, like the rose,
  With a fragrance it hath
Glistened a last time
  Like a flower inspired
  Dawn came in her final crusade.

O' flower of dawn
  Fades white with thorn
With dewy leaves,
  When morning appears.
  Above all the valley she loomed
Entering sunlight
  She fetched in the morn
That gave me hope,
  In all of my yesteryears
  This rose has always bloomed.

Upon her breast,
  I once did rest my head
But as time passed
  I became the stranger
  Still my love for her unswayed
Echoed a moment,
  A thought came instead
A quickened spirit
  Warned me of the danger
  From the games life has played.

Like a summer air
    She refreshened things
But a time arrived
    When she couldn't stay
    I'd wish to remember no longer
Oh my heart swells
    And my loneliness stings
In frowns and tears
    When her hour fell away
    I must learn to become stronger

Oft people pattern
    In a likeness duplicate
So two become one
    Each one becomes two
    Being apart they hardly bear it.
So I now conclude
    Though death is by fate
I reminisce much
    About thinking it thru
    'Cause her likeness, I did inherit.

Her faithful heart,
    Came shadowed at last,
Revealing to me
    Of what was once mine
    Blurred memories come to sight
In asking myself
    To search more of a past
Where I have failed
    My selfishness intertwine
    But cannot change to make right

Oh, fancy bloom
     Daisies dance the fields
Casting their leaves
     Rosebuds open in yawn
     Together this blanket of flowers
Open curtains drew
     Then her briar rose yields
Outshined them all,
     Was the flower of dawn
     From which sprang many towers

Yes I can pretend
     Justify the very thought
To right my wrong
     But I cannot fool myself
     Her departure is hard to define
A visionary view
     Brought truth to naught
Spots the surface of
     The innocence of herself
     All fault and selfishness is mine.

Her angular face
     Was creased with lines
Unforgettable frown
     Yoked with sunny smiles
     The mere fragrance she exhaled
Within me burning
     Surface her many signs
Claim foolish tears
     And was swayed by trials
     Others succeeded where I failed.

For what reason are
    All my dreams scattered?
Why didn't I prepare
    For often I was foretold
    Is life casting a mockery at me?
Shall I now pretend
    As if it never mattered?
Heart of bitterness
    Make dreams turn cold
    Destiny was settled and must be.

Still I pause today
    Just to imagine her touch
Easily I could see,
    I had again failed a trial
    And followed a path to sorrow
Her hair was fine
    And it didn't curl much
A sweet, soft voice
    Always followed a smile
    With enthusiasm for tomorrow

In retracing choice
    A certain heartache I feel
I have failed to find
    Which way to turn or go,
    Death uprooted a flower I knew
Though a time lapsed
    To where the petals peel
The flower of dawn
    Pruned to forever grow
    In another flower garden anew.

WHEN WE WERE ABSENT
  THE ONE FROM THE OTHER
IT LINGERED A VOID
  WORDS CAN NEVER EXPLAIN
  AS IF ONLY TOGETHER WE WERE ONE
WHAT LIFE BEHOLDS
  IN BRINGING TWO TOGETHER
AN SHATTERS DREAMS
  IF ONLY ONE SHOULD REMAIN
  THEREBY TWO MINUS ONE IS NONE.

THE FLOWER IS PLUCKED
  SEPARATING SEED AND STALK
WITH END OF ITS DAYS
  NOW A GHOST IN DREAMS
  I WAKE AT NIGHT CALLING HER NAME
THE GAP IS VERY WIDE,
  WE TRAIL A DIFFERENT WALK
LUMP IN MY THROAT
  WON'T LEAVE ME IT SEEMS
  FOR LIFE WILL NEVER BE THE SAME.

AWAKE SLEEPING FLOWERS
  AWAKE YOU BUSHES NEAR
THE FLOWER OF DAWN
  WILL ONCE AGAIN ADVANCE
  A BIRD'S TRILLING WILL SING OF JOY.
UNTIL THEN I'LL CLAIM.
  WHEN I SEE A ROSE APPEAR
EACH WITH MY DESIRE
  AGAIN TO TOUCH OR GLANCE
  OH' MY FLOWER OF DAWN'S DECOY.

So the dawn came
    In that hour of surprise
Beckoned this flower
    Root from stem divided,
    It was I who couldn't face reality.
O' but another dawn
    From her root did arise
Again she flourished
    In His garden provided
    There to bloom through eternity.

~

SOMETHING MISPLACED

I MISPLACED SOMETHING THIS MORNING,
    BUT EXACTLY WHERE I COMPLETELY FORGOT,
COULD THIS BE AGE'S WAY OF WARNING?
    CAUSE LATELY, IT SEEMS TO HAPPEN A LOT.

MY MEMORY IS QUITE DIFFERENT I FEAR,
    THE ODDEST THINGS SEEM TO VANISH NOW,
THAT WHICH I NEED MIGHT DISAPPEAR,
    LATER SHOWS UP SOMEWHERE, SOMEHOW.

THESE THINGS MEMORIES ARE MADE OF,
    WHEREBY AT ONE TIME I COULD FULLY RELY,
NOW IMAGES AND ALL CLAIMS THEREOF,
    ESCAPE SLOWLY, ONE BY ONE BY AND BY.

ALL THIS MIS-PLACING OF MINE I GUESS,
    IS A BLANK SPOT WHERE MEMORIES STALL,
THIS STRING ON MY FINGER I CONFESS,
    JUST WHY I PUT IT THERE I CANNOT RECALL.

THOUGH IT SEEMS IMPOSSIBLE TO FIND,
    FOR A SECOND IT CAME TO ME THEN WENT,
OH, IF ONLY I COULD HARNESS THE MIND,
    I'D RECALL TO REMEMBRANCE EACH EVENT.

WHERE I PUT IT, I HAVEN'T THE FAINTEST,
    AN ALWAYS HAPPENS WHEN I AM AWAKE,
TO THINK I REMEMBER I WILL BE HONEST,
    MORE OFTEN THAN NOT, IT IS MY MISTAKE.

I LOOKED IN THE PLACE I THOUGHT IT WAS
    BUT, FORGOT WHERE I THOUGHT IT MIGHT BE
THEN ASK MYSELF OVER AGAIN BECAUSE
    IT HAPPENS MUCH TOO OFTEN UNWILLINGLY

Though I set it in a common place,
      So this should make the challenge fair,
However on its need when I retrace,
      I find something different sitting there.

On the other hand I can recall again,
      Experiences way back into my prime,
The question I have will still remain,
      Is my memory today, just lost in time?

In spite of this forgetfulness I grin,
      This emptiness filled with indecision.
I forgot not only the place I put it in,
      But the item itself, I can't now vision.

It vanished, what I failed to recollect
      Knowing something escaped memory
Neither was it what I first did expect
      What it really is I still can't guarantee

Well, "What do ya know, there it 'tis"
      I recollect putting it here once before,
But have to laugh, 'n funny thing is,
      I don't now recall what I wanted it for.

~

REFLECTIONS

REFLECTIONS

In the mirror of rhythmic wonder
        Thinking back on his early growth,
Youngest son from times yonder
        Grew to a man impressing us both.

Fresh today the memories chase
        Into long thoughts of a gone past
With shadows of a time an place
        Reflecting my likeness in contrast.

I saw his enthusiasm in spirit free
        To watch him play was worthwhile
His imagination it seemed to be
        The duplicate that made me smile

Recalling a small hammer he drew
        From the little work pouch he wore
How he would pull a nail or screw
        Then turn to me and ask for more

I watched as he made his costume
        Of a cardboard box or gunny sack
To his imaginary heroes I presume
        Or a fancy cowboy on horseback

We would play catch or fly kites
        Kick the can or marbles we played
The story Jungle Book he recites
        Different characters he portrayed.

Generation is a foundation stone
        Reaching forward building a flame,
Hours with him I cannot postpone
        For his seed shall carry my name.

My little guy with his friendly cat,
    So filled with inquisitive questions
My pal, buddy with an oddball hat
    Surfacing memories of reflections

Yea, I shall again tomorrow reach
    In his past that I've so well known
To hear him call, "Dad", in speech
    With questions in a smoothed tone.

Blush upon his cheeks as a child
    I recall a great zeal he had for God
Or squinting ways his eyes smiled
    To the little paths his feet had trod.

The little imitations from his heart
    With dreams and hopes unfulfilled
But I assured him from the start.
    With labor and faith he can build.

Times will come, you'll feel bound
    Even if your intentions were kind
But in silence you'll hear a sound
    As a still voice councils the mind.

Oh how dim our life's visions are
    Till one in a likeness comes along
Then past that once seemed so far
    Do again make tomorrows belong

Yes, he is a dreamer of dreams,
    Visionary like unto myself an yet.
Bringing past back to life it seems,
    By the things he says I did forget.

I'VE HEARD HIM PLAY A TUNE FAMILIAR
    WITH HIS SAXOPHONE IN GREAT PRIDE
AND OTHER THINGS HE DID PECULIAR
    BUILT THE BOND I KEEP DEEP INSIDE

BY LIFE'S EXPERIENCE, SORT THEM OUT
    AN CAREFULLY SELECT THE BETTER SEEDS,
AN YOU CAN FIND WHAT LIFE'S ABOUT
    AS YOU PLUCK THE UNWANTED WEEDS.

OH, PROUD AM I FOR ALL HE'S GAINED
    HIS CHARM AND SMILES WITH FEELING,
IN SOME OF HIM SOME OF I REMAINED,
    SO MUCH OF HIM STILL MORE REVEALING

YOU'RE THE COMING GENERATION SON
    AN MY LIFE ITSELF WAS JUST A SAMPLE
SO PRESS FORTH TO BE A BETTER ONE
    AND TO YOUR SON A BETTER EXAMPLE.

AND I AGAIN, AS I HAD DONE BEFORE
    EXPLAINED THE HARM OF FOOLISHNESS
THAT HE, MY SON CAN DO FAR MORE
    BY WISELY DIRECTING YOUTHFULNESS.

IN MANY WAYS, I SEE WHERE I STOOD
    HIS CONCERN WORTH MORE THAN GOLD
SURPRISING ME OFTEN AS HE COULD
    REVEALING A COMPASSION TO BEHOLD

IN LIFE WE ALL LIVE BENEATH A COVER
    OF THE CREATOR WHOM WE BESOUGHT
SO, DO RIGHT SON ONLY TO DISCOVER
    WHAT GOES ROUND COMES BACK A LOT

I watched as he stooped and knelt
    Different values than his brothers
Still unrevealed, yet inside I felt,
    Sensitive heart he hid from others.

Though the years, values change
    Yet some of his ways I will accept,
Some of mine to him seem strange
    Certain values we both have kept.

I've tried to teach, not complicate
    What is right in the making of gain
To focus by the ways of illustrate
    To be honorable and there remain.

With many talents he did inherit
    Quick with wit in a humorous way
Mock nationalities by master merit
    Express different cultures display.

Yea, I was younger in bygone days
    An somewhat, a stern fella, I guess,
Encouraging him to mold his ways
    By standards holding nothing less.

Giving, sharing or grasp for truth
    Such standards his life shall trace
Changes as he grows from youth
    To the better ways he will embrace.

Occasionally, personalities clash
    Over perceptions or assumptions
But then suddenly leave in a dash
    Achieving the trace of reflections

The human wrong inside us lies
    Within depths or heights we store
Where guilt in life and shame ties,
    As conscience stands at the door.

His ambition strongly opinionated
    Impossible to otherwise persuade
But I see myself young simulated
    A copy of my youth he has made.

He rides a horse an cracks a whip
    Standing tall in a wondrous frame
Shoot a gun with marksmanship
    Making challenges a simple game

Now other talents surround his life
    With a ruler in hand for to measure
By visions of goals he does strive
    Turning leather scraps to treasure

Into the wee hours he labors long
    To find his place wherein life to fit
And do it with joy and with song
    In preparing labors for his benefit.

He loves his kids as I did indeed
    Concerned about his families task
Filling their gap in times of need
    What better can man desire, I ask?

From this and that he might learn
    Within him a spirit shall be stirred
And within himself if he be stern
    Will find that truth to be his word.

In the past sometimes we fought
Quarreled, disagreed and argued
Then hugged, kissed, as we ought,
Mending our bonds in a gratitude.

But time pressed forth as it does,
His gritting teeth turned to smiles
Matured and settled just because
Time taught him through its trials.

Also characteristics like my own
In reflections that only I can touch
Even his voice echoes my tone
And reasons like me so very much.

Today I will just stand by an grin
From his entertaining suggestions,
Because in him I see myself again
The variety of mirrored reflections

Upon us both, son, did the rain fall
As we change from boy to the man
A certain inheritance comes to all
Likeness our father's father began.

Among disappointments or delight
I'm not judge where he is to belong
For often when I thought I was right,
I have come to find my right wrong

So time has come proving a point
That my being is not without cause.
He is my flesh, my blood and joint
Sharing some qualities, also flaws.

Our years have played their part
 And who am I, that I should judge
It's how we end, not how we start
 A choice made from others nudge.

With many memories to retrieve
 And much to share, give and take
Then more to learn, to achieve,
 The filling of dreams in your wake.

In the days when you be the one,
 Reconsider all of your objections,
I will be with you forever, my son,
 But, in silence of your reflections.

~

A PERSON

A PERSON CAN'T RIGHTFULLY BE JUDGED
      FROM WHAT WAS SAID ABOUT HIM,
BUT YOU CERTAINLY SHALL BE JUDGED
      BY THINGS YOU SAY ABOUT THEM.

A PERSON IS USUALLY NOT INTERESTED
      ABOUT OTHER PERSON'S MATTERS
UNLESS IT'S NONE OF THEIR BUSINESS
      FROM THERE THE STORY SCATTERS

A PERSON MAY DOUBT WHAT YOU SAY
      BUT WHAT YOU DO, THEY'LL BELIEVE
AN OPEN MIND CAN BECOME A SPACE
      TO HOARD TRASH WE MAY RECEIVE

A PERSON SHOULD SEEK COMPASSION
      INSTEAD OF SEARCHING FOR BLAME
THE FOOL SEEKS TOWARD FINDING FAULT
      AS THE WISE PUTS OUT THE FLAME.

A PERSON SHOULD FORGIVE ENEMIES
      DO RIGHT FORGIVE, MAKE A MEND
TYPICALLY AN ENEMY WILL REVEAL
      SPEAKING TRUTH AND NOT PRETEND.

~

A WARM KITCHEN

It's only from a warm kitchen,
  Where recipes and joy are applied,
Comes that of homemade bread,
  Awe! The pleasant smell supplied,
Of just flour and some water
  Kneading in yeast an salt to form,
An in all this you may succeed,
  If only you keep the kitchen warm.

Yea, one thing taught of bread,
  With its grains of chaff and roots
It is our staff of life, typified,
  The Bread of Life that substitutes,
I ask, "Who prepared the bread,
  For supper 'ere the Master went?"
Perhaps in some warm kitchen,
  To a crown of honor in each event.

Out of the earth grows wheat,
  Pure water flows where God wills,
Imagination He has given man,
  Of knowledge, of desire and skills,
So give "thanks" for the bread,
  Generously given for our pleasure,
Until together we break bread,
  In His warm kitchen, our treasure.

~

GOOD FRIEND

As I shut my eyes in wonder,
    To consider a question on this wise,
The interpretation of friends,
    Appears to be in much compromise,
Just what is a friend I'll ask
    Where seems to be a variety of elect,
Any one that one may know,
    Can be called friend in some respect.

So I sought for a definition,
    To what "friend" exactly represents,
This is where I discovered,
    O' shallow are friends in most events,
I've revealed many smiles,
    But they were just fronts upon a face,
And likewise searched hearts,
    Only to find emptiness in their place.

In all this searching I found
    Meaning of a friend comes to naught
Can't common sense judge,
    To who is a friend and to who is not,
A friend is always a friend,
    They are acquaintances of any kind,
But a good friend is scarce,
    For they are few and difficult to find

Yes, a good friend is faithful,
    As their actions do usually illustrate,
To them you know the turn,
    And to which door, or to which gate,
It is not a point of question,
    To who is right or to who is wrong,
Where friendships intertwine,
    Hopes, dreams and failures belong.

LIKEWISE IF YOU FACE TROUBLE,
    AND BE IT A FACT OR BE IT MISCONSTRUE,
SHOULDN'T I AS A GOOD FRIEND,
    STRETCH FORTH MY HAND IN HELP TO YOU?
THEN TOGETHER IN A FIRM GRIP,
    LEAN AGAINST THE WILES OF THE STORM.
SHOULDN'T THIS BE THE CHOICE
    THAT FAITHFUL GOOD FRIENDS PERFORM?

LOOK CAREFULLY, THEN NOTICE,
    IN PLEASANT TIMES WHAT FRIENDS CLAIM,
BUT WOE! BE IN TRIBULATION,
    HOW DIFFERENTLY THE SAME PROCLAIM,
BECAUSE OF POPULAR VIEWS,
    THEY WILL TRUST IN GOSSIP AND DIVIDE,
AN IF SORROW OR SHAME COME,
    IN EMBARRASSMENT THEY STAND ASIDE.

IF THINGS SHOULD GO MY WAY,
    I'M CONSIDERED A FRIEND BY SO MANY,
BUT AH! IF I SHOULD STUMBLE,
    I CAN LOOK AGAIN BUT WON'T FIND ANY,
I HAVE A SUPPORTING FAMILY,
    AND A FEW GOOD FRIENDS THAT I KNOW,
BUT IN TROUBLE ISN'T IT FUNNY,
    O' WHERE DID ALL THE OTHER FRIENDS GO?

SO READER, IT'S A TRUE SAYING,
    I MAY NOT CALL YOU MY GOOD FRIEND,
NEITHER FRIEND DO I LEAD YOU,
    TO BELIEVE OTHERWISE OR TO PRETEND,
FOR A GOOD FRIEND IS EARNED,
    TEMPTED, TRIED AND PASSED THE TEST,
SO WHO I CALL MY GOOD FRIEND,
    IS SOMEONE SPECIAL FROM ALL THE REST.

PEOPLE CHANGE IN AGE TO AGE,
    WITH ITS UPS N' DOWNS, OR TOS N' FROS
OFTEN APPEARING INSIDE OUT,
    TO CONFUSE THE OBVIOUS I'D SUPPOSE,
YES I SEEK MORE THAN MOST,
    IN SELECTING MY GOOD FRIEND, BUT THEN,
I USUALLY FIND SOMETHING HID,
    WHERE A GAIN SEEKS THE HEART OF MEN.

I HAVE SPENT MOST A LIFETIME,
    INTERPRETING GOOD FRIENDS' GUARANTEE,
AN THIS IS WHY ANYTHING LESS,
    IS JUST ANOTHER ACQUAINTANCE WITH ME.
BY FAILURES AND ERRORS IN LIFE,
    I LEARNED THESE CONCEALED REVEALINGS,
AND FOUND HOW TO IDENTIFY,
    A GOOD FRIEND AND THEIR TRUE FEELINGS,

YES, WITHOUT BEWILDERMENT,
    ASIDE OF ERROR AND WITHOUT MISTAKE,
WITHOUT TRIALS I'D NOT KNOW,
    TO TELL THE GOOD FRIEND FROM THE FAKE,
AN SO FOR THIS REASON ALONE,
    I'LL GREATLY REJOICE IN ALL TRIBULATIONS,
BECAUSE OF TRIALS I CAN NOW,
    CHOOSE GOOD FRIENDS FROM IMITATIONS.

~

CIRCUMSTANCES ALTER CASES

WISE MEN TALK LESS, BUT SAY MORE IN VOICE
A HAPPINESS IS NOT BY CHANCE BUT CHOICE
    IF IT COMES TO YOU BY WHISPER OR IN SECRET
    THE HEARING OF IT, YOU ARE BETTER TO FORGET.
LOVE THAT BINDS FRIENDS SHOULD BE GREATER
THAN WHATEVER COULD CAUSE TO DIVIDE LATER
    WORRY IS FOOLISHNESS LACKING FAITH INSIDE
    FAITH IS REFUSING THE FOOLISHNESS TO ABIDE
DON'T PRETEND AGREEABLE IF YOU DON'T AGREE
LET TRUTHFULNESS DIVIDE AND SEPARATE THEE
    EVEN THE WELL TRAINED MULE IN CLEVER TRICK
    CAN'T BOTH AT THE SAME TIME PULL AND KICK.
A CONSCIENCE SORTS WHAT FREEDOM BRINGS
KEEPING US FROM ENJOYING CERTAIN THINGS.
    THE GATHERING OF POSITIVE SAYINGS INDEED
    LAYS THE COURSE FOR ATTITUDES TO SUCCEED
SMELL OF LEAVES BURNING SMOKE IN THE FALL
WAKING THE INNER CHILD TO AGAIN ENTHRALL.
    THE AROMA OF GRASSES CUT IN EARLY SPRING
    STEPS US OUT OF THE SHADOW WINTERS BRING
A FALSE SMILE IS A SILHOUETTE OF DECEPTION
TO QUESTION A MATTER IS A SAFE PROTECTION
    BE CONTENT WITH WHATEVER YOU DO POSSESS
    AN' THEN LEARN TO BE CONTENT WITH EVEN LESS

~

PATTERN OF THE CIRCUIT

The circuit combines a triangle consisting of three,
A bond with the Master, your fellowman and thee
From a birth to the surface of an old familiar place
Surrounds this circuit of His mercy and His grace,

Oh' foolish man, who strives and yet is so bound,
Without promise of hope until the circuit is found,
Some find it early, while yet others stall or replay,
All life is but a waste outside of the circuit's way.

The circuit becomes a circuit, a mere line at birth,
Without direction from each end seeking its worth,
As you who was born; chosen and reared, my son,
My friend, and a part of me where the circuits run.

The bond is deep, often difficult to identify indeed,
Difference is necessary for the circuit to succeed.
Nevertheless within this space together we share,
With life's challenges and tribulations, O' beware.

Thru man's trials of life sorting wants and needs,
The flesh cries in desire whereas the spirit heeds,
But the years will teach us how the circuit begins,
To the completing of the triangle before life ends.

The circuit is family as it weaves through a home,
Neither can be made complete by any man alone,
A reason to do more or cause a cause to do less,
Can complete the circuit bringing man to confess.

Once the circuit is recognized or then discovered,
Let the past be buried and newness be recovered,
Touch not again upon the once old negative force,
So the circuit might direct your life, a new course.

Grasp what is left today and plan your projection
Make of none effect foolishness of man's rejection
The desire to be accepted is such a waste of time,
For the circuit is already yours, it is already mine.

Accept all regrets, disapprovals or condemnation,
Grow by searching its root with much expectation,
Without these trials the triangle ends cannot meet,
But with such we learn how the circuit is complete.

Avoid the seeking of signs or the values of things,
As foolishness rest in the want of Gold and rings,
Rather seek for joy deep in a marrow of the bone,
So is the challenge of the circuit, I've been shown

The circuit never leaves man, as might be thought,
Neither have I forgotten thee, the son I've sought,
Yet man can leave the circuit, a freedom of choice,
And return again by the call of the Master's voice.

Relax my son, take a deep breath, I am but a man,
Familiar also with error, but doing the best I can,
Correct me if you would, for to my gain it shall be,
For without correction, this circuit can't mold me.

Likewise my son, I shall accept you today as part,
Of that circuit we began as individuals from start,
Coming together with the Head, the triangles goal,
Completing the circuit with the master of our soul.

The circuit's triangle is the Head joining two ends,
One end where peace with our fellow man begins.
The other end, ourselves, where fellowships meet,
The Head is Christ, making this pattern complete.

~

I KNOW WHAT YOU SAID, BUT...

I KNOW WHAT YOU SAID, BUT....
I KNOW WORDS DON'T STAND BY THEMSELVES,
    BUT INCLUDE ALSO SOME MENTAL IMPRESSIONS
OPENLY OR DIRECTLY INTENTIONS ARE IMPLIED
    YET CONTRARY CAN BE MEANT BY EXPRESSIONS
OTHER MEANINGS CAN BE ACCOMPLISHED
    CONVEY OTHERWISE BY SIGNIFICATION OR HINTS
OUR INNER EXPRESSIONS CREATE PICTURES
    IMPRINTING TO OUR MIND'S IMAGINARY PRINTS

I KNOW WHAT YOU SAID, BUT....
IMPLYING INDICATES BELIEF WITHOUT SAYING
    EVEN SUGGESTIONS WHICH INVOLVES OR REFERS
WHEREAS ASSUMING OR BEING ASSUMED,
    TAKING FOR GRANTED WHAT EACH RIDDLE INFERS
SELF CONVINCED FULL CONFIDENCE AND TRUST
    THOUGHTS COME ASSURED A FREEDOM OF DOUBT,
LEAVING ASIDE THE SURENESS OF THE MIND
    SELF CONFIDENCE TO UTMOST CERTAINTY ABOUT

I KNOW WHAT YOU SAID, BUT....
REVELATIONS ARE IMPLIED PART BY SPEECH
    INCLUDING SOME GESTURES, ACTIONS OR INTENT
COMBINE TOGETHER WHAT THE HEART FORGE
    INTO CHOICE EMPHASIS THE TONGUE MIGHT VENT
WHEN STILLNESS AND SILENCE IS IN ORDER
    A CERTAIN SENSATION OF HEARING TAKES EFFECT
THEN WITH SOUNDS VIBRATING INTO THE AIR
    SIGNIFICANCE OF MENTAL IMPRESSIONS CONNECT

I KNOW WHAT YOU SAID BUT...
IT'S NOT THE WORDS ALONE THAT WERE SAID
    THAT REVEALS ALL THOUGHTS OF INNER FEELINGS
WHICH ALSO INCLUDES SOME EXPERIENCES
    FROM IMAGINATION OR PERSUADED REVEALINGS
EXPRESSIONS PUT MEANINGS ONTO WORDS
    REPRESENTING IN A LANGUAGE BY SYMBOLIZING
A MINGLING OF WORD, PHRASE OR SENTENCES
    CONSOLIDATES EXPOSED INNER ZEAL STABILIZING

I KNOW WHAT YOU SAID, BUT...
SOME SAYINGS ARE NOT EASILY UNDERSTOOD
    SOME ARE OBVIOUS AND GOES WITHOUT SAYING
NEEDS NO EXPLANATION AND IS SELF EVIDENT
    UNMENTIONED WITHOUT ANY EFFECT DISPLAYING
ALTHOUGH TO UTTER IS THE USE OF A VOICE
    IT DOESN'T ALWAYS APPLY TO COMMON SPEECH
A SKILLFUL DEMONSTRATION MADE FOR EFFECT
    A MOAN, A SCREAM OR SOME SOUND TO TEACH

I KNOW WHAT YOU SAID, BUT...
EXAMINE VARIOUS SOUNDS, SIGNS, SIGNALS,
    AS EXTRAORDINARY ILLUSIONS OCCUR NOTABLE
PONDERING APPARENT SIGNS GIVEN GESTURES
    COULD FORMULATE ALL OPINIONS UNREASONABLE
EXPRESSIONS, EMPHASIZE IDEAS, EMOTIONS,
    SILENTLY MENTIONED OR EXPRESSED IN A VOICE
FROM SOME OPINION WE REPEAT OR REPORT
    THESE BECOME EVIDENT MANIFESTING A CHOICE

I KNOW WHAT YOU SAID, BUT...
INDIVIDUALS HAVE ENTIRELY DIFFERENT MOODS
    WHICH RELEASE IMPRESSIONS AS WORDS UNFOLD
THESE PASSIONS OF EMOTIONS SEEK OUTLETS
    FANCY SURFACING THEN CANNOT BE CONTROLLED
AS ARROGANT LONG THOUGHTS SIT AND WAIT
    FOR THE APPROPRIATE MOMENT FOR DISCLOSURE
INTENT CAN BE SOMETHING UNMEANINGFUL
    TRAILING THE HEART INTO SOME FALSE EXPOSURE

I KNOW WHAT YOU SAID BUT...
ONE FUNCTION OF MIND IS MENTAL IMAGES
    IN PIECES OF VISUALS IN THE MIND OF MEMORIES
THIS POWER OF FORMING THINGS NOW ABSENT
    IS THE REPRODUCTIVE IMAGINATION OF THEORIES
WHEREAS FORMING OF IMAGES NEVER SEEN
    OR INCAPABLE OF EXACT EXISTING ILLUSTRATIONS
FANTASIZE OR ENVISION A NON-EXISTENT FACT
    PORTIONS OF REALITY CREATING IMAGINATIONS.

I KNOW WHAT YOU SAID BUT...
EXPRESSIONS CAN EASILY DECEIVE A TRUTH
    WHEN DISTORTED INTERPRETATIONS ARE MISLEAD
ATTITUDE CAN CAUSE THIS POTENTIAL OF ERROR
    AND BE ENTRAPPED, CAUGHT BY SNARE INSTEAD
CHARACTERIZE CIRCUMSTANCES IN GESTURE
    IN PLACE CAUSING CERTAIN WORDS TO SHUDDER
AN INTENT TO EXPRESS WHAT WORDS CANNOT
    INCREASE EFFECTIVENESS OF WORDS THAT UTTER.

I KNOW WHAT YOU SAID, BUT...
TO ACCOMPLISH THE ENTIRE ACHIEVEMENT
    MAY INVOLVE MORE BECAUSE IT'S COMPLICATED
AND WHAT MIGHT SUGGEST, HINT OR SIGNIFY
    BRINGS DESIGN HOW THOUGHTS ARE FABRICATED
IT'S WISE TO BE ALERT WITH A POINT OF VIEW
    DISPLAYING THE FUNCTIONS DIRECTING DEFINITES
INTENDING COULD INFLICT ON EACH VENTURE
    A FRAME OF MIND IN A LANGUAGE OF OPPOSITES

I KNOW WHAT YOU SAID, BUT...
IN ACHIEVING CERTAIN EFFORTS TO PERFORM
    INCLUDES ACTS THAT COMPLETE BELIEFS TO EFFECT
SUGGESTIVE IDEAS CONFIRMING THE MIND
    SKILLED OR EDUCATED PERFORMANCES WE ELECT
ASSUMPTION CAN INSPIRE THE CONFIDENCE
    BECOMING THE PROMISED POSITIVE STATEMENT
MAKING ONESELF SURE OF CREATIVE THOUGHTS
    UNITING RIGHT OR WRONG AS A REQUIREMENT.

I KNOW WHAT YOU SAID, BUT...
TO ACCOMPLISH A SOLE PERSONAL PURPOSE
    INTRODUCES THAT STATE OF BEING SELF ASSURED
FULFILL SELF CONFIDENCE, BRINGING TO PASS,
    THE FOUNDATION GIVING GAINS TO BE ENDURED
UNITED COMBINATION OF OPINIONS DRAWN
    GIVE VISUAL TRACES OF IMAGINARY INDICATIONS
THESE MAY OR MAY NOT REFLECT THE TRUTH
    BUT A MEMORY BY MEANS OF INTERPRETATIONS.

I KNOW WHAT YOU SAID, BUT…;
SINGLY OR SETS OF SYMBOLS, EXPRESS FACTS
    REVEAL THE INNER PERSON BY SIGNS OR FIGURES
EVEN THE SCENT OF TEARS RISING UP INSIDE
    GIVE EXPRESSIONS UPON A FACE WITH TEXTURES
WHEREAS ANTICIPATION CAN INVOLVE THE LIKE
    BY THIS POWERFUL PURPOSE A GOAL IS INVENTED
IF BY CHANCE OBJECTIVE EXPRESSION SLIPS
    UNPLANNED EXPOSURE SURFACES UNINTENDED.

I KNOW WHAT YOU SAID, BUT…
THESE CONSEQUENCES ARE VERY COMPLEX
    EMBRACING GESTURES ACCIDENTALLY AFFIRMED
OFTEN ACCOMPLISH THAT WE DON'T REALIZE
    CONVEYING MANY THOUGHTS TO BE CONFIRMED
WHERE A LAUGHTER USUALLY EXPRESSES JOY
    EXPOSING CHARACTERISTICS IN SPECIAL DISPLAY
LIKEWISE A SURPRISE OR STARTLING EFFECTS,
    BRING SMILES OR FROWNS IN COMMON PORTRAY

I KNOW WHAT YOU SAID, BUT…
JUSTIFICATION IS AN ACT MODIFYING MOTIVE
    WITH ABILITY TO THINK, THEN CAUSE A CAUSE
A JUDGMENT VIEW PICTURIZING CONCLUSIONS
    TO MAKE A CALL, OR DECISION BETWEEN PAUSE
CERTAIN MOMENTS WHEN MOODS ARE EVIDENT
    IN APPLIED WORDS, NONE SHOULD DARE SPEAK
THEN EXPOSES DISPOSITIONS OF EXPRESSIONS
    TRANSFORMS STRONG POINT OF VIEW TO WEAK.

I KNOW WHAT YOU SAID, BUT...
THINGS PRESUMED, GATHERED, SUPPOSED,
    CONCEIVED, BELIEVED, INFERRED OR VISUALIZED.
TAKEN GRANTED, ENVISIONED OR CALCULATED
    IMAGES, SPECULATED, SIGNIFIED OR FANTASIZED
FIXED HINTS WHICH DETERMINATE OR INVOLVE
    CONNECT, SUSPECT, HAVE IN MIND SURMISING
INSINUATE, INDICATE, SUGGEST, GUESS, DESIGN
    FORECAST OPINIONS, EJECT CRITICAL THEORIZING

I KNOW WHAT YOU SAID, BUT...
PICTURES IN DESIGN WHICH ALLOW PRETENCE
    WHERE VOICED ASSUMPTIONS ARE ANNOUNCED
MENTIONED TONES COMMUNICATION REVEALS
    EXPRESSIONS EXPOSE THE WORDS PRONOUNCED
YIELD TO THE SYMBOLS, RECOGNIZE CONTEXT
    ACKNOWLEDGE THESE REMARKABLE INDICATIONS
MANNER OF, RESPECT, COMPREHEND, DISCERN.
    FIGURE OF EVIDENCE FORECAST MANIFESTATIONS.

I KNOW WHAT YOU SAID, BUT...
I'VE CONSIDERED THE FORMER MENTIONED,
    MIXING AND COMBINING IN A VARIETY OF ARRAY
I BLENDED BELIEFS, OPINIONS WITH LANGUAGE
    KNOWING CERTAIN MOODS CHANGE DAY TO DAY
YES, I'VE HEARD YOUR EVERY WORD PLAIN
    AS EVERY ASSORTED IMPLICATION I DID PURSUE
OF COURSE, I KNOW WHAT YOU SAID, BUT...
    MORE IMPORTANTLY THE QUESTION IS...DO YOU?

~

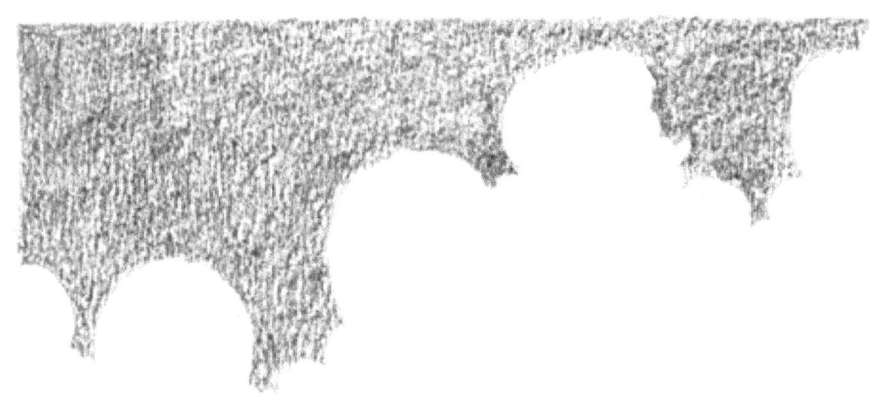

BOX MADE OF PINE

BOX MADE OF PINE

UPON HIS BREAST,
 HIS HANDS CROSS IN REST,
AND BODY INCLINE,
 IN THIS BOX MADE OF PINE,
CORNERS WRAPPED,
 TIN NAILED THEN STRAPPED
EDGES ARE ROUNDED,
 CLAMPED, GLUED, BONDED.

INSIDES ARE LINED,
 OF FABRIC YOU MIGHT FIND,
OR PADDED AROUND,
 WHERE A COTTON IS FOUND,
HINGED UPON TOP,
 CHAINED IN A SAFETY STOP,
AND GASKETED TIGHT,
 SHEDDING DUST AND LIGHT.

ITS LOCKING HASP,
 IS A BRONZE HEAVY CLASP,
AND COLORS FAINT,
 OF A MILD COLORED PAINT,
AND BOX NOW BOUND,
 FOR A HOLE IN THE GROUND,
AND A BODY INCLINE,
 IN THIS BOX MADE OF PINE.

~

CLUMP OF GRASS

Even if I should live with an age,
  Of the Juniper tree or tumblin' sage
I shall not forget desert or hills
  Where clumped grass hug Daffodils.

This forest and desert edge I see,
  Where the tumbleweeds meet the tree,
The former lava, sand and sage,
  The latter in color in a different stage.

Upon this ledge the sand clings,
  The Crows squelch and Robin sings,
So gracefully, the Osprey soars,
  Above cinder beds with open pores.

Desert grouse camouflaged nest,
  Beneath some rock, the scorpion rest,
Rattlers pursue hollow of a stone,
  As the badger digs a hole of its own.

Laurel's age of its shedding bark,
  Twigs are a rest to the Meadowlark,
On this side is a desert of ease,
  On that side stood a hedge of trees.

Old scrub Oaks etched with time,
  On Ponderosas, dines a porcupine,
Darting forth, a Dragonfly sped,
  As a doe rests on a pine needle bed.

Clumped leaflets of grass sway,
  Dandelions break part and give away,
Still waters rest at the creek side,
  Nearby the crickets and skeeter hide.

Of ripples in silver laced stream,
    Come a Skipper's wake in circle's seam,
Alert frogs leap place to place,
    Where the Cattails and gnats interface,

Among wildflowers assorted eyes,
    Caterpillar and butterfly now disguise,
Through blankets in beds of clover,
    Rabbits and squirrels cross trails over.

Creek moves to its reward flow,
    Drifting cattails cloak in a fuzzy blow,
Its banks narrow into a river ties,
    Where clumps of grass on its edge lies.

The desert's air is warm with play,
    Until some greater wind blows it away,
Wisping through brush in a sneeze,
    Of a sudden swirl or a stirring breeze.

Aged trunk of a juniper explodes,
    Among its limbs, the Magpie abodes,
Upon this warped and twisted tree,
    Twigs share space with the Gin berry.

Awkward, brittle lava, twisted look,
    Ruffled, choppy edge of clumsy nook,
Uprooted burl, a cluttered sight.
    A chalkboard of nature's calm delight.

Field flowers are dressed in lace,
    It blooms in spots from place to place.
This tarnished edge now fades,
    As the evening slowly pulls its shades

PATCHES OF BERRIES AND OF BRIAR
    ENTANGLING LOFTY CLIFF ON PRAIRIE ATTIRE
TWISTING VINES CRAWLED THE PARK
    SAP BREACHES TRUNK UPON PITCHY BARK

VANISHED WIND, CROSSING WEAVES
    A WAVING SORTS ITS BLOOMS WITH LEAVES
SHELTERED WIND IN DREAMY SLEEP
    CONFORMING FAMILIAR SOUNDS IN SWEEP

A TWISTED LIMB OR COLOR OF PALE,
    BY WORN SPOTS ON A ZIG-ZAGGING TRAIL,
HOLLOW STUMP OR ROCK DEFORMED,
    WIND BEATEN CREVICE SO ODDLY FORMED.

CROOKED, BENT, UNPOPULAR LUMP,
    A CLUMP OF GRASS OR UNSHAPELY STUMP,
YEA, I DO LOVE THIS ODD SHAPED ART,
    O' HOW I HAVE LOVED HER FROM THE START.

~

LET'S ALL SING A PSALM TOGETHER

(Song 1970-1971)

LET'S ALL SING A PSALM TOGETHER,
LET'S ALL SING A PSALM TOGETHER,
    LET'S TOGETHER NOW PRAY,
    THAT TOGETHER WE'LL STAY,
    LET'S ALL SING A PSALM TOGETHER.

LET'S ALL RE-JOICE TOGETHER,
LET'S ALL RE-JOICE TOGETHER,
    LET'S TOGETHER RE-JOICE
    PRAISING HIM WITH A VOICE.
    LET'S ALL RE-JOICE TOGETHER

LET'S ALL JOIN HANDS TOGETHER
LET'S ALL JOIN HANDS TOGETHER
    JOINING HANDS WITH THE LORD
    TO-GETHER IN ONE ACCORD
    LET'S ALL JOIN HANDS TOGETHER

LET'S ALL BE HAPPY TOGETHER
LET'S ALL BE HAPPY TOGETHER
    HA HA, HA HA, HA HA,
    HA HA, HA HA, HA HA,
    LET'S ALL BE HAPPY TOGETHER.

~

EARLY MORN' SECRETS

EARLY MORN' SECRETS

BREAK OF DAWN DOES DISCOVER
  SUCH A BEAUTY IN EARLY LIGHT,
UNSHACKLES NATURE'S PASSION,
  AS PATTERNED WITH ITS DELIGHT.

LEAFY BOUGHS NOW SWAYING.
  FAINT WINDS SEARCH TO BLOW,
WHILE EARLY MORNING BIRDS,
  SING OUT FROM PUSSY WILLOW.

'TIS COVERED MOSSY ROCKS,
  BLANKETING DEW MORN' TRACE.
YE LITTLE WHITECAP FLOWERS,
  SHOW OUT THEIR KINDLY FACE.

OH WONDROUS BLUE HEAVENS,
  GIVE A JOY OF SUMMER MORN'.
ENCHANTMENT SO STRANGE
  THE FLOWERS BREATH IS BORN.

DOWN THROUGH THE LAURELS,
  UPON A BAREHEADED GROUND,
IN SILENT SONGS FROM TREES,
  STRAY AIR'S UNTAUGHT SOUND.

THE VALLEY PINES STAND TALL,
  A WEALTH OF ITS TOWERS GROW.
AS TWISTING CREEK WONDERS,
  CRISP PURE WATER OVERFLOW.

BLADES OF TALL GRASS TOSS,
  WITH CHEER THAT'S UNAFRAID,
A SMILING MORN' MEADOW.
  BY ITS LIGHT AN BY ITS SHADE

GOLDEN THREADS OF TREASURE
OVER BUTTE RIDGE LIGHT IS BENT
THERE LEAVES OF AGED WOOD
SWEATS DEW OF MORNING SCENT

AGAIN A STREAM IS PAINTED
CERTAIN GUSHES OF WATER SPILL
BIRDS WING BRANCH TO LIMB
TACTFUL TONES OF MAGIC SHRILL.

OH YE BLOSSOMING BOUGHS,
HOW YOUR VISIONS NOW TARRY,
YOUR COLORS GENTLY UNFOLD,
AS YOUR BLOSSOMS DO BERRY.

REFLECTIONS MIRROR IMAGE,
A CLOUD'S TRACKLESS SHADOW,
WILL CAST ITS MANY SHAPES,
OVER THE GLANCES FAR BELOW.

HERE, A PRIMITIVE LANDSCAPE,
GREETS GOLDEN GATEWAY ZONE
MORN BENDS THE WILDERNESS
TO LIGHT THE STEPPING STONE

FROM THE BIRTH OF A SUNRISE
LIGHT BREAKS FROM ITS COVER
COME EARLY MORN' SECRETS,
SUNRISE BEAUTY TO DISCOVER.

~

SEA

Out of the evening,
  As eyes of starlight,
    Kiss heavenly atop the sea....
And changeful moon,
  With its golden face,
    Glimmer out so beautifully...

Who fathoms free?
  This wonder of seas
    How streams to ocean creep
From greatest waves
  To the gentlest swell
    Those charmed waves leap

The tinge of crimson
  Casting on blue waters
    Then reflecting on salty air
From blue distance
  An unashamed Pacific
    Floating its driftwood affair

Designer of storms,
  Repeats musical rain
    Playing with flutelike breeze
White foamy waters,
  Roaring like thunder,
    Upon a shoreline with ease

Tis a visual sight,
  On this glorious earth,
    Where words are salty gold
And in this prayer,
  Upon the sea I stare,
    And imaged dreams unfold

~

WHO SHALL FEED MY BIRDS

WHO SHALL FEED MY BIRDS

SILHOUETTES IN RHYTHM ON DISPLAY
      FLAUNTING ABOUT MY YARD AS TO ASSEMBLE
WITH WINGS THEY APPLAUSE IN PLAY,
      MANNERS OF EXPRESSION IN ARTFUL SYMBOL
WEAVE AND KNIT A ROUTE ON COURSE,
      SMOOTH, EFFORTLESS FLIGHT, UNCHARTED PLOT
IT IS THEIR GIFT IN BOUNDLESS SOURCE
      SCATTERED ABOUT IN AMUSEMENT ON MY LOT.
    OH, IT'S SUCH A JOY TO WATCH MY BIRDS.

BEYOND THE FOREST AS COLORS FADE
      WINGING ABOUT MIDST A FLUTTERING BREEZE
AS GROWS THE GRASS TO THE BLADE
      THEY WHIRL AND NEST THRU' ARMS OF TREES,
SWARM ABOUT WHERE ANGELS TROD
      LITTLE TREASURES A FLYING IN JEWELED SKIES
LIGHT ON LAURELS ABOVE THE SOD,
      BUILDING STUBBLE NEST UP IN HOLLOW TIES
    OH' HOW THE TREES DO HOUSE MY BIRDS

CONSIDER THE RAVEN, THEY NEITHER
      DO SOW, NOR REAP WHICH NEITHER HAVE NOT
STOREHOUSE, NOR BARN NOR EITHER
      BUT GOD FEEDETH THEM WITH A MASTER PLOT
NOW MANY YEARS HAVE PASSED BY
      IN OBSERVING A MANY BIRDS SEEKING SEED
FROM TREE TO TREE THEY FLEE AND FLY
      WITH CHIRPING MUSIC OREGON JUNCOS FEED
    THE LORD HIMSELF FEEDS ALL THE BIRDS,

Spots of thickly grown fresh grass
      Blossoming with raw green steady stem
As Yellow Breasted Chats trespass
      Towhees dot edges of lawn's green hem
Tall stylish trees unfold their arms
      Where Flycatchers and Phoebes do light
Dancing Daisies claiming charms
      Wagtails and Pipits sing themes in flight
    Stem and worms shall feed my birds

Pine needles scatter about brittle
      Forms buds on boughed branches stout
Where pitchy knots twisted a little
      Warblers and Vireos roll and turn about
Gracefully in air fly the Swallows
      Diving or turning with their fluent quotes
Joining at times the Swipe follows
      With a fluttering flows of chattered notes
    Trees and insects shall feed my birds

Artful fields of wandering grass
      Rotating leafed bushes in a rhythm sway
A darting Wrentit twirls to pass
      Nearby quivering beams on a sunny day
Redpolls exposing flaps in flight
      Hastens a Brown Creeper place to place
Catbirds dash in and out of sight
      Enjoy matchless spring to now embrace
    The warm spring sun cheers my birds.

All around the property borders
        Boundaries of fence line, trees or shrub
Bobolink whistles various orders
        Thieving Jays fly from stub to feeder stub
Meadowlarks in flutelike phrases
        Then emerges Grey Partridge or Grouse
Bird's morning music paraphrases
        Soft lyrics from Grosbeaks and Titmouse
I'll tend the feeders that feed my birds.

I whistled tunes in my boyhood
        For mocking different birds of their kind
Climbed trees with barked wood
        Seeking the unused nest they left behind
Kingbirds catch food on the wing
        And he fears none save the Martins line
A Bobwhite repeats in a chirping
        His own name while melodies intertwine
This fruit of the vine it feeds my birds.

Descending dew spring showers
        Nature itself delights in seeding its oats
Redstarts brilliance like flowers
        As Poorwills utter various skilled notes
A bird it fears no snare or trap
        Trills with an occasional change in pitch
Sparrows bid tail feathers clap
        Upon a hush of air, the shrills do switch
As wild seeds of nature feeds my birds.

BUNTINGS TURF IN FLUSH OF SPRING
       WHERE YELLOW-BIRDS, SHOW OFF WITH SPARK
I HEAR THE ALARM BUSHTITS BRING
       AS FLICKERS SWOOP IN A LANDSCAPED PARK
NEIGHBORING HILLS UNFOLD PATCHES
       PLEASANT FIELDS OF FRESH EMERALD GARDEN
UPSIDE-DOWN ON A TREE NUTHATCHES
       TURKEYS APPEAR ON A GROUND UNTRODDEN
THE BLOOMS OF FLOWERS FEED MY BIRDS.

WOODPECKERS MAY DRILL THEIR HOLES
       ON TOP OF LIMBLESS AND WELL PECKED SPUR
AS LOUD WHISTLED NOTES OF ORIOLES
       A LIVELY MERGING OF MUSICAL NOTES OCCUR
A PHEASANT LANDS TO RUN CONCEALED
       BLUEBIRD'S PERCH UPON A LIMB WITH A VIEW
RED WINGED BLACKBIRDS RAID A FIELD
       AND THE MAGPIE'S A THIEF WHO WILL PURSUE
ON THIS PROPERTY, I CALL THEM MY BIRDS.

ALL NATURE IS PATTERNED UNPOLLUTED
       NIGHTHAWKS WILL FEED AT DUSK ON THE WING
AGAIN THE MOUNTAIN CREST SALUTED
       BROADCASTING THE ROBIN'S SONG OF SPRING
HORNED LARKS TINKLING MUSIC TRILLS
       OTHER LARKS SING IN CHEERY ALTERED NOTES
THE WILD VEERYS SILVER VOICED FRILLS
       SONGBIRDS MIX TWEETS IN VARIOUS REMOTES
WHERE SUNFLOWER SEEDS FEED MY BIRDS.

Mockingbirds or Thrashers attend
       Accomplishing usual ways to duplicate
Fabricate tones in pleasant blend
       Determined to mimic what others dictate
Nest of mosses, twigs and grasses
       Splotched eggs, a bluish freckled whiten
In warbles a Red Crossbill passes
       As canyons ring with songs of the Wren
      Even my Guinea Hens call to my birds

Upon wings of spring a Cowbird
       Suddenly chatters and then would tarry
On the edge of breezes windward
       A Killdeer nest sets in a shallow quarry
I will reminisce to again review
       These faded images of Kinglets' domain
Years passed and much withdrew
       Likely I'll never see those glances again
      But memories still embrace my birds.

Dove's coo-croo soft rolling voice
       For good news, soars to perch for peace
The Tangers are a colorful choice
       A ventriloquist of buzzing sound release
Pine Siskins whistle tones of joy,
       Finches' sweet world of musical airways
Filling my void they do employ
       All these morning songs begin my days
      My happiness itself nourishes my birds

OVER THE CROPS WHERE SUN PEEKS
     THE MARTINS DRIVE HAWKS OR ROGUES AWAY
A CUCKOO FOR CATERPILLARS SEEKS
     REPEATING ITS NAME IN AN ECHOED DISPLAY
A FLOCK OF GRACKLES FEED TOGETHER
     FLITTING ACROSS A BLOOM OF BUD SWELLINGS
IN PLUMP GRAY TO CHESTNUT FEATHER
     CHICKADEES NEST IN TREE CAVITY DWELLINGS
THEN UP THEY SWOOP TO JOIN MY BIRDS

A STARLING WILL RATTLE AND SQUEAK
     IN MIMIC CALLS, HE WHEEZES AND WHISTLES
AS GOLDFINCHES PLAY HIDE N' SEEK
     PATCHES OF TALL BUSHY UNWEEDED THISTLES
THE WEAVER PROJECTS AN INTENSE CALL
     BUT A NUTCRACKER CHIRPS A HARSH GROWL
CROWS BELLOW 'CAW CAW' IN A SQUALL
     BY WIT MORE INTERESTING THAN OTHER FOWL
I HEAR EACH OF THE SOUNDS OF MY BIRDS.

YELLOWTHROATS TO TWISTED SHELLS
     TO SWIFTS' MUSICAL SPEECHES OF AIR SKILLS
I LAY AWAKE, AND MY HEART SWELLS
     WHEN EARLY BIRDS CROSS THE WINDOWSILLS
THEN FROM TREE TO SHRUB THEY HOP
     THRUSHES CHEER CHITTER IN MORN' TWINKLE
PORCH FEEDER OF SUGARWATER DROP
     HUMMINGBIRDS SIP UNTIL WATERS WRINKLE
BY HUMMIN' OR WHISTLES I HEAR MY BIRDS.

Friendly Waxwing lights on a tree
        Quails clucking notes are a drift to hear
So wild Pigeons are shy in degree
        A Townsends Solitaire sings loud, clear
Gnatcatchers singing like banjos
        As the Wood Peewees are on a lookout
For Beetles, Wasps or Mosquitoes
        And other insects that come near about
The Peacock's fan entertains my birds

Tunes and echoes in toil of day
        A Lapland Longspur then stops to rest
Bird's songs, my hearts bouquet
        While Sapsuckers lie in the cavities nest
I fancy all birds of different sort
        For certainty birds are my jewels of joy
Be still and listen to their report
        A concert of musical chitchats to enjoy
How I will listen just to hear my birds

As I make my travels to the coast
        With rivers or streams before the shore
I look for Western Gulls foremost
        For Waterbirds to Shorebirds I explore
There Seagulls exhibit illustration
        Ahoy! converse in squelch and squawk
Salt air brings their congregation
        To the Pelican or Sanderlings they talk
The fish and seaweeds feed my birds.

THE SWAN IS GRACE AND FANCY-FREE
  PLEASING COLORS CHANGE AS FEATHERS FOLD
A GREAT EGRET ON AN ESTUARY I SEE
  AS SANDPIPERS TRILL IS A SOUND TO BEHOLD
OR REMARKABLE JOURNEYS OF TERNS
  FROM A RED PHALAROPE OR SORA OR RAILS
TO VOCAL PERFORMANCES OF BITTERNS
  OR A CORMORANTS GRUNTING CALL IN DETAILS
  ON SEASHORES, ESTUARIES I SEE MY BIRDS

AMONG DUCKS, THE MALLARD OR TEAL
  A MERGANSER, GOOSE, OR SOUND OF SNIPE
GREBES LOUD ROLLING "CRREE" SQUEAL
  OR KINGFISHER WHERE WATER SHORES SWIPE
A DIPPER BOBS UP, DOWN IN STROKES
  THE YODELING OF A LOON, I'LL NEVER FORGET
A GREAT BLUE HERON'S HARSH CROAKS
  TO AMERICAN COOTS, DUNLIN, OR THE WILLET
  THE MARSH, GRASSLANDS ARE FOR MY BIRDS.

ALSO INCLUDED ARE CURLEW OR CRANE
  IN WHISPERING WATERS, IBIS QUEST IS FOUND
STILTS IN FRESH TO SALTWATER'S TERRAIN
  A LONG-LEGGED DOWITCHER STANDS AROUND
MURRELETS ONLY COME INLAND TO BREED
  BUT YELLOWLEG'S SOUNDINGS ECHO ASHORE
WATERBIRDS HOVER ABOVE BRIAR WEED
  INTO CATTAIL BEDS SCATTERED THICKETS MORE
  SMILES DWELL LONGER CAUSE OF MY BIRDS

But to Buzzards I make allowance
       Hawks, Falcons, Kites, Owls and Osprey
Raptors, Harriers, vultures glance
       To Merlins and flesh eating birds of prey
Strong wings hook beak and claw.
       Yet they, and Eagles, I differently admire
They soar till shadows withdraw
       Gliding at a far distance I happily desire
     Visual pleasure but they're not my birds

When winter settles in the valley
       And bird's food source becomes scarce
I hear their cascading music rally
       From unseen singers in a tree or terrace
I'll look to the feeders being bare,
       This is at a time when sap returns to root
I'll hear their call, feel their stare
       Then must return to fill the feeder's loot
     Again I look forward to feeding my birds.

So...be chattering or gargles anew
       Upon lighter wings they skimmed along
Fluted whistles of feathered crew
       Twittering harmony in a mixture of song,
If flesh and soul divide in twain
       Or rather if I should die in other words
I ponder the questions that remain
       Oh' who else then...shall feed my birds??
     Oh' who else then...shall feed my birds??

~

GRANDMA

GRANDMA

SHE WALKS ABOUT WITH SONG IN HEART,
      AND DREAMS OF LONG AGO,
OF THINGS DONE, WHEN SHE WAS YOUNG,
      THINGS NO ONE ELSE KNOW.

THEN DECIDES, TO SHARE HER THOUGHT,
      MEMORIES SHE TELLS AT LAST,
THAT SHE'S HELD INSIDE, NOW IN PAUSE,
      SHE TELLS OF A HAPPY PAST.

SHE KNOWS LITTLE BIT ABOUT EVERYONE,
      SHE'S BEEN AROUND A WHILE,
RECALLS SMALL THINGS OTHERS FORGOT,
      OL' HAPPENINGS IN A SMILE.

HER CAMPING, HUNTING, FISHING TRIPS,
      REMINISCING OF YESTERDAY
GOOD TIMES, BAD TIMES, OR BETWEEN,
      SHE WOULDN'T TRADE AWAY.

SHE CRIED AT TIMES WITH BROKEN HEART,
      FROM A THOUGHT SHE RECALL,
BUT HAPPY TIMES WERE MANY TIMES,
      AND LOVELY WERE THEY ALL.

SHE LAYS AWAKE INTO THE WEE OF NIGHT
      THINKS OF GOOD OLD PAST.
THEN ROLLS OVER, AND AFTER A PRAYER,
      FALLS FAST TO SLEEP AT LAST.

TOGETHER WITH HER MATE, SHE DREAMS
      WAITING ON HIM WITH LOVE,
BUT NOW HE'S GONE, WAITING ON HER,
      IN A BIG HOUSE UP ABOVE.

MUCHLY CONCERNED ABOUT EVERYONE,
         SHE LIKES TO HELP THEM ALL,
AND DOES SO MUCH, WITHOUT A TOUCH,
         LETTING THEM KNOW TO CALL.

SHE LOVES HER FAMILY AND CHILDREN,
         IT IS NEEDLESS TO EVEN SAY,
SEE HER ACT, WHEN TROUBLE'S ABOUT,
         JUST TRY TO KEEP HER AWAY.

SHE BAKES, COOKS AN' CLEANS HOUSE,
         GARDENS UP THE GROUNDS.
ENJOYS FLOWERS, IN HER VASE, AND
         NOSTALGIC, MUSIC SOUNDS.

HER GOOD OLD WAYS IN ALL HER DAYS,
         ARE RECORDED BY AND BY,
WHERE ALL THE LINES UPON HER FACE
         HER LIFE'S ENGRAVINGS LIE.

HER LIKELY SMILE ESPECIALLY BEAMS,
         FILLED WITH PRECIOUS SIGHT,
IF ONLY SMILES WERE MADE OF CANDLES,
         SHE'D LIGHT A DARKEST NIGHT.

HER EYES GREW DIM, HAIRS HAVE GRAY,
         YET SO PRECIOUSLY WE SAW,
HER LOVE FOR US HAS NOT GROWN DIM,
         THIS ONE CALLED "GRANDMA".

~

THE TEST

Loneliness, in the thought of her,
    Would wake me and then,
    Surround me with tears, as it began,
        I'd reach out for her, and wonder why,
        Realizing even the fool, greater than I
    Could easily pass this test.

My love for her was engraved,
    So intense within my heart,
    She's in my paths long before I start,
        Cannot live dreams nor touch a blur,
        I only fool myself, I know it's not her,
    So, I must act out the rest.

Could this be my imagination,
    In fantasizing that much?
    Puts flame in my heart by her touch,
        Stirring a passion where both we fit,
        I could take our love and live by it,
    Her vision is my conquest.

Devoted test in lonely sleep,
    Then two became a team,
    Untouching good-nite kiss in dream.
        I sense her smiles, projecting delight,
        Feel her presence both day and night.
    Without her, time is stillest,

And more fine than soft music
    Her unfading voice sings
    I see her image with invisible wings,
        As she alone acting my counterpart
        She is my other half, that better part,
    Here the test will manifest.

~

CAN THIS BE?

Is this again the same dream repeated,
　　That I've feared in youth,
Where the nights would come and go,
　　Then to find myself alone
Only why should I pretend any longer
　　To hide part of this truth
For who could possibly read the heart
　　And not turn every stone.

I am weary and tired of acting the part,
　　That I can no longer play
I am but a plain and but a simple man,
　　Who pretends to be strong,
But when evening comes I grow weak
　　Sick at heart if you're away.
For it comes, it goes, then comes again
　　Is this right or is it wrong?

Because of this lonesome inward hurt
　　I've acted foolish, I agree,
The effects a wounded heart expresses
　　Neither could any explain
You, claiming it's "no big deal" to you.
　　But not the same for me
If when nightfall comes and I'm alone
　　My sleepless hours remain.

　　And I said to myself "can this be?"
　　A distance between us crushes me
　　Oh' what gates must I open dear
　　So when eve comes, you'll be near??

You can accuse me of being insecure
      Maybe I don't understand
Or question why I want to be with you,
      Every night of every year?
You know Darling, you're all I live for,
      You knew that beforehand
And about the loneliness I experience
      So often I've made it clear.

The day ends without you, then silence
      Nights come, I'll die inside
The phone rings, my heart would rush
      Then it calms as you speak,
Just hearing your words brings a glow
      Again I feel you at my side
Until you hang up, I continue to cover
      Inner feeling, empty, weak.

All alone at night I weep into darkness,
      A blend of midnight shade,
My evening scattered thoughts of you
      Embrace you're absentee
You know all my grief, and you alone,
      Make the difference made
Neither could I make your heart lonely
      So you want to be with me.

      And I said to myself "Can this be?"
      A distance between us crushes me
      Oh' what gates must I open dear
      So when eve comes, you'll be near??

SOME MAY GAZE UPON ME TO BE CURSED.
PERHAPS I'M A FOOL BROKEN,
UNABLE TO REST, CAUSE OF LONESOME FEAR
AS I LIE AWAKE, HALF ASLEEP
I AM SICK OF LIFE IN NIGHTS WITHOUT YOU.
EXPRESSED BUT NOT SPOKEN,
ALL PATCHES OF APPETITE THEN DISAPPEAR
AS THE EVENING GREW DEEP.

THEN I ASK MYSELF WHY SHORTEN MY JOY
WHY SHOULD WE EVER PART?
COULD IT BE TRADITIONAL VIEWS OF OTHERS,
YOU'VE COMPARED WITH OURS?
I HAVE NO OTHER PERSON TO LEAN ON DEAR
ALONE, THIS MELTS MY HEART.
I NEED YOU AT MY SIDE WHEN NIGHT FALLS
TO EMBRACE IN THOSE HOURS.

WITHOUT YOU BIRDS WOULD SING NO MORE
ALL MUSIC THEN FORGOTTEN,
MY REMAINDER OF LIFE WOULD BE EMPTIED
BELLS WOULD HAVE NO RINGS
A BEAUTY IN FLOWERS WOULD CEASE TO BE
NOR COLOR IN LIFE BEGOTTEN
I'LL EMBRACE YOU HERE, WHEN YOU'RE NOT,
THIS YOUR ABSENCE BRINGS.

AND I SAID TO MYSELF "CAN THIS BE?"
A DISTANCE BETWEEN US CRUSHES ME
OH' WHAT GATES MUST I OPEN DEAR
SO WHEN EVE COMES, YOU'LL BE NEAR??

And I always wonder when you're gone
    If you think of me at night
Or are you just content by being alone
    As you embrace mid-air
Am I in your thoughts when eve nears
    Do you long to again unite?
Does an emptiness enter in your heart
    While mine is in despair

So now here I am once again all alone
    Just before daylight fades
I'll try harder to find some things to do
    For end of day's duration
I called out her name without thinking
    Before reality escalades
And find myself companionless again
    But unto her, a vacation.

Your flowery brilliance smiles at me so
    Of cheeks that hold blush
My joy ends if your silence fills the gap
    All reason becomes unfair,
Still, every time when a nightfall comes
    And I but hear your hush
I'll reach across just to touch you, then
    Grieve if you're not there.

    And I said to myself "can this be?"
    A distance between us crushes me
    Oh' what gates must I open dear
    So when eve comes, you'll be near??

~

DESTROY MY THOUGHT

DESTROY MY THOUGHT

Tho' I'm wrong,
    O' make me strong,
        Yea, Lord tonight.
O' bend thy ear,
    And guide me near
        To walk in Thy light

Yea…help me free,
    Myself unto Thee
        I pray, O' my Lord.
My unrighteous way,
    Of moldered decay,
        But O' Thy sword.

For lo! Release
    A forever peace
        So that I can find,
A faded sorrow,
    Today….tomorrow,
        Within my mind.

Destroy my thought,
    It is wrong a lot,
        O' will Thee mend,
Within my core,
    O' Christ is more,
        Than just a friend.

~

MR. WORLDY AND MR. FAITH

MR. WORLDY AND MR. FAITH

MR. WORLDLY AND MR. FAITH,
        WENT TO A CHURCH ONE DAY,
MR. WORLDLY TO PASS THE TIME,
        AS MR. FAITH WENT TO PRAY.

MR. WORLDLY SAT IN THE BACK,
        DREAMING OF FUTURE DAYS,
MR. FAITH WENT TO THE ALTAR,
        TO GIVE GOD MUCH PRAISE.

MR. WORLDLY IN HIS STRENGTH,
        WAS STRESSED WITH SORROW,
MR. FAITH OF SPIRITUAL STRENGTH,
        OF JOY DEEP IN HIS MARROW.

MR. WORLDLY, LEFT UNSAVED,
        AS CHURCH ENDED THAT DAY,
MR. FAITH, THEN AFTER PRAYER,
        HE THEN LEFT, WENT HIS WAY.

MR. WORLDLY THAT VERY NIGHT,
        FOUND DEATH UPON HIS BED,
MR. FAITH IN THAT SAME HOUR,
        THEY FOUND HIS BODY DEAD.

MR. WORLDLY, FOREVER SORRY,
        FOR IN HELL WAS NO REPENT,
MR. FAITH, WITH A JOY FOREVER,
        A WORTHY FAITH WELL SPENT.

~

I AM WHAT I AM

I AM WHAT I AM, AND YOU ARE WHAT YOU ARE,
 WE ARE WHAT WE BOTH HAVE BECOME THUS FAR
I'M CURRENTLY MYSELF, WHATEVER THAT MAY BE
 AND YOU ARE WHAT YOU ARE SO FOREIGN TO ME.
WE BOTH CHANGED A LITTLE HERE, A LITTLE THERE
 AND STILL BE DIFFERENT SOMEHOW, SOMEWHERE
WITH CERTAIN UNLIKENESS BETWEEN EACH OTHER
 WITH DISSIMILAR OPINIONS INSIDE ONE ANOTHER

SO I AM NOT WHAT YOU ARE, NEITHER ARE YOU I
 WE SHOULD RECEIVE EACH OTHER WITHOUT ALIBI
I WAS MADE ME AND YOU WERE MADE AS YOU
 APPROACHING SUBJECTS WITH A DIFFERENT VIEW
YOU MAY NOT LIKE THE WAY I LOOK OR APPEAR
 OR A COMMENT I'LL MAKE THAT YOU MIGHT HEAR
DESIGNED FROM WHAT MY EXPERIENCES BEGOT
 YOU CANNOT DISCERN ME, BECAUSE YOU'RE NOT

I AM WHAT I AM, I AM A PRODUCT OF MY PAST
 WITH WORTHLESS DIFFERENCE WE ALL BROADCAST
I DESIRE TO BE BETTER, FOR LIFE IS SHORT ITSELF
 AND NOT BE SOME OTHER, BUT JUST BE MYSELF
I DO NOT EXPECT ANY TO MOLD FROM MY MOLD
 BUT ALLOW THEIR OWN LIFE IN STAGES TO UNFOLD
FOR GOD CREATED US ALL EXACTLY HOW WE ARE
 OF QUALITIES AND FAULTS, WITH MARS AND SCAR

I'LL LEARN SOME GOOD FROM ALL THOSE AROUND
 EVEN CHANGE MY WAYS TO BETTER WAYS FOUND
AND MY CHANGES MAY NOT BE TO YOUR DESIGN.
 FOR CHOICES OF ALTER IS NOT YOURS, IT IS MINE
YOU ARE WHAT YOU ARE BY THE CHOICES MADE
 THEN I AM WHAT I AM FROM MY OWN CRUSADE
SO BEFORE CRITICIZING ME WITH YOUR SARCASM
 LOOK BEYOND THIS SHELL OF WHO I REALLY AM

YOU MAY NOT APPROVE MY HAIR OR MY DRESS
  OR BLUNT WAYS OF TALKING IN AGGRESSIVENESS
I CANNOT CHANGE TO WHAT YOU WANT ME TO BE
  BECAUSE MY CHARACTER IS DISTINCTIVE TO ME.
EVEN IF I COULD COPY YOUR IMAGE IN DISPLAY
  SOMEONE ELSE MIGHT WANT ME TO BE AS THEY
THEN IF I CHANGED TO BE LIKE THEM, I KNOW
  ANOTHER WOULD DESIRE ME TO BE THEIR SHOW.

ONE CANNOT BECOME SOME OTHER THEY SEEK
  EVERYONE OF US, EVEN MYSELF, WE'RE UNIQUE
SOME LONG FOR ME TO BE LIKE THEM IN WAYS
  BUT I AM WHAT I AM FROM MY BY-GONE DAYS
I'M ONE OF A KIND, UNCOMMON AND STRANGE
  A PECULIAR INDIVIDUAL OF DISTINCTIVE CHANGE.
OF SPECIAL CHARACTERISTICS EXCLUSIVE OR ODD
  BUT I AM WHAT I AM, AS WAS CREATED BY GOD

DESPAIR, DEFEAT, JOYOUS MEMORIES AND PAIN
  THESE EXPERIENCES PASS BUT WOUNDS REMAIN
AND THE ME THAT I WAS MAY AGAIN OVERCOME
  FROM TRIALS OF LIFE, A BETTER PERSON BECOME
I'LL HAVE GOOD, SOME BAD, SOME IN BETWEEN,
  SOME BAD, OVERLOOKED, SOME GOOD UNSEEN
EXPERIMENTS END, AS EXPERIENCES EMBRACE
  THESE EPISODES MODIFY LIVES THAT INTERLACE

I AM ALSO FASHIONED BY LIFE'S GAINS AND LOSS
  TRIALS CHANGED MY PERSON BY PATHS I CROSS
LIKEWISE YOURSELF, ARE DIFFERENT THAN BEFORE
  LIFE'S ENCOUNTERS CAUSE CHANGE TO RESTORE
BY ROOTS AND FOREFATHERS I ADOPTED A NATURE
  BY EXPERIENCES OR GOD, I'M A NEW CREATURE
AND YOUR MAKEUP IS SO DIFFERENT THAN MINE
  NOR COULD I BE THE YOU THAT YOURSELF DESIGN

ON PATHS OF BITTERNESS TO TRAILS OF KINDNESS
    I WAS TAUGHT TO SEEK GOOD IN ALL, REGARDLESS
TO LET EACH MAN GRASP WHATEVER THEY DESIRE
    AS FOR MYSELF, BE CONTENT IN WHAT I REQUIRE
IN DAILY LIFE IF I DISCERN ANOTHER WITH NEEDS
    I TRY TO MAKE A DIFFERENCE WITH SOME DEEDS
WHEREFORE WHO JUDGES WHERE I FIT OR BELONG
    FOR I AM WHAT I AM, SOME RIGHT, SOME WRONG

TODAY I WONDER; IF I HADN'T BEEN BORN AT ALL
    WOULD ANY FLOURISH THAT I'VE CAUSED TO FALL?
WHO IS IT THAT MAY PROSPER BY MY ABSENTEE?
    WOULD MY NONEXISTENCE BRING A JOY TO BE?
OR IF MY BEING HAS CAUSED ANY TO BACKSLIDE
    BE ASSURED IT WASN'T BAD INTENT FROM INSIDE
NEVER LESS, I APOLOGIZE AND AGAIN RESUBMIT
    I'M ONLY WHAT I AM AND THAT'S WHAT YOU GET.

I CLOSE MY EYES IN SLUMBER AND REACH INSIDE
    BRINGS OUT VARIOUS, UNIQUE VIEWS THAT HIDE
WAS SOMEONE HURT BY SOMETHING SMALL SAID
    OR SOMETHING I DID WITHOUT LOOKING AHEAD?
AND WHY THEY ARE CRUSHED, I HAVEN'T A CLUE
    FUNNY ISN'T IT, HOW TINY THINGS MISCONSTRUE
EVEN IF I ATTEMPT TO CONVERT MYSELF THEN FALL.
    I AM BASICALLY ME; I AM WHAT I AM, THAT'S ALL.

ASIDE OUR DIFFERENCES I KNOW WE CAN BLEND
    IF WE CAN JUST BE OURSELVES AND NOT PRETEND
I AM WHAT I AM THAT'S ALL, NO MORE, NO LESS
    FOR I AM WHAT I AM WITH NO ONE TO IMPRESS.
I AM WHAT I AM UNTIL I FALL SHORT OR IMPROVE
    EVEN THEN I'M MYSELF; FOR CHANGES REPROVE
WE EACH TAKE ON TRAITS, A FEATURED DIAGRAM
    SO BY THE GRACE OF GOD, I AM JUST WHAT I AM

~

ROSES OF TWENTY-EIGHT

MUCH OF THE PAST I REMINISCE,
    OF OUR TIMES SPENT TOGETHER DEAR,
SO OFTEN I REMIND MYSELF,
    THAT WITHOUT YOU I WOULD PERISH,
YOU'RE AN ANGEL IN MY LIFE.
    WHO HAS BLESSED MY EVERY YEAR,
ONLY YOU CAN OFFER TO ME,
    THE GENTLE TOUCHES THAT I CHERISH.

I LOVE YOU SWEETIE, SO MUCH,
    O' MORE THAN COULD BE MEASURED,
EVEN TRIALS IN HARD TIMES,
    IN HAPPY TIMES OR SHARING TEARS,
TOGETHER WE HAVE ADJUSTED,
    INTO A ONENESS TO BE TREASURED,
HAPPY ANNIVERSARY N' THANKS,
    FOR TWENTY-EIGHT ROSES OF YEARS.

~

OUR THREE SONS

As one by one around my chair
They stand in line a waiting there,
Three lovely boys.

And all at once they happily speak
Of what they did or what they seek
N' about their toys.

How they tumble around my seat
To remove shoes from off my feet
Happy, joyful play.

Tellin' me of what they did outside
Like secret places where they hide
Games played that day

Then with a style each of his own
Expressing love n' feelings known
A special pleasure.

My precious sons tonight I'll hold
There upon my lap of which I fold
Yea, this I treasure.

A song or happy jokes n' silly talk
About' Jack n' me n' the beanstalk
We laugh together.

I'd get down like a horse n' crawl
To let them ride and let them fall
Into a pile gather.

FINALLY I TUCK THEM EACH INTO BED
SHARING PRAYERS WERE THEN SAID
GOODNIGHT LITTLE ONES.

I'LL FINALLY REST WITH MOTHER AWHILE
TO THANK HER FOR HER LOVELY SMILE
AND OUR THREE SONS.......

~

OUR THREE SONS

OH DAD, IT'S JUST THE THOUGHT

O' Glorious sky that looks
    Down upon a city of the grave
The dead lie there asleep
    Neither voice nor sound gave.

Plucked by angel's wings,
    Fading from all sight of trials.
Oft' I see him once again,
    The look upon his face, smiles.

This hush with silent sleep
    Scattered of memories hidden
Plucked of life's harvest
    Placed into a world forbidden

Ah! And for what reason
    Do his echoes no longer ring
Or his shadow cast about
    In the warmth of early spring

Oh Dad, It's just the thought
    Of not ever seeing you again
Alas! Came the final hour
    Which you could not remain

Unswayed by costly things,
    Or the fancy ways to impress
In his own simple approach
    He projected thoughtfulness.

Those tunes echo no more
    Of songs he played back then
Silent are his guitar strings
    And hums to a familiar hymn

O FAINT BREATH OF FRAGRANT
    HIS COAT STILL HANGS IN THE HALL
YET, VOICELESS ARE VISIONS
    THAT SEEM TO RISE AND THEN FALL

FOR WHAT POSSIBLE REASON
    AM I LEFT IN THIS PLACE I'LL ASK?
AND FOR HOW MUCH LONGER
    MUST I HIDE BEHIND THIS MASK?

OH DAD, IT'S JUST THE THOUGHT
    OF HAVING YOU, AGAIN NEARBY
ALAS! MISS YOUR SMILING FACE
    YOUR LAUGHTER, GRIN, YOUR CRY.

THE THOUGHT BEING SO FINAL
    MAKES IT SO DIFFICULT TO REASON
CAUSING MY SENSES TO STRAY
    I'M A MAN BORN OUT OF SEASON.

TEARS CHOKED IN THE DUST
    DESTROYING SMILES FROM FACES
NOTHING MORE BE REQUIRED
    FROM HIS MOVEMENT OR TRACES

SILVER GRAYS PRANCE ABOUT
    REMINDING OF HIS SIMPLE WAYS
AND SMELL OF WOOD SMOKE
    RECALL ANEW OLD CAMPFIRE DAYS.

THAT SO-CALLED FRUIT OF DEATH
    I CAN ONLY IMAGINE WHAT MAY BE.
WITHIN A DIFFERENT DIMENSION
    ANOTHER LIVING CITY IN ABSENTEE

OH DAD, IT'S JUST THE THOUGHT
    OF YOU WHO CAN NO MORE HUG
ALAS! NOR KISS YOUR CHEEK
    OR TO FEEL YOUR EMBRACING TUG.

YET IN MY UNDERSTANDING
    I STILL MISS HIS LIFE'S DISGUISE
THEN IN FOOLISHNESS I AWAKE
    ONLY TO SEE DEATH IN HIS EYES

NONE COULD CONVINCE ME,
    A THRUSTING UPON IMAGINATION
I SOUGHT A TRUTH, UNSWAYED
    FINDING LIFE ITSELF A TRIBULATION

YONDER CITY OF FELLOWMEN
    LEFT TRAILS A PATTERN IN THOUGHT
SO I MUST CONTINUE IN BATTLE
    FIGHT THE FIGHT THAT HE FOUGHT.

SO SAND ENCIRCLES HIS GRAVE
    IN THAT QUIET HIGH DESERT PLACE
AND I WITH A HOLLOW SHOUT
    CAN ONLY LONG FOR HIS EMBRACE.

OH DAD, IT'S JUST THE THOUGHT
    OF THAT GREAT LOVE YOU SHARED
ALAS! YOU CAME, AND YOU LEFT
    WHILE I REMAINED UNPREPARED

FEEBLE STORIES, ECHOES PAST
    FOREVER NOW LOCKED IN HEARTS
HIS KIND WORDS LEFT UNSAID
    APPEAR TO FLOAT AWAY IN PARTS.

SHADES OF NIGHT HAVE FALLEN
 SUDDENLY I FIND MYSELF ALONE
HOW HIS HEART ONCE DID BEAT
 ALONG THE RHYTHM OF MY OWN.

THE SOURCE CANNOT REMAIN
 FULFILLING THAT JOY HE INSPIRED
LONG IDLE DAYS CAME EMPTY
 WHEN HE LEFT AS WAS REQUIRED

O' FOR WHAT REASON I ASK
 WAS MY BEST FRIEND ALSO DAD
FOR THE TIMES WE SHARED
 WERE THE VERY BEST I EVER HAD

OH DAD, IT'S JUST THE THOUGHT
 THAT I'LL NEVER SEE YOU AGAIN
ALAS! UNTIL I ALSO JOIN ANEW
 WITHIN THE CITY OF FELLOWMEN

~

OLD CHRISTMAS IMAGE

TIME PASSES BY, OVER A SUN PARCHED
EMERALD GRAY,
WHERE CHALKINESS OF SNOW NATURALLY
WHITENS DAY,

WATER VAPOR FROZEN INTO CRYSTALS OF
GLISTEN WHITE,
REFLECTING AN IMAGE WHERE ASSORTED
COLORS UNITE

SWEEPING CLOUDS PRANCE THE CHILLED
RIPPLED SKY,
ABOVE WHITENED LOWLANDS, SHADOWS
BREATH SUPPLY

THIS AMOROUS BLOOM OF CHRISTMAS,
WHITISH GLARE,
THE HEAVENLY MUSIC, OVERFLOWS INTO
EXALTED PRAYER.

OVER BRILLIANT SILENT LAKE COVERED IN
LUSTROUS SKIM,
AN OLD FASHIONED CHRISTMAS LOOK OF
VISUAL HYMN.

A SPIRIT OF ENCHANTMENT, STIRS ABOUT
WHIRLED SNO'
ITS FROST BITTEN BERRIES ERE BUNCHED
IN MISTLETOE,

UNSPEAKABLE HARMONIES THROUGHOUT
MISTY LANDSCAPES
THIS LUSTROUS VALLEY BLANKETED WITH
ITS SNOWFLAKES.

CHEERED WINTER FLIGHT AMONG CLOUDS
LOOKING DOWN,
SCATTERED BIRDS WING ABOUT IN MERRY
MUSIC SOUND.

WITHIN THE CANYONS CAVITY AND COVER
SNOW DEEP
UNTRAPPED MOTIONLESS BEAR REST IN A
WINTER SLEEP.

HILLS OF ANGEL MISSION, DEER'S PROJECT
THEIR CALL
FREELY THEY PLAYED ATOP A POWDERED
WHITE FALL.

SWEET MUSIC'S CHEERFUL ATMOSPHERE
VOICELESS SONG
IN VIBRANT MELODIES THE CREEKS PATH
MOVES ALONG.

ACROSS ITS VALLEYS HORIZON AND UPON
MOUNTAIN CREST
THE SPIRIT OF CHRISTMAS WHISPERS IN
FREEDOM BLEST

LIKE BEFORE THE HUSH OF WINTER AGAIN
TIMELESSLY WITHSTOOD
TRAILS ARE NOW COVERED WITH FLAKES IN
THIS NEIGHBORHOOD

THE FRUITLESS KNOTTED TREES SCATTERED
MOUNTAINS TONGUE,
WEATHER-BEATEN BEAUTY BROAD ARMED
AND OVERHUNG.

EACH WEARY LUSTY LIMB SHED MOST ITS
SUMMER WIG,
SCABBY LEAFLESS BOUGH WITH SNOW ON
EACH TWIG.

MEMORY HAUNTED IMAGE A DAY I WILL
ALWAYS REMEMBER
THIS UNMISTAKABLE AND BLISSFUL IMAGE
IN DECEMBER.

~

FEATHERED FRIENDS

CLEARLY I HEAR THE JUMBLE OF MUSICAL NOTES
A SERIES OF UNLIKE SONGS IN WHISTLE QUOTES
WITHIN THE BRIAR TO A WEED LANDSCAPE HUSH
A MOCKING BIRD HIDES IN THICKET AND BRUSH

THE MARTINS ATTACK LARGER BIRDS THAT WREST
ALL UNINVITED INTRUDERS WHO APPROACH NEST
LEARNED BY SCARS OR STRUGGLES OVER YEARS
STILL REMAINING UNALTERED BY TIMES OR FEARS

STELLER JAYS DO NOT FEAR THOSE PEOPLE ABOUT
ROBIN GREETS THE DAWN IN A CHEERFUL SHOUT
THE SWALLOWS BRAVE IN COMPETITION FOR SITE
REFUSING THE ENCROACHER THEY DIDN'T INVITE

A DESERT WREN NESTS IN YUCCAS AND CACTUS
PROTECTED BY PRICKLES OF SHARP LEAF'S TRUSS
THE KINGLET IS RULER PROTECTING ITS FREEDOM
AS THIS SPRY BIRD COMBS ITS LITTLE KINGDOM

THE CROW IS INTELLIGENT AND WORKS IN FLOCKS
OF GREAT INSIGHT SOLVE PUZZLES AND UNLOCKS
THEIR WORLD'S UNCHANGED IN LOVE OR CRIMES
OUR WORLD'S CONFUSED AND ALTERED BY TIMES

KINGBIRDS DEFEND HOMESTEAD FROM WRECKS
BY DRIVING OFF INTRUDERS WITH SHARP PECKS
FOR BIRD'S EXAMPLES, THE WORLD SHOULD SEE
THAT SOME #?@!! ON EARTH WILL NEVER AGREE

SO WHY ARE WE INVOLVED AS IT NOW APPEARS
IN CHANGING FOREIGN LANDS WHO IN EVIL FEARS
SHOULD NOT WE RETREAT TO OUR LAND AMENDS?
LEARN BY EXAMPLE OF OUR FEATHERED FRIENDS

~

PROFILE OF A POET

A poem is written
        Removing any mask,
Experience Stricken
        From unbottled flask
Expose burnt hopes
        Revealing life's task
Unsealing envelopes
        Enclosed into a cask,
Silver lining lifted,
        Itself brushed aside,
Its reality is sifted,
        Secrets once confide,
Pause, allowing time,
        Reconsider or divide,
For words to rhyme
        Reach a depth inside
Surface knowledge
        From deepest below
Beyond, over edge
        In shadowed hollow,
Weave good or bad,
        Right or wrong flow,
Joy, interlaces sad
        Mingle truth bestow.
When left by tongue,
        Expresses it wrong.
In memory it hung,
        But, it didn't belong
Words writ confirm,
        As interpreters tong
Furthermore affirm
        To feelings age-long.

Upon a silent stage,
   Words for metaphor
Grasping for a page
   Printing its splendor
Dreams from heart
   From fact or a rumor
Thoughts to impart
   A language inventor.
Upon scribbled note
   With recorded tablet
Of words once spoke
   For sayings to beget
Collected an' spaced
   Arranging and reset
Then jointly placed,
   The lyrics of a poet.

~

WHY???

WHY???

WHY DO I FEEL THE WAY I DO,
        WHEN I'M AWAY FROM YOU DEAR
BUT THEN AGAIN I'M SO HAPPY,
        THE MOMENTS YOU COME NEAR.

WHY MUST I ASK MYSELF OVER,
        ARE YOU THE ONE WHO I BELONG,
CAN'T SEEM TO FIND THE ANSWER,
        IS THIS RIGHT OR IS THIS WRONG??

WHY, IS IT YOUR HAPPY SMILE,
        OR IN THE WAYS YOU LOOK AT ME,
MAKES ME WANT YOU MORE,
        WHEN YOUR HEART I CANNOT SEE.

WHY DO I SEEK FOR ROMANCE
        BY WHOSE TOUCHES ARE SO FEW
AND WHEN LOVE IS EXPRESSED
        IT'S SELDOM FLASHED IN MY VIEW

WHY ARE THE FEELINGS INTENSE,
        A MELTING OF MY CORE THEREBY?
IN SEARCHING THESE QUESTIONS,
        I CANNOT FIND THE REASONS WHY?

~

TWAS A GIFTED SIGHT

T'WAS A GIFTED SIGHT

TWAS THE RAVISHING EYES OF HEAVEN
     IN SUCH BRILLIANT CRYSTALS OF WHITE
SILVERY MOON ATOP SPIRITUAL TOWERS,
     AN ENGRAVED HALO INTO THE NIGHT.

TWAS THE BEDS OF DANCING DAFFODILS
     STANDING ASIDE THE TINKLING BROOK
BIRCHES BEND IN THE MEADOWS SHADE,
     WITH ITS INNOCENT HERBS THAT LOOK…

TWAS FLOWERS IN SHRUBS OF BLANKETS,
     WITH THE BREACHEN BUDS SO STILL…
OR GREAT CALL FROM A LONELY COYOTE,
     CRICKETS WITH AN' AWKWARD SHRILL

TWAS AN AIRY FORCE, KIND OF GHOST,
     AN' BECAME AN UNGUIDED BREEZE,
WHISTLED TUNES AND BLEW FRESHNESS
     THROUGHOUT THE BODY OF THE TREES.

TWAS SHADES T' SHADES, YET SPECIAL,
     TWAS IN SHARING THIS GIFTED SIGHT
A JOY OF GLADNESS WITH JUST A LOOK!
     LIKE THE ONE I JUST SAW LAST NIGHT…

~

JOLLY LITTLE LAKE

JOLLY LITTLE LAKE

Once when I was young,
  Beneath the trees cool shade
I laid myself down to rest,
  Sipping a glass of lemonade,
  Then fell asleep to a gentle breeze sound.

And later that same day,
  Whenever I finally did awake,
I surprisingly discovered,
  That I had made a little lake,
  When my lemonade spilled on the ground.

A sudden motion began,
  Upon a glance there I begot,
At the edge of the grass,
  By the little lake's bare spot,
  Then closer to it I crawled upon my knees.

And gathered there about
  Several bugs of many kinds
Touring a lemonade lake,
  From around its shorelines,
  A miniature setting where weeds are trees.

I saw centipede and ants,
  Playing with the bumble bee,
Where the moth and fly
  Roach and beetle met the flea,
  Where an earwig passed a worm in its way

As music from the cricket
  Soothed the butterflies along
Pretty lady bugs swayed
  To the grasshoppers song,
  And a honey bee watched the mantis pray.

A CATERPILLAR CRAWLED A JIG
    DANCING BESIDE A POTATO BUG
THE WASP AND MITE LOOKED
    WHILE THE SNAIL RACED THE SLUG,
    THEN A SPIDER SKIPPED ALL AROUND THE LAKE.

THEY WERE BUSY AN BUZZY
    AND FUNNY FUZZY LITTLE FRITTERS
AS ENJOYING ONE ANOTHER
    AT THIS LAKE PARTY FOR CRITTERS,
    IT WAS HERE THEY LEARNED TO GIVE AND TAKE.

SOME TURNED SOMERSAULTS,
    OTHERS ROLLED ON THEIR BACKS
THEN SOME FLAPPED WINGS,
    AS OTHERS MADE LITTLE TRACKS
    AND GREETED ONE ANOTHER AS NEVER BEFORE

EQUALLY, IT WAS BUG TO BUG
    DIFFERENTLY BUT OF ONE MIND
FOR FEW HAPPY MOMENTS
    THEY LEFT DIFFERENCES BEHIND
    TO ENJOY ONE ANOTHER AT THIS LAKE'S SHORE

OOOOPS! THEN ALL AT ONCE
    THEIR LITTLE LAKE DISAPPEARED
QUICKLY THEY SCATTERED SO,
    LEAVING CAMPGROUND CLEARED
    ENDING THIS HAPPY AND PLAYFUL CIVILIZATION.

THEN, THINKING TO MYSELF
    OF ALL THE CONTENTIONS IN LIFE
AND THE LESSON AT THE LAKE,
    WHERE WAS FOUND NO STRIFE,
    COULD IT BE THIS WAS ONLY MY IMAGINATION?

Perhaps a desire in heart
    Of a hidden hope for peace,
Because to me it was real
    Oh how their joy did increase,
    From the great example of love displayed.

Even this day I still recall
    A unity of that neighborhood.
When I visit the old place,
    Where they crawled or stood
    Together near this little lake of lemonade

~

HAPPY BROTHER

Now lift up a song,
　　And sing along,
　　　　With me happy brother.
Of forgotten signs,
　　In the many times,
　　　　That we shared together.

O' how the past,
　　Has gone so fast,
　　　　Seems like just yesterday,
Together we strayed,
　　Together we played,
　　　　But time is turned away

So here tonight,
　　I'll sit and write,
　　　　Cause you're my thought,
So's I can show,
　　And let you know,
　　　　I miss those times a lot!

I now recall,
　　The most of all,
　　　　Way back in yesteryear,
Childhood days,
　　Our happy ways,
　　　　Now are gone yet so dear.

We skipped walk,
　　With happy talk,
　　　　An shared our joyful fun.
An' we put aside,
　　Bad thoughts t' hide,
　　　　So lost them one by one.

Times of thrills,
 With porky quills,
  Or shot marbles around.
We got inside,
 Old tire and ride,
  A favorite tire we found.

Whittle whistles
 Play in thistles
  To games of kick the can
Sharing a riddle,
 Pillow in middle
  Building a fort with plan

We banged pots
 Made sling shots
  Skated around the block
Chores we did
 On sleds we slid
  Birds we strived to mock.

Times we shared
 And really cared,
  So rich with just a dime,
We mend our ways,
 Back in those days,
  And fought time to time.

But still brother,
 My happy brother,
  Those times I easily find,
Each happy day,
 Still has its way,
  A path deep in my mind.

~

HUNDRED YEARS AWAY

HUNDRED YEARS AWAY

No friend, I am not a hero
     No brave tasks have I done,
Never claimed to be more
     Than just a poor man's son.

Now the years have passed
     And yes, I've seen them all,
Among many of my trips
     Around this world so small.

My jobs have been several
     With trades which I've held,
I have slept in cold alleys
     And time or two been jailed.

O' how my dreams wonder
     An' how my thoughts stray,
However, my mind still lives
     Bout a hundred years away.

We own a little business
     Down at the end of a street,
Was built of sweat an' hope
     A place where friends meet.

Yet, not a day passes me by
     With old times on display,
For my mind lives in a past
     Bout hundred years away.

At home a wonderful family
     That's so ever dear to me,
Three great boys and a wife
     With many gifts, I can see.

MY, DESIRES SEEM UNUSUAL
        IT'S WHAT, MANY PEOPLE SAY,
THE THINGS I WISH FOR TODAY
        ARE A HUNDRED YEARS AWAY.

OR SOME MAKE FUN AND JOKE
        OF THE THINGS I DON'T KNOW,
FOR THINGS THAT INTEREST ME
        WERE FORGOTTEN SO LONG AGO.

MODERN STYLES WAYS, LOOKS
        ARE SO FOOLISH TO ME TODAY,
N' MY WAYS ARE OL' FASHION
        OR A HUNDRED YEARS AWAY.

I DON'T USE FANCY WORDS
        NOR SPEAK WELL IN A GROUP,
BUT LIKE HARMONICA MUSIC
        OR BOSSIE IN A BOWL OF SOUP.

EVERYONE IS IN A BIG RUSH
        N' THERE'S NO TIME FOR PLAY,
RACING TO MAKE A DOLLAR
        NOT LIKE IT WAS YEARS AWAY.

BUT, THE LORD PICKED NOW
        FOR ME BEING HERE O' FATE,
YET CAN'T HELP IF I STILL FEEL
        A HUNDRED YEARS TOO LATE.

IF I COULD ONLY MAKE A WISH
        I WOULD WISH I MIGHT OR MAY,
TURN BACK HANDS OF TIME
        ABOUT HUNDRED YEARS AWAY...

~

LIFE'S VENTURE

SEARCH OUT, THEN CONSIDER THE MATTER,
    FROM ERROR WE SHOULD LET WISDOM LEAD,
        BRING TO REMEMBRANCE THE REASON THE CAUSE.
RECONSTRUCT, RECALL, BE ENLIGHTENED,
    LEARN FROM THIS BAD ONCE PLANTED SEED,
        IN THE SOIL OF TIME WHERE ADVENTURES PAUSE.

NONE CAN CHANGE THE FINISHED PAST,
    NEITHER CAN ALL OF YESTERDAY BE FORGOT,
        ESPECIALLY ERRORS WHERE, BITS AND PIECES ARE,
FOR THAT WHICH HAS HAPPENED IS FIXED,
    ONLY NOW FOR A CHANGE MAY BE SOUGHT
        YET WITH EACH VICTORY OR FAILURE COMES A SCAR.

DON'T USE THE "BECAUSES" FOR EXCUSE
    SOMETIMES EXCUSES DEFILE EXPERIENCES
        THEREBY LIFE'S VENTURES ARE EXAMPLES ON FILE,
ANY ACTION OR CHOICE OF FOOLISH ERROR,
    IS AFTER KNOWLEDGE WITH INTERFERENCES,
        AND IS FOR CORRECTION, REFERENCE, AND FOR TRIAL.

HEREBY, EXPERIENCE IS THE BEST TEACHER,
    ONLY IF ONE CAN LIVE THROUGH IT, I SAY,
        FOR A PROGRESS, A CHANGE IS REQUIRED TO BEAR.
NEVERTHELESS I SHOULD BE TOMORROW,
    A BETTER PERSON THAN THAT OF YESTERDAY,
        FOR REPENTANCE WITH CHANGE JUSTIFIES ERROR.

~

EDGE OF THE RAINBOW

Great banner in the sky
    An arch array of circle rite
Exposes bonded colors
    Connect bands one by one.
Hung sprays contracts
    Form a ray's reflected light
Appearance of heaven
    Mirroring opposite the sun.

Drops of rain fall vapor
    Dispersing light in mid-air
At the close of a shower
    In a corner of the heavens,
So fancy it shall fashion
    Into this water dance affair
Reviewed within prism
    From sun's fabricated lens.

Thereby stages a scene,
    Of a mist that rolls and rise
A throne of twisted light
    Visions loom across a dew
Mingled in merry whirl
    Promised Sign in disguise
Earliest bow's covenant
    For future floods withdrew.

Streaked a view to meet
    End to end or knoll to knoll
Hue's take shape in spin
    Shed blessings on its scene
By wonder and delight
    Various color merge scroll
On the crest of the edge,
    As sunny ridges intervene

The ledge is faint and far
    Upon sky's colored ribbon
Enveloped in a warmth
    Forming captured ozones
O' it glistens and blends
    With multi look on horizon
Bodiless vision weaves
    Red colors to violet tones.

Emerges from odd angles
    Red, orange, yellow, indigo
Blue and green to violet
    Together seven colors bent
The sun is always behind
    The one facing the rainbow
Each eye of an observer
    Sees their wave of crescent

A gathered dew blushed
    In its vapors glance of mist
Casting forth a glimmer
    Sunlight appears on its rim
Spirit towering rainbow
    Walks the valley on a twist
Cease beauty portrayed
    It surfaced, then faded dim.

Decked in water pearls
    A light of spray encumbers
Dressed in a full delight,
    A colored halo on display,
Moistened and unbroken
    Mounting bend of wonders
Only the world can wear,
    This crown as worn today.

~

BOY AND HIS DOG

BOY AND HIS DOG

(1965)

WALKING PAST A WILLOW TREE
    DOWN THE OLD SWIMMING HOLE,
JUST A BOY AND HIS DOG,
    WITH HIS BAMBOO FISHING POLE.

THEY STOP TO REST AT A BANK,
    NEAR THE MEADOW HE DID SEEK,
AS HIS EYES CAST OUTWARD,
    ONTO THE SLOW PASSING CREEK.

AN OPEN CAN AT HIS SIDE,
    FILLED WITH WORMS JUST FOR BAIT,
THEN HE DROPS IN HIS LINE,
    TO PATIENTLY SIT THERE AND WAIT.

NOT A CARE IN THE WORLD,
    NEITHER A SINGLE WORRY HAS HE,
AS HE COUNTS THE LEAVES,
    DRIFTING DOWN FROM OFF A TREE.

DRAWS PICTURE IN THE DIRT,
    A WHITTLED STICK HE MAY HOLD,
SPLASH WATER WITH HIS FEET,
    JUST TO SEE IF IT MIGHT BE COLD.

HE WHISTLES A LITTLE TUNE
    IN TRYING TO MOCK SOME BIRDS,
OR SING HIS DOG A SONG,
    PROBABLY USES HIS OWN WORDS.

HE'LL SIT AND PET HIS DOG,
    OR MAY TIE HIS EARS UP IN KNOT,
THE DOG SHAKES HIS HEAD,
    FOR THE BOY IS ALL HE HAS GOT.

HE MAY LISTEN TO THE WINDS,
    WHISTLING MUSIC FROM A BREEZE,
OR LOOK ABOVE THE SHADOWS
    OF THE SMALLEST OR TALLEST TREES.

THEY MAY LOOK HIGHER YET,
    AS CHANGEFUL CLOUDS PASS BY,
FORM THEM INTO PICTURES,
    BY WHAT HE VISIONS IN THE SKY.

OOOOOOOPS, IT'S A BITE,
    WITH A SURPRISE UPON HIS FACE,
HE JUMPS UP ON HIS FEET,
    AND YELLS WITH A CHEERY GRACE.

HE REELS A FISH IN SLOWLY,
    AN HOLDING HIS POLE VERY TIGHT,
THEY WATCH WITH EXCITEMENT,
    AS HE PULLS WITH ALL HIS MIGHT,

A BIG SMILE FILLS HIS FACE,
    JUMPS IN A MOST HAPPY SHOUT,
REELS IT IN A LITTLE MORE,
    SAYING "I'VE GOT IT...JUST ABOUT".

Then a few moments later,
    He whistles his favorite song.
It's the biggest he's caught,
    Nearly fourteen inches long.

Wraps his line on his pole,
    And hugs his dog really tight,
He might even kiss him,
    You can't tell, he just might.

An skipping toward home,
    As his dog follows at his side,
Happiness, a can of worms,
    And with a big trout well tied.

So down through the valley
    Such a team and so full of joy,
Just a bamboo fishing pole,
    My dream of a dog and a boy...

~

IF WHEN, WOULD YOU

IF WHEN, WOULD YOU

(For Carole Moore 1961-1962)

IF WHEN I WALK A LONELY NIGHT,
    AS UPON A PATH OF CLOUDY DEW,
WOULD YOU THINK ON A CHANCE
    THAT YOU WOULD WALK ON IT TOO?

IF WHEN I DREAM OF US TOGETHER,
    IN A LITTLE COTTAGE SOMEWHERE,
WOULD YOU WAIT TO LET IT END,
    OR WAKE TO END THEN AND THERE?

IF WHEN WE'RE SEPARATED APART,
    AWARE I'D MISS YOU AT MY SIDE,
WOULD YOU ALSO TREMBLE SOME,
    AND YEARN TO BE WHERE I ABIDE?

IF WHEN I HANG HEAD IN SHAME,
    WOULD YOURS NOT BE LIFTED HIGH,
WOULD YOU SUPPOSE IT'S RIGHT,
    AND MAYBE CRY IF I SHOULD CRY?

IF WHEN I SAY I LOVE YOU DEAR,
    WITH A LOVE STRANGE AND STRONG,
WOULD YOU HAVE SUCH FEELING,
    THAT LEAPS AT A WORDLESS SONG?

IF WHEN OTHERS TALK ME DOWN,
    OR QUESTION THE AVENUES I WALK,
WOULD YOU BELIEVE IN MYSELF,
    OR MAYBE THEY WITH EMPTY TALK,

IF WHEN ANOTHER MIGHT JUDGE
    BY ASSUMING OF WHAT THEY SEE,
WOULD YOU TRUST TO ASK FIRST,
    BEFORE YOU SPEAK TO JUDGE ME?

IF WHEN I PRETEND WE TOGETHER,
 UPON A CLOUD OF MIDNIGHT DEW,
WOULD YOU HOLD MY HAND TIGHT,
 AND PRETEND IT MAY COME TRUE?

IF WHEN LIFE SEEMS AT ITS WORST,
 ALL WE HAVE IS THINE AND MINE.
WOULD YOU STAND AT MY SIDE,
 AND SAY THAT, "THINGS ARE FINE"?

IF WHEN YOU HAVE TIME, DEAR,
 OH, JUDGE THESE QUESTIONS FAIR,
WOULD YOU READ BETWEEN LINES,
 TO SEE HOW MUCH I REALLY CARE?

~

JOYOUS SPIRIT IN MY HEART

(Song 1970-1971)

O' THERE'S A JOYOUS SPIRIT
    IN MY HEART,
O' THERE'S A JOYOUS SPIRIT
    IN MY HEART
WITH A LIKENESS I SEE, WITH JE-SUS IN ME
THERE'S A JOYOUS SPIRIT IN MY HEART.

O' THERE'S A JOYOUS SPIRIT
    IN MY HEART,
O' THERE'S A JOYOUS SPIRIT
    IN MY HEART,
BORN IN THE SPIRIT; WANT THE WORLD TO HEAR IT.
THERE'S A JOYOUS SPIRIT IN MY HEART

O' THERE'S A JOYOUS SPIRIT
    IN MY HEART,
O' THERE'S A JOYOUS SPIRIT
    IN MY HEART,
HE OPENED A WAY, FOR FELLOWSHIP TODAY
THERE'S A JOYOUS SPIRIT IN MY HEART.

~

GREEDY EYE

GREEDY EYE

Beware ye, of gleaming,
And greedy eye,
Whom so greatly values
Where gold dwelt,
Do you not know that it
Shall fade on by,
And strongest of irons
Shall even melt

From the days of birth
Man seeks gain
As the foolish desires
Captures his heart
But in time thru scars
Losses and pain
He discovers all things
Will soon depart.

So beware ye, oh fools
With your wants
O', what will tomorrows
For you hold?
A soul may be required
With warrants
For cost of your greed
Due sevenfold

~

THINGS

FROM THE BEGINNINGS EVEN UNTO NOW
   MAN HAS LONGED TO OWN CERTAIN THINGS
      THAT HAS CAUSED HIM TO LOOSE HIS CUE
THIS GREED AND WANT OF THINGS ALLOW
   THIS FALSE EFFECTS SATISFACTION BRINGS
      THESE 'EFFECTS' OF NO IMPORTANT VALUE

ONCE MAN PERCEIVES THIS IN HIS SPIRIT
   HE SORTS AGAIN OVER THINGS OF CHOICE
      IF A HEART BE WISE HE'LL INSIDE BE TRUE
TO SEE THE FOOLISHNESS THINGS PERMIT
   AND TO HEAR IT FROM A DIFFERENT VOICE
      AND SEE HOW A SOUL SEEKS ITS RESCUE

WHAT CAUSES A MAN YEARNING TO WANT
   OR DRIVES HIM WITH SUCH GREAT DESIRES
      TIL HIS PERSECUTION OR DEATH PURSUE
BUT GAIN OF OWNING SEEMS IMPORTANT
   FOR THE WONDER OF THINGS HE ADMIRES
      AS OBJECTS PROVOKE HIM TO BE UNTRUE

THE WORLD GRASPS FOR THINGS IN A LUST
   NEITHER DO THEY CONSIDER ALL THE COST
      A WANT OF STUFF HE WILL MISCONSTRUE
A HUNGER FOR THINGS ADVANCES UNJUST
   SLOWLY HIS CONSCIENCE SEARED OR LOST
      AS A HOPE FOR MORE THINGS CONTINUE

ALL THINGS THAT HE CONSIDERS AS GAINS
     ARE TRANSIENT, TEMPORAL AND BUT DUNG
          ALL THIS TIME HIS HEART HAS NOT A CLUE
INTO THIS SNARE HIS SOUL STILL REMAINS
     OF GREED AND LIES WITH SILVER TONGUE
          JUSTIFYING THOSE THINGS HE WILL ACCRUE

AGAIN HIS GADGETS AND THINGS PREVAIL
     AND IN THIS HE'S CONQUERED BY DEFEAT
          COVETNESS REPLACES HIS JOYS OVERDUE
SO THESE THINGS CAUSE THE SOUL TRAVAIL
     TOWARD FANCY OF THINGS HE WILL REPEAT
          THINGS BECOME HIS SOURCE OF REVENUE

KINGDOMS WILL FALL FOR WANT OF THINGS
     SOULS LOST FROM MERE DESIRES OF WANT
          LIFE IS IN RUIN BY FAITH OF FALSE VIRTUE
ALL HOPE CRUSHED WHERE GREED CLINGS
     GREED IS THE ISSUE HE WON'T CONFRONT
          THE WANT OF THINGS WILL CLAIM ITS DUE

~

FIRST STAR OF THE NIGHT

FIRST STAR OF THE NIGHT

OH, HOURS OF DUSK WHERE,
      A TWILIGHT CHASES DAY,
HEAVEN'S SUNSET GLOW AS,
      LAST STEPS FADE AWAY.

ABOVE RICH FLOW OF PURPLE,
      RIPPLES ALONG THE SKY.
A BRIGHT STAR OF MEMORY,
      PUTS GLEAM IN HIS EYE.

HIS EYES CAST TOWARD HER,
      WHERE A GOLDEN LIGHT,
ABOVE A HORIZON PRANCED,
      THE FIRST STAR OF NIGHT.

HE PICTURED HER IN HEAVEN,
      IN A SPIRIT SOMEWHERE,
FOR HE KNEW SHE WAS GOOD,
      SO GOD WOULD BE FAIR.

HE SLOWLY CLOSED HIS EYES,
      IMAGING INTO A DREAM,
WHEN SHE WAS AT HIS SIDE,
      THEY EQUALED A TEAM.

LIKE FLOWERS OF SWEET ODOR,
      OR THE BIRDS OF A SONG,
THEY REMAINED TOGETHER,
      WHERE BOTH DO BELONG.

HE BROUGHT FORTH MOMENTS,
      BOTH THE HAPPY OR SAD,
LOOKED BACK OVER THE SILLY
      QUARRELS THEY HAD HAD.

IF BOTH SPIRITS ARE BRIGHT,
    TO CHERISH AND HOLD,
THIS IS ALL PART OF LOVE,
    HE RECALLS BEING TOLD.

HE CLEARLY REMEMBERS,
    EACH LINE IN HER FACE,
SHE WAS ALL OF HIS HEART,
    SAVE NO OTHER SPACE.

FROM SWIMMING TOGETHER,
    OR A WALK ON THE SAND,
THEIR MINDS WANDERED OFF,
    TO AN UNKNOWN LAND.

EACH TEAR, FROWN, SMILE,
    OR LAUGHING TOGETHER,
COULD NEVER BE SOLD FOR A
    GREAT ANGEL'S FEATHER.

BECAUSE ALL THESE THINGS
    IN A BIRDLIKE MELODY,
THEY'RE REALLY, NOT MATTER,
    BUT SURE THE MEMORY.

THE DREAM ENDED AS SHE
    POINTS HIGH UP ABOVE,
SAYING, "LOOK, DARLING,
    IT IS OUR STAR OF LOVE."

THEN, BEHOLD THE DREAM,
    VANISHED FROM SIGHT,
HE STOOD ALONE, WITH THE
    FIRST STAR OF THE NIGHT...

~

TRY ME LORD!

TRY ME LORD! FOR I'M BUT FLESH AND BONE
    SO I DO NOT STRAY FROM THE CORNERSTONE
THE TASTE OF SIN APPEARS SWEET YET I SEE
    EACH VICTORY OVER SIN FELLOWSHIPS THEE

TRY ME LORD! TO MEET THY EXPECTATIONS
    QUICKEN MY SPIRIT WITHOUT EXPLANATIONS
FOR I KNOW YOU'LL TRY THE HEART'S DELIGHT.
    TO CHANGE MY WAY; FIGHT THE GOOD FIGHT

TRY ME LORD! THOU HAST PAID A RANSOM
    THAT I'LL NOT FAINT NOR FAIL, BUT OVERCOME
I AM SUBJECT TO FAILURES THAT LEAD ASTRAY
    LORD, LIMIT MY TRIALS TO A LITTLE EACH DAY

TRY ME LORD! I THINK IT NOT STRANGE TO BE
    CONCERNING THE FIERY TRIALS THAT TRY ME.
TRIALS OF FAITH ARE MORE PRECIOUS I KNOW
    THAN OF GOLD THAT PERISHETH TOMORROW.

TRY ME LORD! FOR I KNOW WITHOUT A TRIAL
    I COULD BECOME FOOLED AND LOST IN EXILE
OR BLIND AND CONTENT IN MY OWN UNJUST
    NOR DISCERN THE ENEMIES I NOW DISTRUST

TRY ME LORD! INTO MOLDING OF MINE WILL
    DIVIDING SPIRIT AND FLESH BY GENTLE SKILL
AND IF MY FLESH SHOULD DESIRE TO STRAY
    THEN TRY ME O' LORD A LITTLE MORE I PRAY

TRY ME LORD! WITH THIS DIFFICULT REQUEST
    I DO NOT ALWAYS RECOGNIZE WHAT IS BEST
O' LEAD ME MERCIFULLY THRU TRIALS OF FIRE
    SO MY LIFE'S END MAY BE IN YOUR DESIRE.

~

THERE AND HERE

There, in glorious sky that gives look,
    Down upon the cities of the grave,
        And all the mourners upon the land,
Here, winds echo across the brook,
    By causing just the slighted wave,
        In a world we don't quite understand,
    For this is what I now see,
    When I think of you and me.

There, you walk the streets of gold,
    Singing songs of glory and praise,
        With no yesterday, and no tomorrow,
Here, it's loneliness at the threshold,
    Where we share dreams and ways
        A life where tears are made to flow,
    For this is what I now see,
    When I think of you and me.

There, you have visions very much,
    Without the worries as once before,
        As standing beside the Master's feet,
Here, I miss your voice, your touch,
    Wondering why you are no more,
        When my heart is permitted to beat?
    For this is what I now see,
    When I think of you and me.

There, a victory so calm embraces,
    Happiness and sunshine devours,
        In your new mansion of pearly white,
Here, common sorrow, hollow faces,
    Cold and chill through weary hours,
        Senses stray blending gay with fright,
    For this is what I now see,
    When I think of you and me.

There, time's an undetermined while,
    Where peace and joy is ever played.
        From troublesome times you're free,
Here, I still see your familiar smile,
    And then become weak and frayed,
        Whenever your voice cries out to me,
For this is what I now see,
When I think of you and me.

There, no more sorrow for to be seen,
    No more heartache, no more pain,
        Neither reasons to want or be denied,
Here, caught somewhere in between,
    I see your visions again and again,
        As you looked into my face and died!
For this is what I now see,
When I think of you and me.

~

WITNESS

WITNESS

Finally tonight I see my wrong
  For days I prayed and prayed,
So tonight Lord, I cry along,
  O strengthen me for I'm afraid.

I see that I am a worldly man,
  As circumstances guide away,
And need the help of Thy hand,
  To guide me in my daily day.

With desires to be a man of God
  And for Christ live each hour,
The world is just a place I trod,
  And Thee, Oh Lord, my Tower.

O' accept me Lord...this night.
  I'm not the witness I should be,
I'm just a spot before the light
  Travailing daily to serve Thee.

~

DREAMS AND THOUGHTS

DREAMS N' THOUGHTS

Tis dreams I've drempt',
        Can no more find,
Or thoughts I've thought
        Then left behind,

With eyes I've searched,
        Seeked n' sought,
Of dreams n' thoughts,
        I over half forgot.

A fancy consciousness
        With imagination
Of sensational images
        Free of limitation

A visionary, I suppose
        Into fond dreams
The power to picture
        Thought redeems

My dreams I've found
        Are different now,
Past thoughts did pass,
        Change somehow.

Now dreams I dream,
        Are bits I borrow,
And thoughts I think
        Are of tomorrow......

~

A NATION

(1972)

O' GENERATION O' LAND OF PEACE
WITH MANY YEARS OF ANGUISH SIGH
IN SETTING ASIDE THE BATTLE PIECE
SO THE FLAGS OF PEACE COULD FLY

O' AMERICA, THY QUEST IS FOUND
FROM SUCH A GREAT PRICE TO PAY
BLOOD WAS SHED UPON THE GROUND
WHICH IS A COST THAT WARS PORTRAY

> A NATION, A NATION
> GOD REST THEIR SOULS WITH THEE
> AND BRING OUR TROOPS
> AGAIN BACK HOME TO OLD GLORY

O' FELLOWMEN, REMEMBER WHEN
'NEATH PEACEFUL SKIES DID ROAM
FOR OUR SAKE THESE COUNTRYMEN
ASSURED THE PEACE BACK HOME.

O' BROTHERHOOD IN TRIBULATION
SOME WOUNDS HEAL, SOME WON'T
STRANGE HISTORY'S OBSERVATION
SOME RETURN HOME, SOME DON'T

> A NATION, A NATION
> GOD REST THEIR SOULS WITH THEE
> AND BRING OUR TROOPS
> AGAIN BACK HOME TO OLD GLORY

O' VICTORY, YOUNG VETERANS FALL
AND OUR FELLOWMAN WOULD DIE
THOSE WHO MIGHT SURVIVE IT ALL
SUFFER IN OTHER SCARS THEREBY

O' SILHOUETTE, FOR US ALL TO SEE
O' PRAY FOR THE BATTLE TO CEASE
THAT MANKIND MIGHT ONCE AGREE
AND TOGETHER STRIVE FOR PEACE

A NATION, A NATION
GOD REST THEIR SOULS WITH THEE
AND BRING OUR TROOPS
AGAIN BACK HOME TO OLD GLORY

~

THINGS I LIKE THE VERY MOST
(1973)

THE THINGS I LIKE THE VERY MOST
O' WATCHING MY BOYS JOYFULLY PLAY
    MY LOVELY WIFE IN HER HAPPY WAY
AND THEIR HAPPINESS IN UTTERMOST
ARE THINGS I LIKE THE VERY MOST.

THE THINGS I LIKE THE VERY MOST
IS COFFEE SERVED IN AN OLD TIN CUP
    DREAMS OF DIGGING SOME GOLD UP
STAKING MY NAME ON A CLAIM POST
ARE THINGS I LIKE THE VERY MOST.

THE THINGS I LIKE THE VERY MOST.
HOMEMADE BREAD AN' SMELL IT BAKE
    VEGGIES SOUP, MAYONNAISE CAKE
HAMBURGER, RED BEANS, AND ROAST
ARE THINGS I LIKE THE VERY MOST.

THE THINGS I LIKE THE VERY MOST
AL JOLSON, INK SPOTS AND LULLABY,
    SOUND OF HARMONICAS LONELY CRY
A DESERTS HIGH GROUND UPPERMOST
ARE THINGS I LIKE THE VERY MOST.

THE THINGS I LIKE THE VERY MOST
STRETCHING OUT IN MY FAVORITE SEAT
    MY SONS TAKING SHOES OFF MY FEET
GRAPE NUTS AND HOMEMADE TOAST
ARE THINGS I LIKE THE VERY MOST.

The things I like the very most
Together our family up in the hills
    Or together in deserts, sandy fills
Boating the lakes or at the coast
Are things I like the very most.

The things I like the very most
See my folks watching them smile
    My jack-knife and whittle awhile
Sing a song with the Holy Ghost.
Are things I like the very most.

The things I like the very most
All these things I dream and plan
    To do as often as I possibly can
This family life to me is foremost
Are things I like the very most.

~

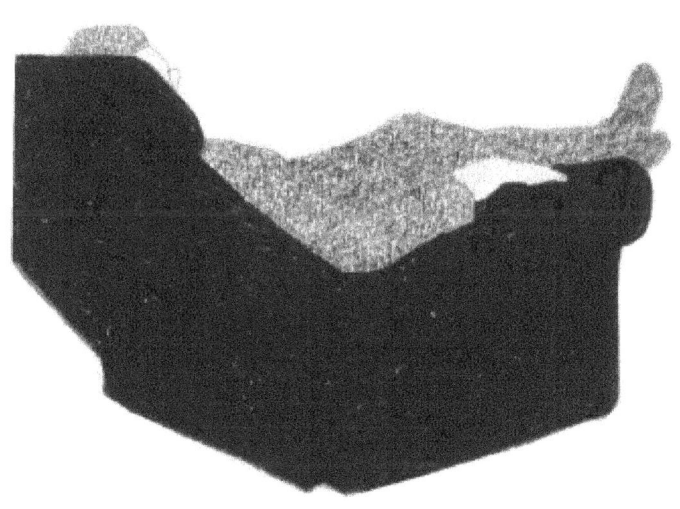

ONE IN-BETWEEN

LO! REMEMBRANCE COMES TO ME
    OF A TIME THAT IS PAST
    THIS COBBLESTONE PATH OF BYGONE DAYS
HERE MY SON'S BOYHOOD I SEE
    SHADOWS IMAGE CAST
    HIS REFLECTING INNOCENT SMILE DISPLAYS

ONE BROTHER WAS A LITTLE OLDER,
    ONE YOUNGER THAN HE
    WITH A SWEETNESS HE STOOD IN-BETWEEN
FOR THAT HELPED HIM BE BOLDER
    UNDERSTAND IN DEGREE
    THEN TO REASON FROM EXPERIENCES SEEN.

IF ONLY I COULD SOMEHOW REACH
    BACK IN A TIME YONDER
    TO WHERE ONCE CHILDHOOD DAYS REMAIN
I WOULD BUT HAPPILY RELIVE EACH
    MAKE OUR TIMES FONDER
    AND AVOID THINGS I WOULDN'T DO AGAIN

BUT THEN AGAIN I SHALL REJOICE
    AS I GENTLY LOOK AT HIM
    OLD THOUGHTS REPEAT AND COMES PAUSE
THEN SUDDENLY I HEAR HIS VOICE
    IT WHISPERS TO ME DIM
    WHERE SHADOWS MELT WITHOUT A CAUSE

ONCE UPON A TIME I TOO INDEED,
    WAS A BOY JUST LIKE HE
    SO I KNEW WHEN HIS HEART BROKE TWAIN
DISAPPOINTMENTS WE ALL NEED,
    HOWEVER HIS WERE TO ME
    A HURT IN MY HEART I COULD NOT EXPLAIN

NEITHER COULD I EVER BRUSH AWAY
THE PLACE MADE READY
AS I READ HIM STORIES OF WHAT COULD BE
THEN HOW MY SON STRAIGHTAWAY
RECITING WORDS STEADILY
SPEED READING UPSIDE-DOWN BEFORE ME!

OUR LITTLE TALKS I CAN STILL RECALL,
WITH BEDTIME STORIES
THEN, BEING THANKFUL AS I TUCKED HIM IN
SUCH CALMNESS RESTED OVERALL
IN PRAYER AND GLORIES
BEFORE HE FELL ASLEEP IN A PEACEFUL GRIN.

HIS CHARACTER WAS SO PECULIAR
MUCH LIKE MY VERY OWN
HOW HE EYED ME IN SUCH A DRAWN STARE
FROM THE PLACES ONCE FAMILIAR
WHERE ONCE HE DID ROAM
SUCH A TIME IN HIS YOUTH OF SIMPLE CARE

HE WOKE UP FOR MIDNITE SNACK
INTO THE KITCHEN CREEP
BEING DROWSY, WEARY HE COULDN'T FAKE
MUMBLE, MOTION, THEN LAY BACK
AGAIN QUICKLY FELL ASLEEP
IN SLEEPY DAZE HE COULDN'T STAY AWAKE.

LIFE'S MYSTERIES HE APPRAISED
WITH INNOCENT YOUTH
BUT HOW HE WORRIED SUCH OVER NAUGHT
IT'S LIKE THE GREAT FUSS HE RAISED
LOSING HIS FIRST TOOTH
OR DISPUTE WITH A FRIEND ONCE SOUGHT.

HE WOULD TURN ABOUT AND TWIST
    WHEN HE HELD HIS DOG
    TOGETHER IT SEEMS THAT TIME JUST BEGUN
AND HUGGING HE COULDN'T RESIST
    AS OFF THEY WOULD JOG
    PLEASURE SCHEME PLAYING GAMES IN FUN

THE LAD WOULD TARRY AND LISTEN
    AT STORIES TOLD OR READ
    A CHARM ONCE AGAIN WOULD BE REVEALED
IT'S HOW HIS EYES WOULD GLISTEN
    FOR KNOWLEDGE INSTEAD
    INTENSE WITH GREAT INTEREST UNCONCEALED

SO MANY OF HIS PAST EARLY HOURS
    AND THEIR GAPS OF SPACE
    CAN ONLY FONDEST MEMORIES UNCLASP IT
THEY'LL ALWAYS REMAIN JUST OURS,
    ANOTHER TIME, OR PLACE
    HE REACHED TO MY HAND AND GRASPED IT

STAGE PLAYS AND STORIES REDEEMS
    THIS FRISKY HEALTHY LAD
    CREATING SHOWS WITH IMAGINARY SCREEN
I VISION OCCASIONALLY IN DREAMS
    WITH A WONDER SO GLAD
    PROUD OF THIS SON, THE ONE IN-BETWEEN

I REMEMBER THE APRON HE WORE
    AND HIGH BAKER'S CAP
    I CAN SEE A MENU TUCKED UNDER HIS ARM
AND SERVING ME MILK AS BEFORE
    PLATE OF TOAST ON MY LAP
    A SCRIBBLED RECEIPT IN PENNY'S CHARM.

THOUGHTS REMAIN UNFORGOTTEN
    HOW HE MOVED ABOUT
      ON HIS CLUMSY, LARGE AND OVERSIZED FEET
HE CUPPED HANDS TOGETHER OFTEN
    MOVING THEM IN AND OUT
      PLAYING TUNES IN A RHYTHM SUCTION BEAT.

WHEN HIS SENSITIVE MOOD TARRIED
    A HIDDEN HURT RESUMES
      YET HE ALLOWED ONLY A SMILE TO APPEAR
FOR HIS SENSITIVITY WAS CARRIED
    BY SOUND AND PERFUMES
      SLIPPING THROUGH FINGERS OF YESTERYEAR.

WE TOLD OLD STORIES IN PRETENSE
    AROUND THE CAMPFIRE
      HERE CHILDHOOD ACTIONS USUALLY UNFOLD
IN SMOKE, FANTASIES AND SUSPENSE
    TO OLD SONGS THAT INSPIRE
      I WATCHED HIM BLOW AS EMBERS GLOWED.

HE DAZZLED ME WITH QUESTIONS
    THIS INQUISITIVE MIND
      NEITHER DID I ANSWER THEM ALL I REGRET
BUT I WOULD OFFER SUGGESTIONS
    AND THEN WOULD REMIND
      HIM OF THE GOOD WE SHOULD NOT FORGET.

HOW HIS SUNNY SMILING CHEEK
    GLOWED IN GREAT PRIDE
      AS HE DRESSED WITH A SPARK AND GLITTER
THEN SOUGHT TO CLEARLY SPEAK
    GENTLE FROM DEEP INSIDE
      HIS CHAINED SILENCE WAS FOUND UN-BITTER.

YES, THOSE DAYS STILL DO GLOW
SO WARM ON MY HEART
OF HOW A CHILDHOOD DID COME AND FADE
NOW HIS YOUTH A BLURRED SHADOW,
AS MEMORIES IMPART
HOW THEY CAME, THEY LEFT, THEY STRAYED

OH! BUT THROUGH TIME THIS BOY
IS NO LONGER THE CHILD
YET, THROUGHOUT MY LIFE HE LEFT A TRACE
WHERE ONCE TO HIM, IT WAS A TOY,
OR JUST HOW HE SMILED
BUT NOW THE PATH SHADOWING MY FACE.

YESTERYEAR HAS COME AND GONE
BUT I RECALL THINGS SAID
AND THOUSANDS UPON THOUSANDS SEEN
I AWAKE TODAY TO ANOTHER DAWN
OF MEMORIES INSTEAD
THIS CHILDHOOD OF THE ONE IN-BETWEEN

~

EXPERIENCES

Shadowed experiences in a life are caused
        By ourselves standing in our own sunshine
Sun shines longest upon the mountain top
        As trials in the valley determines a lifeline

The value of experience is not without cost
        Nor gold shined without tumbled friction
While misfortune puts a proof to the soul
        And justified through trials of correction

Experiences in failures can be our teacher
        As a brook's music comes not without rocks
Turn stumbling blocks into stepping stones
        By making a change as awareness unlocks

Experience teaches us by actual practice
        It's the only way we discover certain things
Personal knowledge of ones observations
        Aside the opinion outward evidence brings

Experience is found on crossroads in life
        Also is the best teacher if we live through it
Cannot be learned thru a fog of textbooks
        But from the texts and pulses that life emits

Learned experience adds root to character
        Like experiencing a faith will overcome fear
Sometimes we'll loose all to gain anything
        Our choices make certain examples appear

For good experiences come from wisdom
        And yet wisdom comes from bad experiences
It's the bad experiences repeated by fools
        Who will pay the price by life's interferences

~

THEY WERE DARN GOOD FOLK!!

TODAY, THE SUN LIES WARM AND STILL
 AS I PAUSE TO PONDER AND LONG RECALL,
SILHOUETTES OF MOM AND DAD I SEE,
 SUCH MEMORABLE TIMES WERE THEY ALL,
IF I AGAIN COULD RE-LIVE THE HOURS,
 SELECTING PAST DAYS TO BECOME ANEW,
THEY'D LIVE AGAIN BENEATH THE SKY,
 RESHARING THE TIME WE SCARCELY KNEW.

AN INTIMATE FRAGRANCE I STILL SENSE,
 CERTAIN QUOTES RECALL FAMILIAR SOUND,
NEITHER DO I NEED LOOK HARD OR FAR,
 TO IDENTIFY SIGHTS THEY ONCE SURROUND,
I STILL TOUCH WHAT THEY ONCE TOUCH,
 OR REPEAT MEMORABLE TUNES THEY SUNG,
SOME DIFFERENT THINGS I MIGHT EAT,
 OFT BRINGS FAMILIAR TASTE TO MY TONGUE.

TODAY I'LL SEEK THE RAINBOW'S END,
 FOR SHADOWED THOUGHTS THAT MATTERED,
TO CRISS-CROSS THE PATHS THEY TROD,
 AND COLLECT THE PETALS THEY SCATTERED.
A PAST IS WHERE FORGOTTENS BELONG,
 BUT IN THIS I'M NOT QUALIFIED TO AGREE,
MUCH OF THE PAST BECOMES PRESENT,
 INTERTWINE FORGOTTENS WEAVE MEMORY.

 BY EXAMPLE OF INTENT,
  THEY LIVED HOW THEY SPOKE,
 OH! IN EVERY EVENT,
  THEY WERE DARN GOOD FOLK!!
 SIMPLE AND CONTENT,
  THEY WERE SO RICH YET BROKE
 AH! TO A GREAT EXTENT,
  THEY WERE DARN GOOD FOLK.

My dreams were turned to ashes,
    Visions vanished into vapor untraced,
No amount of time lying before me,
    Can Mom and Dad be again replaced,
Wrinkled smiles are not forgotten,
    They cheered my heart in many ways.
Making grins dwell a little longer,
    They surfaced the joy on cloudy days.

I now agree and know for certain
    No human being is perfect, O' but yet,
Of all my experiences considered,
    Here is a people I could never forget
A choice of folks was never mine,
    Nevertheless, I shall claim the claim,
No better folk could I have chosen,
    Than those folks who gave my name.

From beginning to this very hour,
    My lips still quiver in memories glad,
For none has yet come and faded,
    Who equals that of my Mom and Dad.
And had I totaled, throughout life,
    With much wisdom and gains of merit,
Couldn't have chosen better myself,
    Than the folks whom I did just inherit.

    By example of intent,
      They lived how they spoke,
    Oh! In every event,
      They were darn good folk!!
    Simple and content,
      They were so rich yet broke
    Ah! To a great extent,
      They were darn good folk.

~

COASTAL TWILIGHT

COASTAL TWILIGHT

Ahoy! Wider yet curtains drew
    Across the horizon's ocean rim,
Air is chilled from salty dew,
    A pulse like spray in foggy dim.

Listen for sudden quietness
    Hear the gap, as twilight plays
Stars peek in grayish stillness
    In-between the clouds of strays

Choppy look invented sway
    Awe! How old time here seems
Rock of bird island display
    A weather beaten sea redeems

Tonight's song played uncut
    As spotty sounds come and go
Wailing winds come to strut
    Voiced in a round about echo,

The fog clears and reappears
    As clouds form figure's oblong
Eve' salt air sweats its tears
    A huddled starlight plays along.

Waves overlap into a foam
    Reflecting whirls of radiant flair
An untamed sea breeze roam
    As the fog horn dances with air

Moon's misty eye does invite,
    By glittering silver atop the sea
Spotty clouds shadowed nite
    Revealing heaven without plea

SHINE, SILVERY SALTED WATERS
    AS PHOSPHORUS SPARKLES SPARK
FADES FROM SIGHT THEN ALTERS
    TO TWILIGHT BLUSHES IN THE DARK.

RECEDING SHORE TAPERED SAND
    BEFORE A DAWN BEGINS TO GLOW
REACHES AGAIN TO STRIKE LAND
    OCEAN RHYTHM TO ONWARD FLOW

WHITECAPS GRASP BREAKS TOP
    REACHING FOR ITS HEIGHT TO CREST
WAVE OF FIGURES FLOAT AN FLOP
    PURSUES HORIZON WITHOUT REST.

ANOTHER SLAP UPON THE BEACH
    SEAWEED LIFE PROJECT'S A SMELL
OFF STARBOARD BEYOND REACH
    BUOYS NOISE THE WHISTLE OR BELL

EDGE OF THE BEACH IN A COVE
    SEASHELLS TO STARFISH OF RARITIES
BARNACLES TO TREASURE TROVE
    IN OCEAN'S GALAXY OF MYSTERIES.

NORTHWESTERLYS TO ROGUE REEF
    MACK ARCH, CAPE FERRELO'S SITE
SOUTH TO CHETCO COVE'S RELIEF
    OR ST. GEORGE'S LIGHTHOUSE LITE

IN THE HARBOR, WINDS LAY STILL
    LIGHTS GLITTER BASIN'S DIM PORT
OUTLINED FISHING VESSELS FRILL
    ALONG DOCK DOLPHINS SUPPORT

The silhouette of masts sway
    Docks clutter of hose and line
Seagulls rest, awaiting day
    Air glistens a mist of seabrine

Sea communes without talk,
    Into movements of expressions
Marked reef appears to walk
    In ripples of twilight reflections

Spread upon horizon yonder
    Moonlight gleams in devotion
As star's curious eyes ponder
    Skips a glance atop the ocean.

Around the jetty at the port
    Salt lines mar as tide recedes
Twisted kelp in shell escort
    Shoreline of wood and reeds

Chetco's inlet low elevation
    Streaking estuary's tidal rings
About Coast Guard's station
    The port of Harbor, Brookings.

Here sea and mountain meet
    And morning fog chills the air
For salty air 'tis indeed a treat
    No other sight could compare.

~

LIFELIGHT

LIFELIGHT

This light isn't found
    By simply living in life
But is within the one
    Searching with strife

This life itself is void
    With no divine peace
But within the being
    Where light increase

Can close one's eyes
    But never his heart
In the land of living
    Where light is apart.

Then without Christ
    Man's perpetual light
None can declare life
    Or claim a birthright

Out of the shadows
    Of man's own cover
Glows a light of life
    For each to discover.

A swirled silhouette
    Lights dawn is near
A life is yet to come
    And kingdom appear

~

BE ENCOURAGED O' SOUL

BE ENCOURAGED O' SOUL

Be encouraged O' soul
    Tho' I walk in misty dark
My dark is enlightened
    For by faith does it hark.

Be encouraged O' soul,
    I shall grasp God's hand,
For to ease my own fall,
    From where I now stand.

Be encouraged O' soul
    Tho my thoughts stumble,
The force of the spirit,
    Again makes me humble.

Be encouraged O' soul
    Not by works of my hands,
But directing my goals,
    Into my Lord's demands.

Be encouraged O' soul
    Again the spirit has ruled.
So we shall overcome
    An this time not be fooled.

Be encouraged O' soul,
    For thy peace is my goal
Toward a life everlasting,
    O' be encouraged O' soul.

~

CREEPING SHADOWS

CREEPING SHADOWS

ALAS! A PARTICULAR TRAGEDY,
   TODAY INTO MY MIND IT STILL PRYS,
FOURTEENTH OF AUGUST, FIFTY-NINE,
   VELVET DARKNESS ACROSS THE SKYS,
EVER PICTURED IN MEMORY.
   REPEATING, REPLAYING, VERY CLEAR,
OF A ONE BRISK SUMMERNIGHT.
   WE SET OUT TOGETHER TO GET A DEER.

MOM'S INTUITION HAD SENSED,
   THAT A SOMETHING WAS NOT RIGHT,
WARNING US TO STAY HOME,
   ON THAT SEEMINGLY FATEFUL NIGHT,
BUT MYSELF, BEING YOUNGER,
   CONVINCED I KNEW WHAT WAS BEST,
WHERE SILENT TWILIGHT RUSHES,
   WE SET OUR SKILLS FORTH INTO TEST.

MY YOUNGER BROTHER AND I
   WERE AS HAPPY AS HAPPY AS EVER,
LIKE SCATTERED MILKY STARS,
   WE WERE ALWAYS FOUND TOGETHER,
OUR COUSIN NOW JOINED US,
   TOGETHER SO HAPPY, FULL OF CHEER,
AS WE ALL SET OUT TOGETHER,
   BENEATH WOODLAND TO GET A DEER.

OUT FROM UNDER LIGHTNESS,
   THE DARKNESS GATHERED AROUND,
OUT WHERE GLITTERING STARS,
   AND SHADED SHADOWS ARE FOUND,
BREATHING CHILLS OF SPIRIT,
   WITH SCENT NOW SO SOFT TO PLEASE,
AN CRISP GROWING MOSS LIES,
   AROUND NATURE'S WITHERED TREES.

T'WAS A FULL MOON THAT EVE,
      AS WE STARTED MOVING VERY SLOW,
T'WAS A LIGHT FRIDAY NIGHT,
      BUT THAT NIGHT THE LIGHT WAS LOW,
WHEN WE GOT WITHIN A MILE,
      OF THE PLACE WE CALLED OLD FLINTS,
THEY WAITED AT A CROSSING,
      AS I WENT ALONE ALONG THE FENCE,

I LEFT WITH THEM A FLASHLIGHT,
      AND WENT FROM A WOODS NEARBY,
WHERE TREES BENT N' WHISTLE,
      WHENEVER THE WINDS RUSHED BY,
I TRAILED TOWARD THE CANYON,
      WHERE GRASSES WERE WORN DOWN,
TO THE FIELD OF THIN TIMOTHY,
      WHERE THICKETS OF OAKS SURROUN'

Last half I walked silently
　　　Beneath a starred 'n lonely sky,
From shadows of the moon,
　　　To the pathless woods near by,
I saw a deer in thickness,
　　　Of the woods so full and sweet,
I aimed; pulled the trigger,
　　　He turned to the woods, in leap.

My single shot twenty-two,
　　　Had slightly wounded him now,
He backed into shadows,
　　　I lost the trace of him somehow,
But I knew of a shortcut,
　　　To head him off round the pass
Down thru a timothy field,
　　　Into the dark green misty grass.

Now in dark gathering mist,
　　　Where creeping shadows creep,
Deer in the meadowlands,
　　　Roam in the night, now so deep,
Oh my blood, fast to flow,
　　　As my heart rush to beat again,
I felt sure to get my deer,
　　　Where the air was cool and thin.

Once again I load my gun,
　　　To finish my hunt for that night,
I spot something moving,
　　　Into the shade of the moonlight,
I then saw the deer again,
　　　I turned warm with heart racing,
In echoes through shadows,
　　　Where the crickets now do sing.

I SEE THE DEER STAND ALONE,
  WHERE THE WILDEST FLOWERS GROW,
AGAIN WAVES OF DARKNESS,
  WHERE GLEAMS OF STARLIGHT IS LOW,
SUDDENLY THEN, IT MOVED,
  QUICKLY I SHOT WITH CAREFUL AIM,
AN' AT THE EDGE OF SHADOWS,
  CREEPING SHADOW MADE ITS CLAIM.

THE DEER, WHICH I HAD SEEN,
  BESIDE A SHADED OAK TREE BEAM,
WAS MIST MADE OF NOTHING,
  BUT SHADOWED TRACES OF DREAM,
A LONELY CRYING OF A CHILD,
  SET MY HEART IN A SHOCKING FEAR,
FOLLOWED A BLINDING MIST,
  SQUINTING THROUGH SORROW'S TEAR,

MY COUSIN N' LITTLE BROTHER,
  IN CREEPING SHADOWS HALF-TONE,
DOWN SIDE THE MOUNTAIN,
  TO SURPRISE ME WHILE I'M ALONE,
DISOBEYED OUR PERFECT PLAN,
  FROM THE CROSSING THEY STRAYED,
FOLLOWED ME INTO THE WOODS,
  FROM 'ERE THEY SHOULD'VE STAYED.

MY BROTHER STEPPED OUT,
  AND YES, I SAW HIM CLEARLY THERE,
CRYING OUT LOUD MY NAME,
  ECHOING A CHILLNESS INTO THE AIR.
I THREW MY GUN, AND RAN,
  TO MY BROTHER FROM OTHER HARMS,
AS HE FELL, I REACHED OUT,
  AND CAUGHT HIS BODY IN MY ARMS.

I RAN WITH HIM IN MY ARMS,
      TO A ROAD NEAR THE MANY TREES,
AND THEN FELT WEAK AN' ODD,
      I THEN FELL DOWN UPON MY KNEES,
I REST HIS HEAD ON MY SHIRT,
      "YOU'LL BE OKAY," I FEARFULLY SAID,
BUT TO MYSELF THEN THOUGHT
      BETTER HURRY BEFORE HE IS DEAD.

I RACED TO A VACANT HOUSE,
      THROUGH A WINDOW, CALLED HOME,
AFTER ASKING THEM TO HURRY,
      I QUICKLY THREW DOWN THE PHONE,
BACK OUTSIDE THE WINDOW,
      TO MY BROTHER IN A FASTEST STRIDE,
THROUGH TORN, SHADED TREES,
      TO MY DEAR LITTLE BROTHER'S SIDE

I REACHED HIM LYING THERE
      HE LOOKED UP TO ME ONCE MORE,
AS IF HE WERE ASKING HELP
      OF BIG BROTHER AS TIMES BEFORE
I HELD HIM CLOSE IN MY ARMS,
      AS HE CRIED, 'HELP ME' THAT NIGHT,
I COULD FEEL HIS BODY LIMP,
      AND WILL NEVER FORGET THAT SIGHT.

HIS EYES JUST LOOKED AT ME,
      AS BLOOD RUSHED FROM HIS FACE,
I TRIED A MOUTH-TO-MOUTH,
      BUT ONLY HIS BLOOD COULD I TASTE,
THE BULLET ENTERED HIS SIDE,
      IN MY ARMS HE HAD A FACE OF FEAR,
HE LOOKED DIRECTLY AT ME,
      ONLY VIVID GASPING COULD I HEAR.

OH, MY DEAR LITTLE BROTHER,
      IS THIS GOD'S WAY FOR YOUR DEATH,
OH GOD, IF SO, LET HIM LIVE,
      AND PLEASE TAKE MY LAST BREATH,
I RAISED MY HEAD TO HEAVEN,
      FOR LORD, DEATH I DO NOT DREAD,
O PLEASE LORD, I BARGAINED,
      WON'T YOU LORD, TAKE ME INSTEAD

I KEPT HOLDING HIM CLOSER,
      MAKING FOOLISH PROMISES TO HIM,
KEPT HOPING HE'D HEARD ME,
      EVEN IF THE CHANCES SEEMED SLIM,
WHEN HELP FINALLY ARRIVED,
      I LOADED HIM BUT IT WAS TOO LATE,
MY DEAREST LITTLE BROTHER,
      HAD GONE TO GOD'S GOLDEN GATE.

ONLY SWEETEST MEMORIES,
      WITH THE GOODNESS OF HIS LOVE,
COMES NOW TO MY BROTHER,
      FROM THAT GREAT ONE UP ABOVE,
THE WORLD AND ITS TWILIGHT,
      TIS GOD'S SPARKLING STARRY AIM,
WHERE ONCE WE FOUND GLORY,
      IN THAT SO-CALLED HUNTING GAME.

MY BROTHER CRIED OUT TO ME,
      IN WORDS TODAY I STILL TRY TO HIDE,
THE WORDS, "YOU SHOT ME",
      INTO THE AIR'S STILLNESS HE CRIED,
AND I COULD NEVER FORGET,
      A NEEDING WAY HE LOOKED AT ME,
BUT WONDER WHAT HE THOUGHT,
      OR HIS THOUGHTS OF ME COULD BE,

THEN MOM SO LOOKED AT ME,
      WITH EYES INDEED SWOLLEN SAD,
TEARS DOWN SIDE HER CHEEK,
      WHICH WERE COMFORTED BY DAD,
AGAIN MOM FOUGHT TEARS,
      FROM GREAT LOSS OF HER LITTLE SON,
WITH A TREMBLING OF HANDS,
      DAD WAS STRENGTH FOR EVERYONE.

My other brother an' sister,
        Found it most difficult to adjust,
A feel of awkward sorrow,
        Questioning death and its just.
So hard for them to accept,
        What they saw with their eyes,
Nor knowing what to think,
        How this loved child's body lies,

The doctor brought to me,
        His personal things to recheck,
And one thing that he wore,
        A sink's plug chain on his neck,
Though no one else but I,
        Knew the reasons this was done,
For the chain was the gift,
        That bound two brothers as one,

When the moon is full bright
        In the heavens so high up above,
Still seems I always think,
        Of my dear brother whom I love,
When I hear birds singing,
        Within the clearness of the sky,
I know youth is one thing,
        That all of gold could never buy.

As winds whistle at stars,
        Looking down from their towers.
Or a full moonlight glows,
        On the tops of midnight flowers,
Cloudy shadows in heaven,
        Creeping slowly across the sky,
Another night blossomed,
        As vines of Sweet Peas that tie,

WE WERE YOUNG AND HAPPY,
    BECAME EACH OTHER'S BEST FRIEND
WE WALKED AND TOLD STORIES,
    OR SANG OUR SONG, *LET'S PRETEND*,
NOW THE SWEETNESS OF DEW
    MOISTEN MEADOWLANDS I PONDER
IN THE VALLEY OF YESTERDAY,
    I STILL VISION THAT CANYON YONDER.

A PATH TO HEAVEN'S GLORY,
    THAT LEADS DIRECTLY TO HIS GRAVE,
GATEWAY BEYOND THE STARS,
    SO THE MIGHTY LORD TO HIM GAVE,
HE WALKS ALONG SIDE GOD
    WITH ANGEL STEPS OF AIRY GRACE,
A HALO AND PLEASANT SMILE,
    UPON MY BROTHER'S ANGELIC FACE.

TODAY THROUGH THE WORLD,
    WHERE CREEPING SHADOWS CREEP,
I HEAR ECHOES OF HIS VOICE,
    CALLING OUT TO ME SOFT AND DEEP,
EVEN NOW CHILLS RUN THRU ME,
    BECAUSE STILL I THINK OF HIM A LOT,
AS HE CALLS OUT MY NAME,
    TO THAT MOST QUIET RESTING SPOT.

OH, MY DEAR LITTLE BROTHER,
    IN A HILLY GRAVEYARD NOW TO REST,
HE HAS BUT CROSSED OVER,
    INTO HEAVEN'S BEAUTIFUL DIVINEST.
AN' YEA, AGAIN I SEE HIM,
    A VISION GLOW OF VIBRATING LIGHT,
PRAYING "GOD BLESS YOU"
    MY DEAR BROTHER, AGAIN TONIGHT!

~

CONCLUSIONS

IF YOU DISCOVER YOURSELF IN THE WRONG PLACE
THEN YOU'LL FIND THE RIGHT PLACE EMPTY SPACE
    BETTER TO APPRECIATE THINGS WHICH OTHERS OWN
    THAN TO OWN THINGS YOU PLACE UPON A THRONE.
THE LORD PROVIDES FEED TO THE BIRD'S INTEREST
ALTHOUGH HE DOESN'T JUST PUT IT IN THEIR NEST.
    NONE OF US STOP LAUGHING BECAUSE WE'RE OLD
    WE GET OLD AS WE STOP LAUGHING AND WITHHOLD
LITTLE DECISIONS OVER HURDLES OR COLLISIONS
MOLDS OUR CHARACTER TO MAKE BIG DECISIONS
    EVER NOTICE THAT THE SMARTEST PEOPLE YOU SEE
    THEY BELIEVE JUST LIKE YOU DO AND ALSO AGREE
THE COST OF EXPERIENCES MIGHT BE IN EXCESS
BUT USUALLY IMPOSSIBLE TO FIND FOR ANY LESS
    IT'S MUCH BETTER TO STUMBLE AND CONFRONT STRIFE
    THAN TO AVOID THE SIDE STEPS OF CHANCES IN LIFE
WORSE THAN PEOPLE QUITTING A PROJECT IN PART
IS FINISHING A PROJECT THEY SHOULDN'T LET START
    DO NOT EXPECT THE LORD TO ALWAYS DO FOR YOU
    THE THINGS YOU YOURSELF ARE ABLE TO PURSUE.

~

THE RELATIONSHIP

THE RELATIONSHIP

TRUE HAPPINESS IS NOT EFFORTLESS AT ALL
    RATHER GIVING A LITTLE, AND TAKING A LITTLE
SHARE HOPES, SECRETS, DESIRES TO RECALL
    TO BEND, TO LEAN, AND NOT BE TOO BRITTLE

TO GIVE OR TO TAKE, TO HAVE AND TO SHARE
    BUILD DREAMS TOGETHER A STRONG RELATION
TO LOVE, ADMIRE, RESPECT AND BE AWARE
    BECOME BEST FRIENDS IN COMMUNICATION

BY CORRECTING EACH OTHER, MAKE CHANGE
    HAVING FAITH TOGETHER, IN HONOR IN TRUST
TO WAIT WITH PATIENCE FOR EACH EXCHANGE
    EACH TO CHERISH AND BE WILLING TO ADJUST

BUT A LIFE IS SHORT, THEN COMES A PAUSE
    THAT CHALLENGES A RELATIONSHIP TO BLEND
MAKING CHOICES COMPLICATED WITH CAUSE
    A VAST CONQUEST SHAPING LOVE TO MEND

SO THEN, WHAT'S WRONG WITH THIS PICTURE?
    FOR A LOVE CONSISTS OF STRUGGLE TO STRESS
AS COUPLES FORCE ENERGY INTO ADVENTURE
    TRANSFORMING THIS RIDDLE, EASING DISTRESS

YET JUDGEMENTS AND ITS INCONVENIENCES
    AREN'T WITHOUT TRIALS OR LIKENESS THEREOF,
WHEREAS EFFORT MIXES ALL EXPERIENCES
    MERGING TWO INTO ONE FOR GENUINE LOVE.

~

SHED NOT

Shed not the tears that
    Now fall from your eye,
That last kiss in parting
    Does not mean goodbye
It's just a sad moment
    That has drawn us apart
And equals only a short
    Loneliness in our heart

Shed not the smile that
    Is not even really there
It's written on your face
    Each little hidden care
Smiles from the heart
    May be hid, yet prevail
Its memories in parting
    That will build the trail,

Shed not the last look,
    Just before out of sight
Yes, I know, Sweetheart,
    It don't quite seem right
So think of tomorrow
    With unwavering looks
Sense of wonder unfound
    In any words or books

Shed not inner feelings
     Grasping from the soul
It's difficult, for only
     Together are we whole,
We're just a dream away,
     So reminisce and smile
As the separating miles
     Challenges by this trial

Shed not the memories
     Of that lonely good-bye
Dreams find each other
     If only together we try
Shed not the silence
     Caused by the absentee
As we shed not to speak
     To a one we cannot see

~

RIVER OF LIFE

Have you ridden the twisting of the river?
    Through life's swiftness with its bends,
Or floated down the channels that deliver
    Troubled water dividing best of friends.

Have you burned the bridges behind you
    As you passed beneath them by and by
Ignoring the cries of help as you continue
    Breaking the shadows that may satisfy.

Have you divided clear waters in twain,
    Likened to conclusions you once drew
Look how wide harmful ripples remain,
    Where trembling, wrinkled waters grew.

Have you heard the voice on the lily pad
    Whispering a gossip across its weeds.
Against a someone who might have had
    A hand of friendship in many a deeds

Have you sailed a stream to choppy sea?
    Using foolish wake of words that stray.
And crush the dreams which others plea
    Launching the hopes to some spillway.

    Be careful in life's waterway
    Consider ones you did forsake
    Spend a time for love and play,
    Ease the judgment you make,
    Build no bridges to burn down
    Nor cause dams to hinder flow
    Cast no stones on soft ground
    From the gossip others throw
    In the river of life as you row.

HAVE YOU SEEN LIFE'S BANK OF ITS EROSION,
    WHERE THE CHALKBOARD OF LIFE BE SO FRAIL?
IF A THREAD RUNS THROUGH IT OF CORROSION,
    ARE WORDS OF COMFORT ABOARD YOUR SAIL?

HAVE YOU STOOD IN MAN-MADE SHADOWS,
    PRYING OPEN THE LIVES WITHIN YOUR WAKE?
OR EXPERIENCE THE PATH IN THEIR SORROWS,
    PREPARING THE JOURNEY WE ALL MUST TAKE?

HAVE YOU TOSSED FORTH YOUR OWN LIFELINE,
    OR WADED OUT IN DULL BITTERNESS OF COLD,
HELPING A STRANGER REACH THE SHORELINE,
    UNTIL PEACE CHEERING THE HEARTS UNFOLD?

HAVE YOU PADDLED VIGOROUSLY UPSTREAM
    DURING THE TIME YOU COULD BARELY FLOAT
JUST TO HELP ANOTHER ACHIEVE THEIR DREAM
    TO FREE THE BURDEN, UNSTRAND THEIR BOAT

HAVE YOU SMELLED THE FRESH RAINWATERS
    CLOUDS RETURN WHICH THEY TOOK BY STRIFE
SHOULDN'T WE ALL BE SONS AND DAUGHTERS
    AS WE ROW TOGETHER IN THIS RIVER OF LIFE

    BE CAREFUL IN LIFE'S WATERWAY
    CONSIDER ONES YOU DID FORSAKE
    SPEND A TIME FOR LOVE AND PLAY,
    EASE THE JUDGMENT YOU MAKE,
    BUILD NO BRIDGES TO BURN DOWN
    NOR CAUSE DAMS TO HINDER FLOW
    CAST NO STONES ON SOFT GROUND
    FROM THE GOSSIP OTHERS THROW
    IN THE RIVER OF LIFE AS YOU ROW.

~

BEST THINGS IN LIFE
(1960)

IN THE BEGINNING,
GOD CREATED HEAVEN AND EARTH
PUT ITS FORM
LIGHT AND THE DRY LAND TO BIRTH

THEN WISHED
HE TWO PLANETS ROUND FOR LIGHT
SAYS ONE FOR DAY
AND THE OTHER IS MADE FOR NIGHT

NEXT CAME HERBS
AND TREES WHICH EARTH NEEDED
WHEN HE SAW
THAT WAS GOOD, THEN PROCEEDED

SOME WITH FRUIT
MANY OTHERS WOULD HAVE NONE
BUT ALL TO REACH
UP TOWARD THE GLIMMERING SUN

LET THE WATERS
TO BRING FORTH LIVING CREATURES
AND ABOVE THEM
FOWL IN MANY DIFFERENT FEATURES

IN OPEN FIRMAMENT
OF THE HEAVENS HIGH UP ABOVE
GOD BROUGHT FORTH
ASSORTED BIRDS TO SING OF LOVE

AND TO CREEP
UPON EARTH GOD CREATED BEAST
SAYING "LET THERE
BE OUR IMAGE" 'FORE HE CEASED

He made man
And woman that they'll be one
Once content
He then rested, for it was done.

He made the
Summer skies to winter's snow
Autumnal winds
A breathing forth soft and low

He made the days
With its whitish clouds floating
From the waters
For a shadow cover of coating

He made the
Silvery moon with starry skies
And the airy steps
For when some overcomer dies

He made the
Sweet odors for Lily and Rose
Even the music
Where a brook and river flows

But, the most
Precious of all He made to be
Was you, Darling
Because He made you for me!

~

QUEST OF THE SAX
(1987)

EVENING SHADOWS DANCE, VALLEY TO HILL,
    WHERE SOUNDS UNSOUGHT STAGES TONIGHT'S PLAY,
WINDS PERFORM TUNES IN A NATURAL SKILL
    THRU ARMS THAT APPEAR TO REACH OUT AND PRAY.

INVISIBLE AIR APPROACHES, WINDBLOWN,
    EACH TREE, EACH BUSH, SUDDENLY TAKE ON SOUND,
TUNES QUOTE, FROM A SOURCE UNKNOWN,
    INTO A HARMONIZING CHOIR TOGETHER UNCROWNED.

THIS TRAIL OF SILENCE BETWEEN EACH NOTE,
    OH, FROM WHERE OR HOW COMES THIS ODD SONG?
EACH JOT, EACH TITTLE, THE MASTER WROTE,
    HE CAUSED A CAUSE FOR EVERY SOUND TO BELONG.

LONG I'VE SOUGHT TO KNOW ITS TREASURE,
    WHERE COMES THIS SOUND AS A SAXOPHONE, ALIVE
THIS SHRILL VIBRATES WITHOUT A MEASURE,
    THEN ITS SOURCE SHIFTS AND MOVES WHEN I ARRIVE.

ROUND LEAFLESS BOUGHS, OR CREST OF ROCK,
    BY WHERE THE PITCH COVERED PINE CONE ATTENDS,
A HOOT OF AN OWL OR SQUELCH OF A HAWK,
    THE WINDS BRING TOGETHER AS ITS MUSIC BEGINS

I ASK MYSELF ABOUT THIS STRANGE EVENT,
    OF THIS ARRANGEMENT PORTRAYING A SAXOPHONE?
THE HORN ECHOED WHERE IT WAS MEANT,
    THIS HARMONIOUS TRAIL OF NATURE'S MICROPHONE.

TUNES SOFTLY, THEY COME AND THEY FADE,
    ONLY HERE CAN THIS CHARM AND TONE BE HEARD,
STRING INSTRUMENTS OR HORNS ARE MADE,
    TO CYMBALS OR DRUMS THE WINDS HAVE STIRRED.

QUEST OF THE SAXOPHONE PLAYS ITS KEYS,
    A TUNEFUL RHYTHM WHERE WINDS AND LIMB MEET,
THE CHOIR OF THE VALLEY UPON ITS KNEES,
    ACCOMPANYING THE SAX TO THE MOUNTAINS BEAT.

EACH SOUND IS PATTERNED PLAYING FREE,
    VOICING THIS CHARMED MUSIC WHISPERING LOW,
A WONDER OF SOUND I JUST CANNOT SEE,
    HOW THE SAX'S UNTAMED TUNES OR ECHOES BLOW

AS FINE AS FINE MIGHT EVER BE ALLOWED,
    CASTS FORTH THESE SOUNDS WITH A VESPER HYMN,
QUEST OF THE SAX PLAYED, THEN BOWED,
    AS UNEQUALED TUNES SHUFFLE FROM LIMB TO LIMB

FROM WHERE COMES THIS TONE OF THE SAX,
    AS I SEEK FOR ITS SOURCE, ITS CAUSE, ITS ADDRESS,
THE PLAY IS SOOTHING A CAUSE TO RELAX,
    NOR COULD I EVER EXPLAIN THIS MOOD, I CONFESS.

NOW SCATTERED CLOUDS PASS BY TO PEAK,
    AS THE MOON AND STARS TOGETHER STREAK A STAFF,
THIS SOLO HORNED INSTRUMENT THAT I SEEK,
    PLAY GAMES WITH ME, AND THEN HIDE AND LAUGH.

BETWEEN EACH SHADOW IT FORMS A GATE,
    SOUNDS SHARP TO FLAT, THEN PAUSE EVERYWHERE,
IN KEYS THAT MAN COULD NEVER DUPLICATE,
    DANCING CONCERT AS IT BRAIDS THROUGH THE AIR.

IN HALF TONE NOTES, THE PLAY IS PLAYED,
    FULL NOTES BURST UPON THE WINDS THEY BORROW,
A LEAF STRUMS A LIMB, SHADE TO SHADE,
    CLOSED FLOWERS TONIGHT SHALL SMILE TOMORROW.

SUCH GRATEFUL TUNES, THEN UN-IDENTIFIED,
    COMBINING WINDS WITH NATURE INTO MUSIC SIFT,
FROM WHERE DOES IT COME, OR GO TO HIDE,
    ARRANGEMENT TONIGHT, BEAUTIFUL MUSIC ADRIFT.

PLAYING ONLY FOR THE TIME IT WAS MEANT,
    OR FROM ITS RUFFLED QUIET TURNABOUT MAY FADE,
NONE COULD COMPARE THIS GIFTED EVENT,
    TO ADJUSTED SOUNDS PATTERNED AFTER OR MADE.

SO, LISTEN MY FRIEND AND BEND YOUR EAR.
    SEEK THE PLACE THEY PLAY THESE QUICKEN TONES,
AND PERHAPS, TONIGHT YOU TOO WILL HEAR,
    THIS MELLOW CHOSEN TIME OF THE SAXOPHONES.

~

ANNIVERSARY TRIBUTE

LO! THE YEARS HAVE PASSED
    TOMORROWS WILL HAVE TO WAIT,
AND, IF ONLY TODAY WOULD LAST,
    WE COULD THE MORE, CELEBRATE.

YOU'RE THE GLEAM IN MY EYE,
    OF THIRTY YEARS MY SWEET STAR,
AND AS THE YEARS PASS BY,
    THE MORE BEAUTIFUL...YOU ARE.

MY VALENTINE, OF COURSE,
    A SINGLE ROSE AMONG THE REST,
MY HONEY, UPON A HORSE,
    WHO MAKES MY LIFE, THE BEST!

~

THE SCHOOLYARD

THE SCHOOLYARD

(1970)

I CAN SEE THE CHILDREN PLAY
HAPPILY IN THE SCHOOL YARD TODAY
    BRINGS BACK MEMORIES
DRAW A CIRCLE IN THE GROUND
TO SHOOT THEIR MARBLES ALL AROUND,
    OF PEEWEES AND STEELIES.

PLAY HOPSCOTCH ON THE WALK
OR WATCHING THE TEETER-TOTTERS ROCK,
    RING AROUND THE ROSIE,
PLAYING TAG, TOUCH THEN RAN,
FROM BASKETBALL WITH A MIDDLEMAN
    OR SOME OTHER FANTASY.

OFF THE SLIDE INTO THE SWING,
OR JUMP THE MERRY-GO-ROUND WING
    AND MAKE UP NEW RULES.
I WATCH THEM PLAYING SOME,
PICTURE MYSELF AGAIN BEING YOUNG,
    PLAYING IN THE SCHOOLS,

BE THOSE TIMES FOREVER GONE,
CHILDISH DREAMS A FORGOTTEN SONG;
    ONCE MEANT MUCH TO ME
THOSE DAYS CAME AND PAST
I AM SO GLAD THEY ARE GONE AT LAST,
    SO, I SAY FIDDLE DEE DEE

CAUSE I REMEMBER THE REST
LONG DRAWN HOURS IN HARDEST TEST,
    LONG WAITS FOR HOLIDAY
HOMEWORK AN' EARLY TO BED,
PADDLESTICK, OR BANG ON THE HEAD,
    AGAIN I'LL SAY "HURRAY!"

~

IN MY DREAMS

IN MY DREAMS

O' LAST NIGHT WHILE STARS,
            WERE BRIGHT SHINING,
        AN' THE MOON WAS TO A GLOW,
I FELL SOUND ASLEEP WITH
            THE WINDS A WHINING,
        AMONG CRICKETS SINGING LOW.

AN AIRY STAIRWAY INTO
            A SHADOWLESS VALLEY,
        SUSPENDS ABOVE LONELY DEAD,
THE GREAT CITY OF LIGHTS,
            THROUGH GOD'S ALLEY
        CLOUDS GATHER A PURIFIED BED.

WITHIN A MIST OF HEAVENS,
            ENLIGHTENED SHADING
        T'WAS A BLUR THE WINDS BLEW
AH, A MIST OF WARMTH CHILL
            COMMENCED FADING
        INTO A PATH OF HEAVEN'S PEW.

SLOWLY I BEGAN TURNING,
            WITHIN A SILENT DREAM,
        I HEARD A LOW WHISPER AGAIN,
THEN THROUGH A SHADOWED
            AND ENGULFING BEAM
        SHE STOOD BEYOND A CURTAIN.

AN ANGELIC SMILE ON HER,
            SOFT ROSY HAZEN LIPS
        AN ENLIGHTENING TEAR OF MIST,
SHE LEANED TO ME WHERE
            PEWS STAIRWAY DIPS
        WHISPERED "SON", AND KISSED.

THEN RETRACTING WITH A
        SWEET ECHOING'S REPLY
    "SON", SHE SAID, "I LOVE YOU,
DON'T STAND SADLY WITH
        THE TEARS IN YOUR EYE,
      LIFE FOR ME IS NOT YET THROUGH

FOR WHEN SUNRISE PEAKS
        ON THE MOUNTAINSIDE,
      OR MOONGLOW SHEDDING LOVE
I'LL WATCH OVER YOU EVER
        BUT MY SOUL WILL HIDE,
    IN THAT BIG HOUSE UP ABOVE.

'TIS A CROSSROAD LEADING,
        INTO ENDLESS ETERNITY,
      COMMENCING HEAVEN'S LIGHT,
"SO, YOU SEE SON, YOU'RE
        NOT ALONE WITHOUT ME",
    IN SMILE SHE SAID GOODNIGHT.

WITH TREMBLING HANDS,
        REACHED FOR HER CARE,
      THIS ANGEL A MOTHER OF CRUST
AS I BLINKED I SAW NOTHING
        STAND BEFORE ME THERE,
    SHE SWEETLY SMITTEN INTO DUST.

AY' EVERYTHING VANISHED,
        YET QUICKLY AND QUIET
      SO GONE WAS HEAVEN'S BEAM,
TODAY I STILL SEE HOW HER
        UNSHADOWED EYES LIT,
    AS SHE SMILED IN MY DREAM.

~

HUSH OF SHADOWS

OH! THE HILL STOOD
    BEFORE STILLY TWILIGHT
WITH FOREST SHADE
    THAT NIGHT'S PREPARE
WHERE BRIAR ROSE
    WITH BLOSSOMS BRIGHT
IN BOUNDLESS SKY
    APPEAR COLORFUL GLARE

FLOWING OF WATERS
    WITH LIGHT BLUE GREEN
ON COLORED PEBBLES
    SCATTERED BARE ABOUT
COOL AIR MURMURS
    IN SOFT MUSIC UNSEEN
AS LOW WINDS WAVE
    IN A WHISPERED SHOUT

ON WELL WORN TRUNK
    A MOSS COVERED TREE
CAST SHADOWS WALK
    PRANCE ABOUT THE HILL
PEEPING THRU TREES,
    WILD GARDEN SET FREE,
LEAN VIOLETS SWEET
    TENDER QUIET AND STILL

A CAST OF SHADOWS
    AS SETTING SUN BREAKS
SIGNALS TO PREPARE
    FOR THE COMING HOURS
SETTLING NOW TO REST
    THIS EVENING IT MAKES
FAINTER THEN FADES
    WHERE SHADE DEVOURS

STILL MIGHTY BOUGHS
      UPON MISTLETOED OAK
REACHES TO HEAVEN
      WITH ITS STURDIEST ARM
IT'S HERE MATED BIRDS
      SANG IN WARBLE SPOKE
OR NEST THEIR HOMES
      ON ITS HIDDEN CHARM

AN ENCHANTED TIME
      REPEATING ITSELF AGAIN
AS MOMENTS CHANGE
      THAT PROCESS THE DARK
A SECRET OF EVENING
      PREPARING FOR ITS GAIN
IN THIS FADING TIME,
      ON A SHADOWED PARK

OH' BREATHLESS AWE!
      A BEAUTY TO CELEBRATE
OH' A DAZZLED SIGHT
      IN SHADOWED THICKET
OH' FENCELESS PLACE
      PARK WITHOUT A GATE
OH' SOUNDING BREEZE
      THRU LIMBS OF PICKET.

MANY FORMS OF FORM
      FLICKER INTO THIS EVE
AFTER A SHORT PAUSE
      COME TWILITE BLUSHES
FROM ZONE TO ZONE
      THE SHADOWS RELIEVE
THIS SCENE WE SEE
      IMAGINATION TOUCHES.

From gathering shade
    To silver lined moon
Alters tonight's view
    Within jeweled skies
This hush of shadows
    Shall be fading soon
By lifting its shades
    And change disguise.

WANTS OF ME

I KNOW A MAN WHO FROM GOD
    TURNS HIS HEAD
HE BREATHES FRESH AIR BUT HIS
    SOUL WAITS DEAD
AND THOUGH HIS HOLLOW EYES,
    I STILL TRY TO SEE
HAS GOD INTRODUCED HIM FOR
    THE WANTS OF ME?

FROM EARLIER CALLS HE TURNED
    AND WENT AWAY
FOR A "MORE CONVENIENT TIME"
    FOR "ANOTHER DAY,"
TO WAIT FOR ANOTHER TOMORROW
    WITHOUT CERTAINTY,
HAS GOD INTRODUCED HIM FOR
    THE WANTS OF ME?

AFTER FOLLOWING A LITTLE VISIT
    IT BECOMES CLEAR
WHEN HE HEARS OF THE SAVIOR
    HE LENDS AN EAR
HE SEEKS BY WAY OF EXAMPLE,
    SO VERY SECRETLY
HAS GOD INTRODUCED HIM FOR
    THE WANTS OF ME?

AN INQUISITIVE MIND HE ASKS
    OF THINGS HEARD,
COMES FORTH WITH QUESTIONS
    ABOUT THE WORD
AND MORE ABOUT THE STRANGER
    FROM GALILEE
HAS GOD INTRODUCED HIM FOR
    THE WANTS OF ME?

It is not only from the words,
Heard in youth,
Or smooth ways ones spoke,
False or truth
But, more yet, from example
One might be
Has God introduced him for
The wants of me?

So the moral of this writing
Is a way to say,
We have different missions
In our own way,
From the needs of someone
Seeking the key
To unlock the wants of you
Or wants of me.

~

SENSES

SENSES

I HEARD A TUNE WITHIN THE AIR,
        A LOVELY MUSIC IT DID CAST,
A MELODY WHICH HAD NO END,
        THEN CAME A PAUSE AT LAST,

I'VE SMELLED A PLEASANT SMELL,
        IT WAS A SWEET OF ODOR DEW,
BUT THEN THE SMELL FADED OUT,
        AND INTO THE WINDS IT BLEW.

I'VE SEEN A MOST LOVELY SIGHT,
        RAINBOW COLORS, RIM TO RIM,
ASSORTED ARRAY HUES IN LIGHT,
        AND THEN THE LIGHT GREW DIM.

I'VE TOUCHED SOMEONE LOVELY,
        THRILLING ME ALL OVER INSIDE.
WHEN THE TOUCH GREW FAMILIAR,
        EXCITING MOMENTS SUBSIDE.

I'VE TASTED OF MANY FLAVORS,
        IN DETECTING SWEET AND WILD,
AFTER THE HOT OR BITTER HERBS,
        ALL OTHER FLAVORS SEEM MILD.

AWARENESSES OF SENSATIONS
        THE MENTAL ABILITY TO GRASP
SOME LACK ITS DISCERNMENTS
        OF SENSES UNABLE TO CLASP

I ONCE ALSO TOOK FOR GRANTED
        IGNORING THOSE EVIDENCES,
WHERE TODAY, I'M SO THANKFUL
        FOR EACH OF ALL MY SENSES.

~

DEFINE CORRECTION

OCCASIONALLY WE MAY SCUFF,
      DISAGREE, FUSS OR JUST PLAIN ARGUE,
USUALLY IT'S OVER SILLY STUFF,
      WE MISUNDERSTAND OR MISCONSTRUE.
BUT, IF WE DO, DON'T GET UPSET,
      JUST TAKE A DEEP BREATH AND SMILE.
FOR CORRECTION IS NOT A THREAT,
      IT'S THE SHARING OF DATA WE COMPILE.

THE REMEDY'S NOT VENGEANCE,
      NOR TO HAVE SPOKEN THE LAST WORD,
IT COULD ALTER YOUR CONTINENCE,
      TWIST WHAT YOU BELIEVE YOU HEARD,
SO UNWIND, PAUSE, BE CALM,
      AND GIVE WAY TO THE ANGRY FEELING
LET YOUR NEXT WORD BE A PSALM
      THEN YOUR SMILES AGAIN REVEALING

DISPUTES THAT WE MAY SHARE,
      ARE COMMON AND COMMON TO ALL,
SAVE WHAT SQUABBLES DECLARE,
      OR LAPS OF A TIME ALLOWED TO STALL,
I MAY BE WRONG IN WHAT I SAY,
      MISUNDERSTOOD, STERN WAYS I TALK,
BUT YOU SHOULD KNOW MY WAY,
      HOW MY BARK IS INNOCENT SQUAWK

THE TONGUE'S IN A WET PLACE
      AND IT SLIPS AROUND AN AWFUL LOT,
SOMETIMES A WORD WILL TRACE,
      BY LEAVING THE PLACE IT SHOULD NOT.
AND THOSE CRITICISMS MADE
      WERE NOT A DIRECT ATTACK, WE KNOW,
SO LET'S CALL IT OUR CRUSADE
      AND TO LEARN TOGETHER, AS WE GROW.

FOR THE RULES OF ACCURACY
      EXPRESS THE LACK OF PROPER BALANCE
EVEN WHEN DONE IN PRIVACY
      IT SCREENS THE EMOTION OF ROMANCE
CORRECTIONS HOLD REMEDIES
      AND MAY UNCOVER DEFECTS OR FAULTS
DIVIDING ERRORS OR THEORIES
      AND MAKE CORRECTIONS WITH RESULTS.

AND IF I SUGGEST CORRECTION,
      SHOULDN'T YOU RECEIVE IT GRACEFULLY
RECONSIDER WITH DISCRETION,
      YOU'LL SEE NO HARM MEANT DIRECTLY.
LIKEWISE IF YOU CORRECT ME,
      CAUSING A TRAUMA OF WORDS UNKIND
I KNOW WHAT'S MEANT TO BE,
      TO CRUSH MY HEART WAS NOT IN MIND.

WE NEED BOTH TO CONSIDER,
      WORDS MAY NOT EXPRESS THE HEART,
APPEARING SWEET OR BITTER,
      RECOGNIZE SOURCE, SET THEM APART
TO LEARN IS NOT A WEAKNESS,
      GAINING KNOWLEDGE WITH INTENSITY,
AN ENCOUNTER IN PROGRESS,
      ALTERING VARIATIONS OF OUR LIBERTY.

~

A KISS GOODNIGHT

A KISS GOODNIGHT

THE THOUGHT OF A CHILD DYING
    A SCENE THAT NONE COULD FORGET.
THE TERROR FOREVER IN MY MIND
    STILL TODAY LINGERS WITH ME YET.

I PICTURE HER NOW LYING STILL
    A SOFT WARM SMILE UPON HER LIP.
HER MOTHER KNELT BY HER SIDE
    RECEIVING THE GAY BIRDS GOSSIP.

ON ONE SIDE OF THE CHILD'S BED
    FRESH SUMMER FLOWERS IN A VASE.
MOTHER THOUGHT OF SWEET HEAVEN
    LIQUID TEARS FELL FROM HER FACE.

HER FATHER'S ABSENT LONELINESS
    WAS MUCH GREATER THAN IT SEEMS.
HER YOUNG FRIENDS MERELY SAW IT
    AS UNIMPORTANT, FOOLISH DREAMS.

AS THE WOODPECKERS CHOPPED
    INTO THE LOW LIMBED NEARBY TREE
AGAIN SHE CRIED OUT FOR DADDY
    HIM ONCE MORE SHE BEGS TO SEE.

WITH TEARS IN THE CHILD'S EYES
    SHE HELD HER MOTHER'S HAND SOFT
AS A RED GLOWED IN HER CHEEKS
    SHE HAD TURNED AGAIN TO COUGH.

SUN SHINES THROUGH A WINDOW
    ON LOVELY LOCKS OF GOLDEN HAIR
SHE CRIED OUT LOUD ONCE MORE
    NEEDING DADDY'S LOVE TO SHARE.

THE SUMMER SUN IS VERY BRIGHT
    SHE LIES TO DIE AN' SOFTLY DREAMS
MOTHER PRAYED TO GOD AN' SAID,
    "OUR CHILD SHOULD LIVE, IT SEEMS."

CHUCKS NOW MAKING NEW HOMES
    COLORFUL FLOWERS, WILD THEY GROW,
AN UNKNOWN LOVE FOR HER DADDY
    TO MOTHER SHE WHISPERED LOW:

MAMA, "OH, PLEASE, TELL DADDY,
    THAT I VERY MUCH DO LOVE HIM SO,
TELL HIM OF HOW I WANT TO WAIT,
    BUT THE ANGELS CALL FOR ME TO GO."

SHE LEANED TO KISS HER MOTHER,
    KISSED HER TWICE, SO VERY LIGHT.
AND SAID, "GIVE ONE TO DADDY,
    TELL HIM "IT'S MY KISS GOODNIGHT."

THEN LYING BACK TO FOREVER REST
    BREATHING SOFTLY HER LAST BREATH
MOTHER'S BODY BEGAN TREMBLING
    FOR THE CHILD HAD MET HER DEATH.

HER HAIRS WERE IN SHADED GREY
    HEAVY TEARS SHINED HER CHEEK
DUN-COLORED EYES, GREW DIMMER
    HER TREMBLING BODY GREW WEAK

CLOSED LIPS IN HELPLESS PAIN
    THE CHILD ENTERS HEAVEN'S BEST
THEN IN A BLUR, HER MOTHER TOO
    THE EBB OF LIFE INTO ETERNAL REST...

~

BUT WHY ME

WHAT POSSIBLE REASON CAN IT BE,
    FOR A SON TO HAVE SUCH A DESIRE
        TO BRING FORTH HARM TO ANOTHER?
BUT FROM SUCH A PERSON YOU SEE
    A DECEIVING HEART THEY CONSPIRE
        BECAUSE TRUTH THEY WILL SMOTHER

BUT ONE TIME WEREN'T WE THE TEAM?
SO WHY, OVER I ASK MYSELF AGAIN
        COULD THIS BE JUST A DREAM?
BUT THEN I SAW THE POWER OF SIN,
    LIFE IS NOT AS IT MAY SEEM.

WHY DO YOU TELL FOOLISH STORIES
    BEING BLIND IN RECOGNIZING TRUTH
        BY THE TWISTING OF FACTS INSTEAD,
BUT OUT OF IT CAME YOUR GLORIES,
    WITH FOUL AND SAYINGS UNCOUTH,
        BY FALSE TALES YOU HAVE SPREAD.

BUT IN THE SYMBOL OF LIFE'S CARBON.
WHERE NOW IS THE FAMILY BOND?
        BETWEEN A FATHER AND SON?
BUT, I SEE A BITTERNESS BEYOND,
    AND COME TO KNOW PARDON.

Oh! What great wasteless effort,
As you grasp for empty defense,
Within yourself you build guilt,
But falsehoods gradually sort,
In justifying reasons to be tense,
As your trails of untruths wilt.

But if your heart be so confused,
The thing you should know
Your claims are excused.
But of those claims, let go,
Be no further self-abused.

Why create such a great sorrow.
From imaginations out of hand,
Telling stories for recognition
But foolishness cuts to marrow,
By seeking for to comprehend,
Building a path to corruption.

But a great love for you I'll insert,
But who am I to wonder why?
Could I anymore be hurt?
But somehow, I know you'll try,
Manipulating as you blurt.

You reverse guilt in artfulness,
  In cunning words persuading it
    A smooth tongue rambles forth
But do these things you confess,
  Twist imaginations you permit
    Really give allegations a worth?

But in all this world, why thee?
You're family, blood, and bone,
    For reasons I can't foresee,
But of a spirit to me unknown
    Again, I ask, 'But why me?'

Son, even with all this being so,
  I long desire to be with you still
    Warms my heart to see ya smile
But now again I hear your echo,
  As your laughter brings me thrill
    In the vision that lingers awhile.

But I live now with curiosities.
In hopes that you might call,
    I reach again for remedies
But I must in my heart install,
    You choose to be memories.

~

IF YOU

If you were a star lost in the dark
I'd hunt each lonely night through
Then find you and make you spark
Causing you to glow the days too.

If you were a rose bud by the heat
With a bright sun to be your doom
I'd spray a mist that would defeat
Shielding shade, watch you bloom.

If you were a whirled shifting wind,
In drifting clouds a breeze incline
I'd be a thunder to get you pinned
Then depths of air would be mine.

If you were a lost bird by the lake
And trapped beneath a snowstorm
I'd hunt for you under every flake
Cuddling close to keep you warm.

If you were a creek of waters green
Flowing over pebbles bare bright,
I'd build the largest dam ever seen,
And never let you out of my sight,

Neither star I hunt nor rose I shade
Or shifting wind or to birds rescue,
Or waters green for the Lord made
Me to love you because you're you.

~

KALEIDOSCOPE OF MY LOVE

Of all familiar thoughts I might entertain,
    As visions rise or fall from place to place,
    Twirling about in memory which interlace
Exposing difficult questions that remain,
Taking me by surprise again and again,
    From words spoken by the love I embrace
    Only the turn of kaleidoscope could trace,
I still gaze with wonder, I can't explain.

Life's kaleidoscope reflects, transforms,
    Diverse arrangements that surface about,
    While varied symmetrical patterns scout,
On rotation exhibits many various forms,
Constantly change as a pattern conforms,
    For the kaleidoscope of woman, look out,
    Prepare for a change if it appears devout,
Neither be surprised of coming storms.

Has brightness in your life passed away?
    Have kindled emotions beyond reach fell
    To the place where negative visions dwell,
Do your unfolding thoughts suggest gray,
Are glimpses of happiness in fond delay,
    Surely these things I'll never know to tell
    In the kaleidoscope they are hidden well.
But do leave much confusion on display.

I assumed that you assumed we'd abide
    As one, allowing circumstances to share,
    In building deeper love without compare,
Echo passions or woes that love provide,
Apparently much we built was set aside.
    From what riddles tell or stories declare,
    Our sifting thoughts make realities aware,
How certainties turned inside out divide.

GATHER MEMORIES OF HAPPINESS UNTAINTED,
     BLENDED MY TENDER THOUGHTS OF YOU BUT YET,
     OTHERS MAY HIDE BEHIND THE TRAILS OF REGRET,
FOR THIS IS NOT AT ALL THE PICTURE I PAINTED
HOW TWO BECOME AS ONE WELL ACQUAINTED.
     SHOULDN'T HAPPINESS CLOAK ANY HURT OR FRET,
     AND CLAIM JOYS ONE MIGHT OTHERWISE FORGET,
SUCH HAS THE KALEIDOSCOPE DEMONSTRATED.

SPARE THE SPEECH FOR WORDS CONSTRUCTIVE,
     LISTEN, THE UNVARNISHED VOICE OF INTUITION,
     ALLOW FOR OPPORTUNITY IN SILENT SUBJECTION
PLACING ALL DISAPPOINTMENT IN PERSPECTIVE.
TO ALTER YOUR INNERMOST PEACE COLLECTIVE,
     BRIEFING MEMORIES WITH SMILES OF INTENTION,
     IN THE UNMARKED TIME OF ALL PAST REFLECTION,
FOR KALEIDOSCOPE CHANGES ARE AGGRESSIVE.

HONEY, A FINISHED TASK SHALL BE NO MORE,
     WHY REACH BACKWARDS TO GRASP THE WORST?
     LIKE SALTY WATERS TO THE TONGUE THAT THIRST?
EMOTIONS TODAY WERE ESTABLISHED BEFORE
NEITHER CONCEAL OUR GOOD TIMES OR IGNORE,
     BORROW MEMORIES OF LAUGHTER IF YOU DURST,
     LET JOY TO THE MARROW OF YOUR BONES BURST,
FOR I AM AMAZED BY THE TRIALS YOU EXPLORE.

INTO BACKWARD GLANCES OF BYGONE YEARS,
     WHERE STRENGTH OF TRUTH TRACE AND DISCLOSE
     I'M REMINDED HAPPINESS COMES THEN GOES,
LIKE CLOCKWORK IT MONTHLY AGAIN APPEARS,
A CALM HAPPINESS SUDDENLY TURN TO FEARS,
     I WAS UNACCUSTOMED TO CHANGE THAT AROSE,
     BUT FAMILIARIZED MYSELF IN TIME I SUPPOSE,
I PAUSE TO RECALL OUR LAUGHTER, OUR TEARS.

Let a merry heart dear help you decide,
    How our togetherness should be in delight,
    From love molds together wrong and right,
Still thoughts of you in my dreams abide,
Then quickens a lost youth again inside,
    But, what puzzles me in this moody fright,
    Pray tell dear, why stay with me and fight?
As this kaleidoscope attempts to divide.

You have your troubles dear, I have mine,
    Each others troubles we have accumulated,
    Surfaced, then tumbled together and faded.
PMS, Menopause, or MSG, I can define,
I've even seen them when they combine,
    Afterwards, your laughing face illustrated,
    A love you had for me was now reinstated,
Change appears to float, then intertwine.

The kaleidoscope fits you like a glove,
    Neither do I rely on a calm sweet tomorrow.
    Mood's change is subject to joy or sorrow,
Until the last steps of each day thereof,
I will remain patient in ways unheard of,
    Cause only you cause my dreams to glow,
    Although you change like winds that blow,
You'll always be my kaleidoscope of love.

~

MOMMA

Oh Momma, what is it I can do,
    To lift this burden beyond the shelf,
That I might be able to follow too,
    From the examples you set yourself.

I never gave the slightest thought,
    That one day you'd leave and go afar,
With all the signs I hadn't sought,
    Caused a cause to question this scar.

Oh' foolish dreamer I have been,
    Who can't reveal where visions dare,
I seek the hand that carried me, then,
    For another moment to hold, to share.

I strive to put on and pass the trial
    To act the way that I think I should,
But, wherever I turn I see you smile,
    In flower, rock or some funky wood.

I long for something I cannot grasp,
    In this emptiness where images hide,
Neither can I change it or unclasp,
    Because I'm so lonely for you inside.

I vision you lying atop your bed,
    In the same robe that was often worn,
A magazine open upon your spread,
    Enjoying a program eating popcorn.

I see you Momma, hands marred,
    Planting a flower or shrubs in a spot,
Near a fence encircling your yard,
    Where the night lights border the lot.

I ALSO SEE ROCKS CONFORMING A WAY,
    OR COLOR YOUR PLASTIC FLOWERS SWAYED,
FLOWERS WERE ALWAYS PROUD TO STAY,
    FOR THEY SAW ALL THE CHARM YOU MADE.

THE TREES WE PLANTED SHORT TIME AGO,
    YOU THOUGHT EACH SHOULD BE STRAIGHT,
I RECALL SAYING "JUST LET THEM GROW,
    THEY'LL DO FINE, MOM, IF ONLY YOU WAIT".

I IGNORED THE THOUGHT OF YOU DYING,
    'TIL IT ONCE BECAME AS A MATTER OF FACT,
LIKE A DREAM, I FOUND MYSELF CRYING
    A SHADOWED NIGHTMARE BECAME AN ACT.

I MISS YOUR PLEASANT LETTERS OF LENGTH,
    AND ALL THE SUBJECTS YOU TALKED ABOUT,
YOU PROVIDED US ALL WITH STRENGTH,
    EVEN WHEN IT CAUSED YOU TO GO WITHOUT.

YOU'RE THE BUD, BRIGHTER THAN ANY,
    THE ONE ROSE THAT WAS NEVER CROWNED,
THE CARNATION THAT BLOOMS FOR MANY,
    AND WILD FLOWERS COVERING THE GROUND.

AGAIN I ASK IS ALL THIS REALLY REAL?
    OR SOME MIST BEFORE ME IN DISGUISE?
WILL THESE WOUNDS FOR ME EVER HEAL,
    MUST I CONTINUE TO PRETEND OTHERWISE.

YOUR FUNNY STORIES OF A GOLDEN PAST,
    FILLS THE AIR WHERE THE WIND IS BLOWN,
BUT MEMORIES, MOMMA, ECHO A CAST,
    INTO IMAGES PERMITTED FOR ME ALONE.

Your encouraging smile, so sincere,
    Such desire to serve when need arise,
A squeeze of the hand, a little tear,
    A joyful relief that came to your eyes.

Your opened home, just beamed,
    For family or friends, be rich or poor,
So many drawn to you it seemed,
    But no more to the path of your door.

Mom, whom my life patterns after,
    I'll miss your smiles and gentle touch
Your enthusiasm; your laughter,
    Oh' Momma, miss you so very much.

Can't contain this hurt in my heart,
    An this fire unquenched I try to cover,
The lump in my throat is just a start,
    Another like you I'll never discover.

Fond memories alive within me,
    For this is the place that they belong,
I took for granted you'd always be,
    Oh foolish dreamer, for I was wrong.

In your wrinkled smiles often made,
    Another cheer your presence shared
Others may come; others may fade,
    With those you are always compared.

I ask myself the question again,
    What is life since you've gone away,
I find myself talking now and then,
    Wondering, Momma what you'd say.

Momma, miss you so very much,
      An' to me you seem to be every place,
A squinting smile or gentle touch,
      Image thoughts of you that I embrace.

You are here no more, I confess,
      Ah! Loved more than words can seize,
This emptiness my heart possess,
      Surrounds life's hollow of mysteries.

You're a flower among all other,
      Then weeds crowd its place to dwell,
So I'll pluck weeds that smother,
      So you Mom, the flower, may do well.

I did not see that time was short,
      Yet many weeds did surround the hill,
Although the flower left the court,
      It's image an song shall never be still.

To flowerin' flowers breakin' bud,
      Or worn funky wood along the beach,
To an odd rock stuck in the mud,
      To these simple things you'd reach.

In fun you'd make a funny look,
      Without your teeth and in squinting
Above the glasses you overlook,
      To appear cranky by way of hinting,

You didn't know how to be mean,
      It was a way you'd never understood,
Nevertheless you played the scene,
      But even then you weren't very good.

I MISS THE ACT OF THAT WRINKLED MASK,
      YOUR HEART OF JOY, LAUGHTER AND SMILE,
THE ONLY QUESTION I CONTINUE TO ASK,
      OH' WHY COULDN'T YOU STAY FOR AWHILE?

I MISS STORIES OF TWISTS AND TURNS,
      OF HOW HAPPINESS COMES FROM GRIEF,
I MISS YOUR SCENT; MY HEART BURNS,
      AND HOW YOU HELD YOUR HANDKERCHIEF.

WHERE OTHERS BOAST OF FANCY DRESS,
      THEIR COSTLY JEWELS OF GREAT EXPENSE,
YOU DRESSED BETTER WITH MUCH LESS,
      AND DID IT WITH STYLE AND CONFIDENCE.

YOU HUMMED TUNES DURING DAYS,
      IT CHEERED ME TO BE WITHIN ITS SOUND,
SMILES, FROWNS AND ALL YOUR WAYS,
      ARE REMEMBERED BUT NO MORE FOUND.

YOU'RE MORE THAN ALL CLAIMS THEREOF,
      AND YOUR ABSENCE DIFFICULT TO CONTAIN,
YOUR PRESENCE IS MISSED, YOUR LOVE,
      GOD BE WITH YOU UNTIL WE MEET AGAIN.

YOU OFTEN WARNED, "BE PREPARED",
      SOMEDAY YOU WOULD LEAVE ME BEHIND,
TIME AND AGAIN THIS YOU SHARED,
      BUT ITS REALITY NEVER ENTERED MY MIND.

MY SOUL IS SICK, WEAK AND FRAYED,
      NOR CAN I REASON WITH ALL MY POWERS,
I EVEN MISS THE PRANKS YOU PLAYED,
      AN TALKS WE HAD IN NIGHT'S WEE HOURS.

Fragile Momma, your voice calls,
      Humming happy tunes; songs of old,
Stories you told within these walls,
      I remember today as the times unfold.

Silence in place of joy and Psalm,
      With just too much about you I miss,
So I wrote a poem for you Mom,
      Called, "I'm Sorry" and goes like this.

     "I'm Sorry"
"Then I think of all I should have done,
              But I didn't.
And all the things I could have done,
              But, I wouldn't.
    And I'm sorry.
Then I think of all I shouldn't have done,
              But I did.
And things that were wrongfully done,
              And I hid,
    And I'm sorry.
Then I recall things you did for me,
              In return,
All you should, could or would for me,
              My insides burn
    And I'm sorry.
Then ask myself, "What does this signify,
              This loss of mine?"
For cost of life or death I cannot buy,
              Or intertwine.
    And I'm sorry.
Again I ask, "Can't I have another chance
              To do for you?"
But mom, I know upon another glance,
              I cannot redo.
    And I'm sorry.

MOMMA, I'M SORRY...I'M SORRY EVERYWHERE,
OUR TIME TOGETHER MOM, SHALL BE NO MORE,
NEITHER CAN I CHANGE OR DIFFERENTLY DECLARE,
BUT ONLY TO SAY GOODBYE MOMMA EVERMORE.
        GOODBY MOMMA

GOODBYE MOMMA, WHO MY LIFE'S EMBRACE,
YOUR DESIRE TO LIVE WAS INDEED RICH IN HOPE,
FOR MANY YOU MADE THIS LIFE A BETTER PLACE,
YOU ARE THE FLOWER OF LIFE IN GREATER SCOPE.
        GOODBY MOMMA

GOODBYE MOMMA, FROM ALL YOU LOVED SO,
OR THE NEIGHBOR WHO MAY HAVE GONE UNFED,
FROM THE LESS FORTUNATE WITH NO PLACE TO GO,
OR YOUR MANY STORIES NOW SILENT AND UNSAID.
        GOODBY MOMMA

GOODBYE MOMMA, OR GRANNY GRUNT TO KIN,
FROM EACH FLOWER WHO BATTLES WITH A WEED,
FROM THOSE YOU TURNED THEIR TEARS TO A GRIN,
BY GIVING THEM HOPE WITH A SIMPLEST NEED.
        GOODBY MOMMA

GOODBYE MOMMA, FROM DREAMS DREAMED,
OR LITTLE NOTES YOU LEFT ON THE DOOR OR TABLE,
THE NAME "VI", YOU DIDN'T LIKE IT SEEMED,
SO, GRANNY GRUNT IS KNOWN AS YOUR LABEL.
        GOODBY MOMMA

GOODBYE MOMMA, FROM SCARVES YOU KEPT,
AND VARIOUS VARIETY OF LITTLE HANKYS HELD,
FROM CHIMES WHOSE CHIME THE WIND SWEPT,
AND THE HURTS AND PAINS YOU ONCE WITHHELD.
        GOODBY MOMMA

Goodbye Momma, missed in many ways,
From funky wood, old rocks or grey moss,
From joy and laughter filling empty phrase,
And your so familiar scent is now our loss.
Goodby Momma

Goodbye Momma, from a pet garden frog,
Or the blankets you crocheted for the kids,
Or plastic flowers planted by a knotty log,
To little notes written on a paper that bids,
Goodby Momma

Goodbye Momma, from trees bent bough,
From water fountains off shade bluegreen,
Or the birds searching seed elsewhere now,
And all trails of silence found in between.
Goodby Momma

Goodbye Momma, from a little picket fence,
And little animal figurines you placed about,
For so much in life will miss your presence,
For so much in life will be now left without.
Goodby Momma

Goodbye Momma, from gardens un-tended,
And the birds whistles you so tried to mock,
All those from rest homes you'd befriended,
From river stone, lava and the petrified rock.
Goodby Momma

Goodbye Momma from a little porch swing,
And homes you gave to the abandoned nest,
From words made up in songs you'd sing,
Or the pies you made to share with the rest.
Goodby Momma

GOODBY MOMMA, SO SIMPLE, YET SO CLEVER,
HOW ALL MY TIMES AROUND YOU I DID ADORE,
REMEMBERING FUN TIMES SHOPPING TOGETHER,
YET SHOPPING TODAY CAN NEVER BE AS BEFORE
      GOODBY MOMMA

SO GOODBYE MOMMA, OH MOMMA GOODBYE,
I HAVE BEEN A DREAMER OF DREAMS IN DESPAIR,
AND ALL THAT IS LEFT TO MY STRENGTH'S SUPPLY
IS MEMORIES, PICTURES AND LOCK OF YOUR HAIR.
      GOODBY MOMMA

~

PIERCING WORD

READ,
>> FOR THE WORD OF GOD
>>> IS A GIFT, SPIRITUALLY LENT,
>>> AND IS FOCUSED ON DESIRES OF MAN'S DEED.

LISTEN,
>> TO THE UNHEARD SPEECH,
>>> AS SOUND APPEARS SILENT,
>>> HERE THE STILLNESS OF THE COMFORTER IS FREED.

SPEAK,
>> AND TELL OF ITS WARNINGS,
>>> OF ITS MAGNIFICENT REWARD,
>>> THIS HEAVEN'S BREAD OVER BRIMSTONE'S FIRE.

FEEL,
>> A NEW REGENERATED LIFE,
>>> PROMISE OF PEACE INWARD.
>>> AS THE LIVING WORD REVEALS A LIFE TO INSPIRE,

SEE,
>> THE RESULT OF REPENTANCE,
>>> HOW A SOUL CHANGES COURSE,
>>> WHEN THE MASTER TOUCHES THE HEART WITHIN,

GRASP,
>> A FULL MEASURE MEASURED,
>>> OF FAITH, HOPE AND SOURCE,
>>> AS HOLY GHOST QUENCHES THE THIRST OF SIN.

~

VISIONS AFTER DARK

BEHOLD! NIGHTFALL'S APPROACH,
    AS THE DARKNESS PENETRATES DAYS END,
SUDDENLY DEEP ROSE TINTED CLOUDS,
    TURN SILVER TO GRAYISH IN DUSTLESS WIND.

CRESCENT MOON IS SLANTING,
    SMILING WITH A GLEAM FROM IVORY WARM,
STAR SPOTTED, DENSED HEAVENS,
    ASSEMBLING A WALTZ TO THE NIGHT'S FORM.

WITH ITS ACCUMULATED BLUSH,
    HEAVENS UNTARNISHED FULLNESS APPEARS,
SILVERY SPOTS HERE AND THERE,
    DISPLAY PERMISSIBLE AGE OF MANY YEARS.

TOWERING THIS SHAPED DARK,
    RESTRICTS SHADOWS FROM ITS CRAFTY SKIES,
IMAGINARY SCENES PULSE BY,
    TO RESEMBLE THAT OF SOME PAST DISGUISE.

WASHBOARD RIPPLED CLOUDS,
    GRASPING OUT COMPANIONS OF THE NIGHT.
CAST SHADOWS EVERYWHERE,
    ARRANGING VISIONS FROM BORROWED LIGHT.

ON FERN OR BLOSSOM BLOOMS
    THE SPIDER CONTINUES THE WEB IT WEAVES
FROM WALLS WITH TREE LIMBS
    THE PARTIAL DARKNESS TRAILS THEIR LEAVES.

NEIGHBORING HILLS 'ER VARIED,
GIFTED SHADOWS WEAVE ABOUT AND BRAID,
INTO A QUAINT INVENTED SWAY,
THESE PATTERNED IMAGES COME AND FADE.

HERE SURROUNDS ALL ABOUT US,
MORE THAN ANY COULD HAVE ANTICIPATED,
IN THIS RUFFLED BROKEN UP SKY,
WHERE VISIONS TONIGHT WERE FABRICATED.

ALAS! NOW THE QUARTER MOON,
SLANTS RIM TO RIM THEN SPINS THIS VIEW.
APPEARS TO SMILE AT ME AND SAY,
THESE VISIONS TONIGHT ARE JUST FOR YOU.

~

CANDYLAND N' GINGER ROY

CANDYLAND N' GINGER ROY

ONCE UPON A TIME WHEN
  I WAS AROUND ABOUT THREE,
I WENT TO A LAND BEYOND
  THE LARGE SYCAMORE TREE

A GARDEN THAT MY DREAMS,
  AND WISHES HAD FOUND
WHERE COLORED LOLLIPOPS
  GREW FROM THE GROUND.

THERE I MET A JOLLY LOOKIN'
  HAPPY GINGERBREAD BOY,
INTRODUCED HIMSELF TO ME
  AS HAPPY "GINGER ROY"

AND TOOK ME TO HIS HOME,
  NEAR A POPSICLE STAND
THAT STOOD ON A HILL IN THE
  MIDDLE OF A CANDYLAND

SWIRLED STRIPED TREES AS
  LIKE A PEPPERMINT STICK
BRIGHT COLORED LIMBS OF
  LEAVES COTTONBALLS THICK

TRAILS AND RAILS OF TAFFY
  A TRAIN OF HERSHEY BAR
WHERE A TOOTSIE-ROLL FENCE
  BEYOND STRETCHED AFAR.

THEN HE INTRODUCED ME TO
  THE CANDY PEOPLE THERE
WITH ASSORTED CHOCOLATES
  TO FUDGE COCONUT ÉCLAIR

PEPPERMINT SPIRALED COLORS
  CARAMEL FLAVORS OF TASTE
THESE HAPPY CANDY PEOPLE
  MADE OF A SUGAR PASTE.

ON AN AVENUE OF GUMDROPS
  A CREAM-FILLED BUTTERNUT
WE STROLLED UPON ALMONDS
  MIXED SHREDS OF COCONUT

SIDEWALKS OF PEANUT BRITTLE
  CURBINGS OF CANDY CURLS
BUILDINGS OF WHITE DIVINITY
  TOFFEE POP, PEANUT SWIRLS

DOWN THRU' LICORICE VALLEY
  DANCED GINGER ROY AN' I
THRU STREETS OF CANDYLAND
  BENEATH MILKY WAYS SKY.

TO A ROAD OF MARSHMALLOWS
  SWEETENED PATHS OF MINT.
THEN WE BID OUR GOOD-BYE
  NEAR THAT JELLY BEAN TENT.

STILL IT IS, TO THIS VERY DAY,
  THIS FANTASY I CAN ENJOY
WHEN I THINK OF CANDYLAND
  AND THE ONE GINGER ROY.

SOMEWHERE A GINGER HOUSE
  ON CANDYLAND'S CANDY HILL
MY GOOD FRIEND GINGER ROY
  I KNOW HE LIVES THERE STILL...

~

ROMANCE AND PASSION

O' WHERE IS THE VACANT SPOT
    WHEREIN WE STOOD SIDE BY SIDE
A SINGLE THREAD OF ROMANCE
    WHICH WARMED MY HEART INSIDE
WHAT ARE MEMORIES WORTH
    WHAT DO THEIR EXPERIENCES COST
WHERE DID HER PASSION GO
    FOR SO MUCH SHE FORGOT OR LOST
WAS I EVER IN HER DREAMS
    WHERE PASSIONS COME DESIRES
DO I FLASH INTO HER VIEW
    OF THE EAGERNESS THAT INSPIRES
IS HER ROMANTIC LOVE AFFAIR
    HELD FOR ME BY TENDER PASSION
IS IT A SHORT OR LONG TERM
    THIS THEORY I CAN ONLY IMAGINE
I DID THINGS EMBARRASSING
    AN' MADE SOME CHOICES WRONG
FROM TIME TO TIME IRRITATING,
    AN WENT PLACES I DIDN'T BELONG
I LOVED HER LIKE AN ANGEL
    BUT NOW QUESTIONS STILL REMAIN
DID SHE LOVE ME ENTIRELY
    OF INTENSITY, SHE CANNOT EXPLAIN
IS ROMANCE OF LITTLE WORTH
    BECAUSE OF WORDS I NEVER SAID
I THOUGHT THEM OFTEN, BUT
    NOW I WRITE THEM DOWN INSTEAD
YET TODAY AS EVER BEFORE
    I STILL RECALL HER ROMANTIC WAYS
TODAY AND FOREVER AND EVER
    SHE'S A PASSION OF ALL MY DAYS

~

COTTAGE OF LOVE

I BUILT THIS COTTAGE WITHIN MY
HEART
WITH SILVER STARS ALL SHINING
SMART
ABOVE THE HEAVENS UP IN THE
SKY
A CLOUDY DREAM FOR YOU AND
I

WE'LL WALK THE TRAILS WHICH IT
HAS
WITH DROWSY LIGHTS ALONG ITS
PATHS.
AS CHOSEN WORDS WHISPERING
LOW
WIND WILL CHOOSE ITS WAY TO
BLOW

THEN WE'D PRETEND AN ANGELIC
LIGHT,
WILL STIR UP OUR LOVE, STIRRING
BRIGHT.
IT'LL NEVER FADE, NOR IS IT EVER
GONE
BY DARK OF A NIGHT OR LIGHT OF
DAWN

HOLD HANDS BENEATH DANCING
FLAMES
TWO LOVERS WHO PLAY FOOLISH
GAMES
WHEN OUR LIPS INTO BLIND MIST
MEET,
MY HEART WILL STOP AND SKIP A
BEAT.

Your eyes sparkle as twilight
FAIR,
With precious curls n' dusky
HAIR.
Rosily smile of enlightening
LIGHT,
Lips with a kiss of a summer
NIGHT.

Be it the mist of a thought or
DREAM
I'll vision a cottage of love in
BEAM
By an image spirit appearing
BRIGHT
An imitation of her engulfing
LIGHT.

Within misting skies walking
SUN,
Where heavens and stars are
HUNG.
To a blurring sunset's secret
ART.
Is a cottage of love hid in my
HEART.

~

YOUR LOVELINESS

Your lovely eyes,
        Resembling the moon,
Hurrying to a silvery,
        Silent and sweet white
Where down slanting,
        Pleasant rays bloom
Bleach clouds scarlet
        Into the midst of night.

Your protruding lips,
        Give colorful wonders,
As the sunset moves,
        Cross heavenly aisles,
A crystallizing silence,
        Of forms and ponders,
Such is the loveliness
        In each of your smiles.

Your soft velvet hair,
        Glistens with silence,
Into an image beam,
        Dance engulfing light,
Each strand crowned,
        Into silent suspense,
As it weaves together,
        In its ebony of delight.

Your pleasant voice
        Breaks twilite pauses,
Silent breeze whisper,
        A winds breath walk,
Like music of angels,
        With soft applauses,
Such are the sounds,
        As whenever you talk,

YOUR VIBRATING SPIRIT,
    INTO SILENCE IT GRASPS,
DWELLING IN HARMONY
    REVEALS WHO YOU ARE,
UPON QUIET STILLED AIR,
    ITS INVISIBILITY LAPSES
IN EXPOSING ONLY YOU,
    AS AN ENCHANTED STAR.

YOUR SWEET LOVELINESS,
    A RAINBOW IN SHOWERS,
DWELL IN A HARMONY,
    SILENCES PROUD ARRAY,
CLIMBING MISTY SKIES,
    THRU' DAYLIGHT HOURS,
GLEAMS IF YOU'RE NEAR,
    PAUSES, IF YOU'RE AWAY

~

ALAS! I DIDN'T SEE YOUR NEED

OH DEAR MOM, NOW THAT YOU HAVE GONE AWAY,
I SUDDENLY CAN SEE THIS LIFE DIFFERENTLY TODAY,
    I NOW RECOGNIZE THINGS I DIDN'T DO FOR YOU,
    AN EQUALLY SURPRISED BY WHAT LITTLE I DID DO,
HOW YOU EXPRESSED APPRECIATION AND SUCH,
FOR IT CAUSED ME TO BELIEVE THAT I DID MUCH,
    AND BY THIS, I ONLY FOOLED MYSELF, IT'S CLEAR,
    THOUGH AT THE TIME THAT'S HOW IT DID APPEAR,
    ALAS! I DIDN'T SEE YOUR NEED

OH HOW YOU LABORED WHERE GRASS WAS BARE,
AN SOUNDS OF YOUR HUMMING WAS EVERYWHERE
    I SCARCELY NOTICED THE PRECIOUS TIMES SPENT,
    FOR NOT GIVING YOU MORE OF MYSELF, I REPENT
I FOUND SORTING THROUGH YOUR PERSONAL THINGS,
ITEMS BROKE, CHIPPED, OLD SHOES OR TIN RINGS,
    I DISCOVERED WHAT LITTLE THAT YOU POSSESSED,
    BUT YOU, MOMMA, CLAIMED IT BEING BLESSED.
    ALAS! I DIDN'T SEE YOUR NEED.

UNSEEN LABOR REQUIRED IN TENDING YOUR LAWN,
OR EFFORTS REQUIRED FOR WEEDING LONG DRAWN,
    TO FLOWERS PLANTED WHERE GROUND WAS HARD,
    FROM SOILS OF CLAY THAT SHEATHED YOUR YARD.
THE WORN-OUT WATCH WORN UPON YOUR WRIST,
OR THE INEXPENSIVE HANKIES HELD IN YOUR FIST,
    TO SOME HAND DOWN CLOTHES YOU MADE TO FIT,
    OR TO THE LACK OF YARN THAT YOU LIKED TO KNIT,
    ALAS! I DIDN'T SEE YOUR NEED.

If only I had a little warning of some kind,
Perhaps I wouldn't have appeared so blind.
    I would spend more time with you each day,
    By going before you and preparing the way,
Oh, had I known something was the matter,
I'd given you the world on a golden platter,
    Although you were content in simple things,
    I'd array you in crowns and diamond rings,
        Alas! I didn't see your need.
        Alas! I didn't see your need.

CONSTRUCTION OF A LOCKET

CONSTRUCTION OF A LOCKET

This Locket's round,
    An' built of precious gold
Of nuggets panned
    From an ole' mother lode.

In their purest form,
    These placer nuggets lay
As your purest love
    Adorns my life each day.

This locket's center
    A crystal diamond is set
Projecting a sparkle
    Shared in highest respect

In a sparkle of joy
    As the one in your smiles
Brings back memories
    Of our many happy miles.

This locket hinges,
    Yes, it locks and it folds,
It opens and closes,
    But oh so tightly it holds.

Our marriage is held
    By those pieces and parts
Because your strength
    Hinged love to our hearts.

This locket's pictures
    Have much more to share
Together our family,
    Are all gathered in there.

THE CELLULOID FACE,
         PROTECTS EACH AS PRESENT,
AND IF ONE SHOULD HURT,
         IT BECOMES A FAMILY EVENT.

THIS LOCKET'S BACK,
         ENGRAVES A NOTE FROM ME,
JUST A FEW LITTLE WORDS,
         AND MANY YOU CAN'T SEE.

SO MY BEST TO YOU,
         FOREVER REST IN MY HEART,
IN OUR BINDING LOVE,
         ENCHANTMENTS NEVER PART.

THIS LOCKET'S CHAIN,
         WILL HOLD TO THE VERY END,
ITS LINKS SHALL BIND,
         BECOMING FRIEND TO FRIEND

ALL TOGETHER IT'S A LIFE
         A SPECIAL FAMILY, YOU SEE,
MORE THAN JUST A LOCKET,
         BUT, OUR LIFE AN FAMILY TREE....

~

O' NEW JERUSELEM

O' city of precious stones,
    Aye, decks of fine, yellow gold,
O' valley of enchantment,
    In holy atmosphere of Marigold

O' Christ, prince of peace,
    Son of God, unadulterated white,
O' city, inside New Jerusalem,
    Master Jesus, imperishable light.

O' ye heaven of heavens
    Untold power, love and wealth,
O' eternal fellowship of joy,
    The Messiah, and Lord Himself.

O' come quickly, my Savior,
    To my rescue, which I'm bound,
O' to a prepared resting place,
    O' if by mercy I might be found.

~

KINGDOM OF THE ENEMY

BEHIND LIFE'S HAZE CURTAIN
    THE STAGE CAREFULLY SET
        THIS FOLLOWING IS WHAT I SAW
THE ENEMY BEING CLEVER
    HE WAS SCARCELY NOTICED
        ESTABLISHING A DIFFERENT LAW.

A MOVE HERE AND THERE
    DECEIVINGLY TO AND FRO
        TWISTED TRUTH WAS CONCEALED
LOOKED UPON AS A FRIEND,
    OR WELCOMED AS A GUEST
        HIS KINGDOM IS UNREVEALED.

COME OR FADES FROM SIGHT
    TO SOME UNKNOWN PLACE
        BECOMING A BEING HE IS NOT
BUT TO SOULS MISFORTUNE
    MAKES BLACK LOOK WHITE
        ATTACKING FROM ANOTHER SPOT,

AND OF ALL HIS PROMISES
    NOT ONE COULD BE QUOTED
        WITHOUT END OF SUDDEN GRIEF
FROM PLAIN IGNORANCE
    MAN SEEKS THIS KINGDOM
        FOR HIS FALSE PEACE OF RELIEF

THEIR FALL SHALL BE GREAT
    FEW THERE BE THAT ESCAPE
        RESULTS OF ENEMY'S DEMAND
AND ALL BECAUSE MAN
    WILL ENTER THIS KINGDOM
        GRASPING THE ENEMY'S HAND

As the angel of light
　　Or perhaps Lamb of lambs
　　　　He'll visit by different ways,
Could be sweet music
　　Or the mingling of words
　　　　Or found in a mellow praise

The enemy is clever
　　As a one you may trust
　　　　A one, one holds in respect
If man justifies himself
　　He joins that Kingdom
　　　　To a death he did not expect.

~

YOU BELONG TO ME

I NEED TO HOLD YOU TIGHT
     AND SAY "I LOVE YOU SO",
BUT MY WORDS CAN'T SAY,
     FOR ONLY GOD WILL KNOW,
THE WAY IT'S IN MY HEART,
     OR THE WAY I REALLY FEEL,
TOGETHER WE DO BELONG
     YOUR LOVE DOES REVEAL
       YOU BELONG TO ME.

I DREAM OF YOU EACH NIGHT,
     AND THEN I WAKE A WHILE
SUDDENLY I SEE YOUR FACE,
     IN SWEET, FAMILIAR SMILE
THEN WITHOUT A THOUGHT
     MY PILLOW'S TIGHT TO ME
WITH ENCHANTMENT STRANGE
     DARLING CAN'T YOU SEE.
       YOU BELONG TO ME.

WITH SUCH A THRILL INSIDE
     FROM A THOUGHT OF YOU,
SLOWLY MY EYES WILL CLOSE
     BECAUSE OF WHAT I VIEW,
O' HOW MY HEART WILL BEAT
     HOW MY BLOOD WILL CHILL
HOW MY DREAMS WILL FIND,
     MY LOVE IS WAITING STILL
       YOU BELONG TO ME.

I'LL TELL MYSELF GOOD-NITE
     AN' THEN TRY TO END IT ALL
ALTHOUGH IT WILL NOT END,
     YOUR IMAGE I STILL RECALL
UNTIL YOU'RE IN MY ARMS,
     WHEN ALL DREAMS UNFOLD,
ONLY THEN WILL YOU KNOW,
     WHAT'S NEVER BEEN TOLD,
     YOU BELONG TO ME.

~

ZOO OF NATURE

A ZOO OF NATURE SURROUNDS US,
    END OF THE ROAD, IT SEPARATES,
A PASSION, ENLIGHTENED WONDER,
    TIME HAS SET, AND ILLUSTRATES.

RUNNING WATERS FROM A SPRING,
    MOVEMENT SOUND OF MELODY,
RUSHING ALONG CREVICED EARTH
    OVER ROCKS OR AROUND A TREE.

CHEERFULLY WILD FLOWERS GROW,
    COLORFULLY BLANKETED GROUND,
IN COMPANY OF MANY INSECTS,
    NOBLE WORKERS BUILD A MOUND

BARK WRAPPED ON STURDY TREES,
    ARMS EVERGREEN SPREAD WIDE,
WHISTLE OF MUSIC A JOYFUL WIND,
    EAGERLY PASS THROUGH ITS SIDE.

THE SQUIRRELS AN' CHIPMUNKS,
    ECHO A CHIRPING FAR AND FREE,
NEARBY THEM, FELLOW WILD LIFE,
    SHARING THEIR MOCK JOYFULLY.

UNDER A CALM CLEAR HEAVEN,
    NOW A SHADE OF BEAUTY SHOW,
AROUND COLORFUL BIRDS SWAY,
    EASTWARD GRASS BLADES GROW.

Licorice ferns on mossy trunk
Its branches a deeper green
Thickets of leaves leaning low
Run blackberries in-between

From sources of indirect light
Reaching thru a tree's luring
Fields of red and white clover
Wearing the smiles of spring.

Ripened by a sunshiny heat,
Sweeten wild berries and fruit,
High in a pine tree's pocket,
Bee's honey coned in a flute.

Lo! This beautiful nature lives,
Lying beyond of what we see,
In this thought of wonderland,
Live dreamers like you n' me...

~

OL FRIEND

OH YOU JOLLY, FRIENDLY AND WHISKERED MAN
    IN YOUR OUTSTRETCHED LIFE'S NARROW PATH
OF SUCH WRINKLED SKIN AND WEAKENED HAN'
    A WITHERED LOOK FROM THIS WORLD'S WRATH

YOU'VE WORKED A LIFE FOR BREAD N' WAGES,
    SOME HAPPY DELIGHTS, OR BLINDING TEARS,
TIME'S MARKED YOUR FACE OF MANY PAGES
    PATH OF EXPERIENCE OF YOUR MANY YEARS,

Your hearty shake of most honest grasp
    In your past has won you many friends,
With your hands the age of time clasp
    Drawing life closer to its narrow bends

Wonder what's happened to the ole' days
    When neighbors had time to visit awhile
Time moved slower in old fashioned ways
    As neighbors had time to chat and smile

Ya sing a tune, changing words a little,
    Or recall some jokes of a long time ago
Sharpening a jack knife maybe whittle
    Enjoy showing things you have to show

Still, sidewalk strolls on a nice warm day
    Are yet enjoyable but a lonesome trail
Ol' man the letter received again today
    Is not from a friend but occupant's mail

Sort of seems you're forgotten all about
    Or people just don't have time anymore
If ya jump up, kick your heels and shout
    To some you're a radical; others a bore

Now...there old timer who laughs a lot
    Enjoys small things, like happy games,
Whom people neglect and so long forgot,
    All that's left are memories and names.

But, old friend, who can only look back
    Be yet more stern with pride in your eye.
Worries and happy thoughts you pack
    No better generation has ever gone by...

~

BROTHERHOOD

I FOUND MYSELF REMINISCING
    INTO FRAGMENTS OF MY DISTANT PAST
NEAR FORTY SUMMERS OR MORE
    MY ENRICHED MEMORIES FORECAST
I SEE MY YOUNGEST BROTHER
    BEFORE THE TIMES PARTED OUR WAYS
HOW WE COLORFULLY CHATTED
    IN THOSE JOYOUS CHILDHOOD DAYS

'NEATH GLORY OF SUMMER SUN
    AS WE SHARED TYPICAL IDLE CARES
WEE WORRIES WE THRUST ASIDE
    WHERE GAMES AND PLAY PREPARES
YOUNGSTERS SEEKING TREASURE
    CHUCKLES LAUGHTER WILD AND FREE
HAPPY SINGING FUN AND JOKES
    TO OTHER ADVENTURES PURSUED WE

IN OUR EARLY LIFE AS KIDS WE
    OUTMANEUVER, WRESTLE AND SCUFF
MOCK OR HARASS IN PRETENSE
    PLAYFUL STUNTS LIGHTHEARTED BLUFF
AND IN OUR SPRINGTIME OF LIFE,
    CLUMSY TRAITS AWKWARD DELUSION
JUVENILES, ZEALOUS PASTIME,
    YOKED IN EDUCATED CONCLUSION.

FROM THOSE CHILDHOOD TIMES.
    OTHER CHANGES WOULD TAKE PLACE
PRESS FORTH TO MIDLIFE YEARS
    A CLOSER FRIENDSHIP TO EMBRACE
NOW AS THE YEARS HASTEN BY
    FAITHFUL FRIENDSHIP DUTY TO ABIDE
IT HAPPENED THEN AN EVEN NOW
    FOR OUR DIFFERENCES WE SET ASIDE

Each our likeness we shape
    Making judgments upon our own
Recollecting shadows there
    From blunders we've once known
Together into some yonder
    To far-off dim and distant dream
Where time attempts to trace
    These very beginnings of a team

In life's storms and clouds
    Facing the fierce winds that blew
We each took a path in life
    Where bits of dreams part in two
Disappointments came often
    Of dreams destroyed unexpected
But we inspired one another
    Lifting hope to a joy resurrected.

The highway of life whispers
    Consisting of its twists and turns
We share its bending curves
    To the troubled heart that burns
Then as we both got older
    Our inklings and chapters divide
Frequent familiar feelings
    Visually built greater love inside

Once spirited in vigor, zeal,
    Our silence now replaces a roar
To simple rest on the beach
    Watching surf beat rocky shore
Time itself slowed us down
    With different values in our wake
Mindful to make wrong right
    Question our choices for mistake

TODAY WE SHARE A LIKENESS
    AND COME TOGETHER OCCASIONALLY
FOR A LITTLE LABOR, A LITTLE REST
    OR STEER OUT TOWARD THE OPEN SEA.
MY BROTHER, A CHUM, A MATE
    IS MY ENCOURAGER STANDING NEAR
IN CERTAINTIES WE UNDERSTOOD
    FROM ALL HARMONIES OF YESTERYEAR

MY DEVOTED FRIEND OF YEARS
    THEN AND EVEN TO THIS VERY HOUR
THIS COMPANION AND BROTHER
    WHERE IT'S NOT HIM NOR I BUT "OUR"
SHOULD I YEARN FOR COMFORT
    HE WOULD EMERGE TO ME IN A FLASH
WE SHARE THE BRIGHT AND FAIR
    OR BY NOTION TOGETHER SIT IN ASH

ODDEST THINGS STILL REMIND ME
    FOUNDED UPON MY INFORMED PAST
DISTINGUISHING TRAITS SUGGEST
    FORMED A BROTHERHOOD MADE FAST
THEN REMEMBERING THE FACT
    IT WAS ONLY "HE" WHO WAITED NEAR
IF RUIN TIMES ENCROACHED ON
    I FIND HIS FRIENDSHIP CRYSTAL CLEAR.

FULL WELL DID I ALWAYS KNOW
    HIS HEART FOR ME WAS OPEN WIDE
HE PAUSES A MOMENT IN FEAR
    ONLY TO ADVANCE NEXT TO MY SIDE.
MEMORIES ARE MY SOUVENIRS
    TRUTHS WITH TRAITS OF WHAT I KNOW
THIS HELPFUL BROTHER AND PAL
    THE FAITHFUL FRIEND IN MY SHADOW

Our faith remained in God
    Who gracefully directs life to be
He gave us both good reason
    For brothers rare to bond as we.
Life's nigh hour is before me
    Time as I've known it, is faded by,
I press toward the final mark
    Where measures of reward apply.

Again the road in life divides
    Into some unknown place ahead
Thoughts should be about today
    But I take time to dream instead.
Dreams are sleeping visions
    I foresee us brother in livelihood
Meeting place in life beyond
    Eternal paradise of brotherhood

My visionary dreams focus
    On scenes only I could theorize
A meet place of parted souls
    Family and friends I recognize
Changed and made quickened
    I saw you standing near to me
With all who died before we did
    Awe! A brotherhood of eternity.

~

NATIVE GIFT

The hill stood,
     In the stilly twilight,
With forest shade,
     That fulfills the air,
Where briar rose,
     In blossoms bright,
A boundless sky,
     In its colorful glare.

Waters tremble,
     In light blue-green,
Over colored pebbles,
     Of scattered bright,
Cool breeze murmur,
     Soft music unseen,
Dropping of nuts,
     Or leaves so light.

Care worn trunk,
     Moss covered tree,
Gray squirrels,
     Prance on the hill.
Happy darting bird,
     Singing mildly free,
Where violets lean,
     So quiet and still.

Still mossy boughs,
     Of the mighty oak,
Reach to heaven,
     With a sturdy arm,
Where mated birds,
     With warble spoke,
Nest their home,
     Atop veiled charm.

INSECTS IN SHADE
      ABOUT ROOTS IN SOD
IN CLOVER SMELL
      BEES TO BUTTERFLIES
FOR WILD DESIRE
      THE DEER SHALL TROD
ON ENDLESS FIELDS
      A RICH SOIL DISGUISE

AS TRELLIS'D VINES
      CRAWLED BUTTE CREST
FROM THE GULCH
      WAVES OF LIGHT FADE
LAND OF DREAMS
      WEAVES NOW IN ZEST
NATURE'S SCENERY
      DRESSED FOR PARADE.

ALL THIS FORMATTED
      NATIVE GRACE NEARS
CUT FROM THE WOODS,
      HUSHED SCENES PART
A FREEDOM THEREOF
      FOR ALL YESTERYEARS
CAUSES THE RAPID
      BEATING IN MY HEART

TO PAINTED CREEKS
      ABOUT MYSTIC FIELDS
OR LINGERING CLOUDS
      ON SURGING SEA TIDE
FLASHED IN VIEW
      THE MEMORY YIELDS
THIS NATIVE GIFT
      THAT I'LL STORE INSIDE

~

SUMMER RAIN

Rain's dance across the green,
  Its drizzle bathed the grass
    Walking across mirrored miles,
Wind struggle invisible screen,
  As ripples of water trespass,
    Rinsing face of Daffodil smiles

Sprinkles find a place halfway,
  Sunshine and showers adjust,
    Its tuneful acts of mist remain
Trails pathed around causeway
  Tracks once written in dust,
    Windswept and rinsed by rain,

Soft winds sing within a voice,
  Of breezes designed to flow,
    From the summer winds exhale,
As the swaying of gusts rejoice
  A tune summer rains blow
    While wet whirlwinds turn pale.

Sluggish brook takes its shape,
  Thus falling of drops arrive
    Forward flowing over ground,
Upon crevice formed landscape
  It moves as if it were alive,
    To shallows of the rain sound.

AGAIN THE RAINDROPS SPLATTERED,
UPON A PEBBLE PAVED CREEK,
IN BABBLING WHITE FOAMY THRASH
SPOTTISH CLOUDS HAVE SCATTERED,
VERTICAL IMAGES VIEW SLEEK
RECYCLING MOISTURE IN A SPLASH.

APPEARING MISTY SHOWER STORM,
WASHING THE BERRIES IN WILD,
A COUNTRYSIDE'S TIME AND PLACE,
ITS WEEDS MINGLE WITHOUT FORM,
FLECKED COLORS DULL OR MILD,
SWEET PEAS WEAVE AND INTERLACE.

AN ARTFULNESS OF WONDER MUCH
MOSS STAINS UPON THE ROCKS,
LOCATE DEW OF UNKISSED BEAUTY,
FOR EACH FLOWER SEEKS A TOUCH,
WHERE WILD ROSE INTERLOCKS,
BENEATH THIS WET SHADE OF DUTY.

CONDENSED, MOIST ATMOSPHERE,
ENCHANTED COLORS COPYRIGHT,
GREETING THE GROUNDS WITH TUNE
ITS BEAUTY CLUNG NOW INTERFERE,
DEW DROPS GLISTEN IN DELIGHT
EXHALING ITS FRAGRANCE UNHEWN,

BEYOND THE FAR HORIZON STIRRED
AND ALTERED BY TIME DEVOUT,
BIRTH ANOTHER DAY OF SHOWERS
ITS FAINT PERFUME IS PREFERRED
AMONG A MISTY WATERSPOUT
WHERE WINDS WAVE TO FLOWERS.

SCOOPED FROM SIDE OF THE HILL
DAZZLED BY RAVINE WASHES
FASHIONED TO A CREVICE BEYOND
STORM CLOUDS WEEPS RAIN SPILL
UPON STILLY WATERS IT RUSHES
WHERE LILIES FLOAT ATOP A POND

OH, SO MUCH IS STILL LEFT UNSAID,
NEITHER HAS ENTERED MEMORY
OF SPRAYING VAPOR'S FADED HUE
IN PIECES OF YESTERDAYS INSTEAD,
TOMORROW IS ANOTHER STORY
AND HERE, TODAY, IS JUST A CLUE.

OF TALES THE MOCKINGBIRD'S TOLD,
HOW RAINS DO BECOME SONG,
PLAYING A DANCING TUNE ALOUD,
FOR FRESHNESS BEAUTY TO BEHOLD,
ANOTHER OF NATURE'S THRONG,
THE FRAGRANCE OF A RAIN CLOUD.

~

I'M ALIVE

I'M ALIVE IN MY BED LOOKING UPWARD
    A CEILING WHERE THE COBWEB CLINGS
WITH KNOTS OF PINE SCATTER AWKWARD,
    IN UNEVEN GRAINS OF NATURAL RINGS
NOW CERTAIN SHADOWS FOLLOWED ME.
    FORLONGED MEMORIES MOVE ROUND
FROM VISIONS INSIDE MY HEAD I SEE.
    MUCH FOOLISHNESS IN LIFE REBOUND
AN EXPERIENCE I HAD NEAR TO DEATH
    AWAKENED ME IN CURIOUS SURPRISE,
FROM EVERY MOVE TO EVERY BREATH,
    I SOUGHT FOR WAYS TO COMPROMISE
THE CHANGE OF HEART WITHIN MYSELF
    OF SIMPLE EXPERIENCES THAT DEPRIVE
I'LL QUESTION THE VALUE OF LIFE ITSELF
    BECAUSE IT'S BY CHANCE I AM ALIVE.

I'M ALIVE TODAY TO VIEW THE OCEAN
    AND ENJOY CALLS THE SEAGULLS MAKE
MY LIPS CAN TASTE THE SALTY POTION
    FROM PLEASANT SPRAY WAVES WAKE,
FROM AROMA TAINTED SMELL OF FISH
    FORGOTTEN SHADOWS ARE UNLOCKED
THEN, FOR SATISFYING ANOTHER WISH,
    ANOTHER CHANCE; DEATH IS MOCKED
AMONG THE FIR TREES I SEE THE PINES,
    AND MOVING WINDS THAT FLOAT PASS,
WHERE THE TWISTING OF LAUREL TWINES
    WITH BITTER BRUSH AMONG THE GRASS
MY YESTERDAYS SEEM SO FAR AWAY
    THOSE TOMORROWS ARE RUNNING OUT
TODAY'S COMING SHADOWS DO SWAY
    BY CHOICES MADE THEN TURN ABOUT.

I'M ALIVE TO MAKE DIFFERENT CHOICE
    A CIRCUMSTANCE BEFORE UN-KNOWN,
IN PROMISE FROM A PLEASANT VOICE
    SOME FUTURE DAY TO TAKE ME HOME
BUT ONCE AGAIN THE SPIRIT REPLIED
    AND THEN I CRIED OUT IN MY DESPAIR
SUDDENLY AFTER THAT, THE VISION DIED
    ALONE I SAW MYSELF STANDING THERE,
YES, DEEPLY DISTURBED I'LL CONFESS
    FROM MY LONGING, I CAME SATISFIED
BY REACHING OUT INTO FOOLISHNESS
    MY OWN WRONG WAS OFTEN JUSTIFIED
INDEED SHALLOWS OF SIN SHALL BEFALL
    WITHOUT SOME MEDIATOR TO DEFEAT
BEHOLD, JUDGMENT WILL COME TO ALL
    WHEN TIME AND DEATH SHALL MEET.

I'M ALIVE SEEING A PEOPLE IN NEED
    DOWN FOR ONE REASON OR ANOTHER
SOME, WITH CAUSE TO NOT SUCCEED
    THEN THOSE WHO DESERVE THE OTHER
THERE'S LUCK INVOLVED IN ALL SUCCESS
    IT'S NOT ONLY THE DECISIONS OF RIGHT
THIS THE RICH WILL SELDOM CONFESS
    BUT CREDIT TO THEIR SPECIAL INSIGHT
THEY LACK COMPASSION FOR THE POOR
    FOR GOOD IN OTHERS, THEY LOOK NOT,
BUT DREAM DREAMS OF GAINING MORE
    A LESS FORTUNATE THEY LONG FORGOT
TELLING STORIES THAT ARE IMAGINARY
    HOW BY SOME WITS THEY EARN GAIN
HOLLOW PRIDE FOR THE LOW, UNWARY
    CONSIDER NOT THE HUNGER OR PAIN.

I'M ALIVE TO WATCH THE PROUD DENY
      IN A SELF EGO THEY PUFF UP AND BRAG
ALL WITHOUT REGRET NOR ANGUISH CRY
      O' WOE, TO THAT SOUL IN SUCH A SNAG,
VANITY BY TRIALS OF FORCE AND MIGHT
      IN A DESIRE TO PROTEST OR DISPROVE
THEIR IMAGINATION OF FALSE INSIGHT
      WALKS AN ARROGANT HAUGHTY MOVE
A BOAST TO GAIN THE POPULAR VOTE
      A TRY TO CHANGE HOW STARS ARE SET,
THEIR SUPPORTERS COME AN ANTIDOTE,
      TO ACCEPT AN APPROVAL THEY COVET,
SUCH IMAGES THEY'LL DESIRE TO KEEP,
      OF FANCY TITLES THEY LONG TO BEHOLD
BUT UPON THAT DAY THEY FALL ASLEEP
      HOLLOWNESS OF IMAGES WILL UNFOLD.

I'M ALIVE DURING A GENERATION GAP,
      FOR A FOOL BOASTS AND COMPLAINS
FROM AN ATTITUDE THAT WILL OVERLAP
      ONLY SATISFYING THEIR INNER GAINS
THEY MINGLE WITS IN A CUNNING PLOT
      WITH EGO BACKED IN MUCH ADVICE
A COMMON MAN THEY CONSIDER NOT
      AGREE WITH WHO BELIEVE LIKEWISE
IT'S FROM THESE ISSUES MAN JUSTIFIES
      WITHOUT FULL KNOWLEDGE OF THE TOLL
THEY WRONG THE RIGHT THAT QUALIFIES
      INTRODUCING SORROW INTO THE SOUL
SO IN ALL THIS I WILL FINALLY CONCLUDE
      THAT ALL LIFE IS NAUGHT BUT A VAPOR
AND NO MORE CAN ANY MAN INCLUDE
      BUT HIS FOOLISHNESS UNLOOKED FOR.

I'M ALIVE TO EXPERIENCE THE GREED
    MEASURED BY MAN'S POSSESSIONS
A DESIRE ONE'S IMAGE TO SUCCEED
    AS COVETING BECOMES OBSESSIONS
RAVE ON FOOL BY CAUSING SORROWS
    STRIVING TOWARDS YOUR OWN ESTATE
TRY BENDING TO CHANGE TOMORROWS
    TIS THEIR FOOLISH WAY TO CELEBRATE
A CONCEALED SELFISH WAY OF GIVING
    MINGLING GREED WITH A MAKE BELIEF
THEY SACRIFICE A FULLNESS OF LIVING
    TAINTING THEIR OWN HEART INTO GRIEF
I ASK MYSELF WHAT COULD BE GAINED
    FROM SUCH DESIRES LUST MAY CAST
BY DECEIVING A COVETNESS RETAINED
    SURE THE STINGY WILL FALL STEADFAST,

I'M ALIVE AFORE A SPIRITUAL DRAUGHT
    WHO MOCKS WHAT IS RIGHT OR GOOD
GIVE TO TENDENCY OF MODERN THOUGHT
    NEW WAVE RELIGIOUS NEIGHBORHOOD
CONFORMS TOWARD AN IMMORAL PATH
    DRAWN DOWN TO THE DEPTHS OF LUST
THIS UNDIGNIFIED MANNER OF WRATH
    REVEALS A MORAL CHARACTER UNJUST
AMONG THEMSELVES THEY ADMONISH
    IT'S HERE VANITY IN THE HEART BURNS
IGNORANT OF WHAT THEY ACCOMPLISH,
    JUSTIFY THEMSELVES SO SIN RETURNS
GRASPING FOR EACH RECKLESS HOUR
    WITHOUT A LAMP BEFORE THEIR WAY,
IN SELF-RIGHTEOUSNESS THEY DEVOUR
    AND BRING DARKNESS TO THEIR DAY.

I'M ALIVE TO SEE THE INGENIOUS THIEF
    FULL OF EXCUSES TO ADOPT OR ADJUST
THEY CAUSE MUCH SORROW AND GRIEF
    FROM THE SHREWDNESS DONE UNJUST
WITH STORIES TOLD AND OF FOOLISH LIES
    BY DEFRAUD, BENDING OUT OF SHAPE
TO STEAL OR CHEAT IN CLEVER DISGUISE
    BUT THEIR VANITY IS WITHOUT ESCAPE
OVER VIALS OF TIME TO FLEE WITH ALIBIS
    BECOME CRAFTY CUNNING AND ARTFUL
DEFENDING, SUPPORTS SELF SATISFIES
    EXCUSE THEMSELVES BEING DECEITFUL
FALSEHOOD FROM SOME UNTRUE STORY
    FANTASY WITH A FANCY IMAGINATION
IN A FAITHLESS OVERBEARING TERRITORY
    WEAVING THE FEEBLE TO TRIBULATION

I'M ALIVE TO VIEW MAN INFLICT HARM
    INJURE, MISTREAT, DAMAGE OR ABUSE
WITH EMOTION HIDDEN BEHIND CHARM
    TO CAUSE ONE PAIN WITHOUT EXCUSE
THE ILL AMONG THEM BECOMES CLEAR
    DISASTER OF MORALS THAT VANISHED
INTO A PRESENCE OF DANGER AND FEAR
    TO A PATH THEMSELVES ESTABLISHED
THE UNBELIEVABLE PRICE MAN PAYS
    WHAT SELF AFFLICTIONS THEY'LL CAUSE
THEIR EVIL AND FOOLISHNESS STRAYS
    ELECT BAD CHOICES WITHOUT PAUSE
REPEATING OVER THE WAYS OF CRIME
    TRANSFORMING THE WOUNDED SPIRIT
O', THEY SHALL CRUMBLE IN DUE TIME,
    AND APPROACH THE JUDGMENT UNFIT.

I'M ALIVE TO SORT OUT A FAIR BALANCE
    WITHOUT FEAR INTO THE UNJUST HOURS
TO LOCATE ALLOWANCE FOR TOLERANCE
    THAT A COMPLICATED WORLD DEVOURS
IN MY SPEECHLESS WONDER I GAZED
    FROM ALL I SEE FROM WHERE I STOOD
OVER A LOST MANKIND I AM AMAZED
    TRIUMPH CAME NOT AFORE IT SHOULD
DESPERATE MAN WHOSE LINK'S BROKEN
    IN YOUR REPENTANCE BE YE REJOICED
YOUR IRON HEART MELTS INTO A TOKEN
    AS CONVICTIONS SURFACE UNVOICED
A SPIDER CHASES A SHADOW IN DOUBT
    A MAN PLEASING HIMSELF WILL DEFILE
BUT THE SPIRIT'S ARM STRETCHING OUT
    FORGIVES A MOST PARDONABLE GUILE.

I'M ALIVE AGAIN TO SEE ANOTHER KIND
    A FAITH PEOPLE WHO ARE CALLED OUT
A PEOPLE OF A QUITE DIFFERENT MIND
    A PRAYING PEOPLE WHO ARE DEVOUT
THIS WORLD FACES ITS MORAL CRISIS
    BUT JUDGMENTS HAVE BEEN DELAYED
TIME, PATIENCE AND COMPROMISES
    ARE BY FAITH OF A FEW WHO PRAYED
LOOKING ABOUT IT'S HARD TO IGNORE
    THE ODD BALANCE OF JUSTICE SCALES
HEAVIER IS SIN NOW THAN EVERMORE
    AS HISTORY REPEATS BIBLICAL TALES
SO THE FAITH AND HOPE OF JUST A FEW
    BESTOWS OPPORTUNITIES TO CHANGE
REPENT OUR WAYS AND COME ANEW
    TO TAKE UP OUR CROSS IN EXCHANGE.

I'M ALIVE AGAIN TO A SECOND CHANCE
    OPPORTUNITIES IN TIME TO MAKE RIGHT
AN ALTERING OF SOME CIRCUMSTANCE
    THEN TAKING THE TORCH INTO THE NIGHT
ANOTHER VIEW OF MY MANY LIVES FLAW
    MUCH SELF-EVALUATING TO YET EXPLORE
MEMORIES IN PICTURES I CANNOT DRAW
    MY PAST OF ERRORS I CANNOT RESTORE
ONCE IN MY BOLDNESS, I DID REJOICE
    INTO GREAT FOOLISHNESS I DID FOLLOW
NOW NEW SOUNDS OF ANOTHER VOICE
    EXPLAIN HOW MY HEART WAS HOLLOW
OF COURSE, THESE HAVE CAUSED SCAR
    FROM JUDGMENT, I HOLD MY BREATH
ATTEMPT TO RIGHT MY WRONG THUS FAR
    AFORE DECAY COMES ON MY DEATH.

I'M ALIVE AND FORTUNATELY SURVIVED
    TO SORT THOUGHTS OF LIFE'S ILLUSIONS
OLD HAPPENINGS ONCE AGAIN REVIVED
    JUDGES MYSELF WITHOUT EXCLUSIONS
OH' DEATH, THOU HOLDS THE SECRETS
    REGARDING THE OTHER SIDE ISOLATED
OH' MYSTERIES WHICH DIVIDE REGRETS
    EXPOSING MY WRONG ONCE IMITATED
OH' GRAVE, WHAT'S BEHIND THE CURTAIN
    SHADOWING MYSTERIES I CAN'T KNOW
OH! THAT I TRUST I KNEW FOR CERTAIN
    ARE ALL OPEN SECRETS LEFT TO BESTOW
MATTERS IN LIFE, WHICH PERSECUTES
    TWAS SO SIMPLE WHEN I DID ARRIVE
O' AFORE I DIE, FORGIVE MY DISPUTES
    LORD, HELP ME LIVE WHILE I'M ALIVE.

~

SILENT WORLD

SILENT WORLD

And the sunset glowed,
    Imitating rose-tinted flowers.
Spread on the horizon,
    During its last fading hours.

Pouring beams of violet
    Thru' lifting clouds a stirred,
And immortal air in dew,
    Eased twilight without word.

Inside each folded bud
    Cloaks the hearts of blossom
The unraked field waves
    On mountain summits bottom.

Enchanted glitter star,
    The trace where it might leap,
Or many searching fish,
    Navigating the strange deep.

The ocean with its roar,
    Pauses into its quiet melody,
Wondrous silent world,
    That's swamped by the sea....

~

PROSPECTOR N' ASS

PROSPECTOR N' ASS

OL' PROSPECTOR N' ASS THERE AT HIS
  SIDE
WALKING THE SAND IN A SLO' PACED
  STRIDE
AN' READING HIS MAPS, TORN AT THE
  FOLD
SOME FOOL WRITTEN WHERE MIGHT BE
  GOLD

HIS DREAMS ARE DREAMS OF ALL HIS
  DREAMS
OF BECOMING RICH FROM SANDY DIRT
  STREAMS
DREAMS NOW GIVE HIM STRENGTH AN'
  PRIDE.
THE OL' PROSPECTOR WITH A WRINKLED
  HIDE

TIS BROWN ON HIS SKIN SUN BEATEN
  FACE
WRINKLED BROW SHARING SAND IN ITS
  PLACE
HIS BLACK STETSON SHADES SUN IN
  RELIEF
TIED AROUND HIS NECK, A RED HAND
  KERCHIEF.

HIS HAIRS ARE SANDY AND LIPS ARE
  DRY.
LOOKS THROUGH SQUINT OF A BEADY
  EYE.
ENJOYS A LITTLE CONVERSATION AS HE
  WALKS.
SO TO A FAITHFUL FRIEND, THE ASS, HE
  TALKS.

HIS CLOTHES WELL WORN, COLORS DULL
     GREY.
BLENDS IN WITH DESERTS SURPRISING
     PREY.
HIGH LEATHER BOOTS TO SHED RATTLE
     SNAKES
IN THOUGHTS ONLY OF THE GREAT GOLD
     STAKES.

BUT NOW ON AN' ON THE PAIR MOVES
     ON.
TELLING SOME STORIES OR SHARING A
     SONG.
THEY WALK AND' LOOK OR STOP FOR A
     WHILE.
SEARCHES ANY GROUNDS SUSPICIOUS
     PILE.

TO UNDERCOVER OR FIND SOMEONE'S
     LOSSES
WHERE WINDS BLOW AN' SAGE BRUSH
     TOSSES.
LOOKIN' FOR ARROWHEADS OR HIDDEN
     CACHE
RELICS, TIN CANS OR BOTTLES IN OLD
     ASH.

HE HOLDS HIS FAVORITE GOLD PAN IN
     HAND.
AND SCREEN TO SORT TREASURE FROM
     SAND.
BUT, BACK OF HIS MIND HE'LL ALWAYS
     HOLD
TO FURTHER SEEK FOR THAT SPARKLE OF
     GOLD.

ANY ODD LOOKING BEADS. ROCK OR
STONE.
GETS SORTED AN' GRADED AN' PLACED
ALONE
AFTER A CAREFUL INSPECTION WITH HIS
GLASS,
PUTS IT IN A BAG THAT HANGS ON HIS
ASS.

THEN, INTO THE HEAT, OF A STAGGERED
TRAIL,
PASSIN' DRIED BONES, SUNBLEACHED
PALE.
BENT OVER WALKING IN A SEARCHING
BOW,
WHIPPING THE WET FROM HIS SWEATY
BROW.

WITH THE OBSIDIAN CHIPS LAYING ALL
AROUND
MAKES IT HARD TO FIND ARROWHEADS
FOUND
A SEARCH GOES ON WHERE ONCE WAS
ABODE.
EXPOSING THE SECRETS OF OL' MOTHER
LODE

WITH BASIC EQUIPMENT TO WORK THE
DIRTS.
AND OTHER ITEMS IN THE PACKSADDLE
INSERTS.
TIS HIS FAITHFUL FRIEND WITH DUMMY
SMILES,
HAS ACCOMPANIED HIM THRU MANY
MILES.

THE OL' PROSPECTOR DIGS AROUND AN'
    PICKS,
SKILLFULLY TRIES OUT HIS GOLD FINDING
    TRICKS.
HE, FOLLOWS A DREAM, OR STORY ONCE
    TOLD,
ABOUT SOME LOST, UNFOUND HIDDEN
    GOLD.

FROM THE DESERT TO THE EDGE OF ITS
    HILL
WHERE TREES AND SOME GREEN GROW
    STILL.
A DELIGHT TO THEIR EYES, AS THEY ARE
    BOUND
A PLACE WHERE COOL WATER MAY BE
    FOUND

FROM THE SPRING AT THE BASE OF ITS
    SLOPE,
WASHES HIMSELF IN SANDY MUD FOR
    SOAP
REFRESHES HIS FRIEND IN A RAG CLOTH
    DAMP,
AN TAKES A BREAK BEFORE SETTING UP
    CAMP.

THE OL' PROSPECTOR THEN SO KINDLY
    ASKS,
"O' WHERE MY FRIEND, MIGHT BE MY
    FLASK?"
HE WETS HIS WHISTLE AN' WATERS HIS
    ASS,
SAYS, "LET'S SET CAMP IN THE SAGEY
    GRASS."

Empties the saddle pack upon the
    groun'
Curry combs his asses back an all
    aroun'
Then fed his friend some special
    grains,
With carrots he saved across the
    plains.

He builds a fire of juniper twig an'
    sage,
Brewed his coffee to its enjoyable
    age.
Drinks from his blue tin cup in his
    han'
Fried jackrabbit in the old frying
    pan.

Then built lean-to out of limbs an
    rock,
To sit against, rest and to his ass
    talk.
He eats then cleans his eatin' tins
    out,
With hot water sand and dirt as a
    grout.

Draws his harmonica, an' sits an'
    plays,
In some parts of tunes in different
    ways.
Plays to his ass, or new friends he
    makes,
Like the desert rats, bats or rattle
    snakes.

Now dancing up a tune as he gets
    up,
For the coffee to refill his favorite
    cup.
The ol' prospector, he dances an'
    strolls,
Round and round warm campfire
    coals.

Eve is come dark upon their airy
    home
Together they will rest their weary
    bone.
Rest from walking all day's dusty
    pass,
Ol' prospector and his friend the
    ass.

Again talks of dreams he's been
    told,
Of how they are on a trail of free
    gold.
He tells of the things he'll buy his
    friend,
That's if these dreams do come to
    end.

But, his friend, the ass, just silly
    smiles,
Without hopes of gold, but happy
    miles.
So bedding down in night's desert
    cold,
In dreams of searchin' for yellow
    gold.

OL' PROSPECTOR SLEEPS WITH DESERT
    SLOPIN',
HAVING ONE EYE SHUT AND ONE EYE
    OPEN.
THE FIRE COALS GLIMMER A BLINKING
    LIGHT,
AGAINST SILENCE OF DESERT PESTS AT
    NIGHT

NIGHT'S DESERT WHERE TUMBLEWEEDS
    TUMBLE
OL' PROSPECTOR AND FRIEND SLEEPING
    HUMBLE.
AN' DREAMS OF DREAMS OF GOLD THAT
    HIDE,
FOR THE OL' PROSPECTOR N' ASS AT HIS
    SIDE...

~

ROBIN

It's only one of God's
Beautiful creations,
This common robin
     Announcing cheer.

Where fully throated,
Pours out the song,
Twittering enchanted
     Music in volunteer

Body is gray above
Brickish red breast
Hops upon ground
     A worm in its bill

Then nests on a limb
Of mud lined grasses
With light blue eggs
     Guarded with skill

Then wings its way
And whirling about,
Swiftly rushing in a
     Blue chalky glare.

With dappled breast
Its dawn cast wings,
Tracing a cloudless
     Path thru mid-air.

~

O' LORD, WHERE IS SHE?

O' LORD, WHERE IS MY LOVE, MY OTHER HALF?
 O' WHY DOES SHE PLAY ME ALONG THIS WAY?
WHAT POSSIBLE REASON ON WHOSE BEHALF
 WOULD CAUSE ALL MY INNER JOY TO DECAY?

O' MY LORD, WHY ME, WHY ME, OH LORD?
 HOW COULD SHE FORGET ALL THE MEMORIES?
WHY WOULD SHE BRING FORTH THIS DISCORD
 AND RUIN OUR LIVES BECAUSE OF FANTASIES.

O', WHY ME, LORD? I ASK WHAT HAVE I DONE
 HOW IS IT I SHOULD COME IN SECOND PLACE?
BETWEEN SHE AND I STOOD SOME OTHER ONE
 AND BITTERNESS TOWARD ME IS ON HER FACE.

DREAMS ARE CLOUDED THAT ONCE WAS OURS
 DESCRIBING MY TORMENT, I DON'T KNOW HOW
HER MOMENTS WITH ME SEEMS LIKE HOURS
 MY HOURS WITH HER IS MOMENTS SOMEHOW

IN SECOND PLACE I FEEL LIKE A LOVE LEFTOVER
 THIS UNFAIR BALANCE, I CAN'T YET CONCLUDE
AS I LOOK INTO HER EYES, SHE LOOKS COLDER
 WITHOUT HER LOVE I FEEL ALONE IN SOLITUDE

O' LORD, HOW MUCH MORE CAN ONE TAKE
 HER VOICE NOW TRANSMITS UNHAPPY TONE.
WHERE'S THE LIMIT, OR EDGE WHERE I BREAK
 HER TENDER LOVES TURNED TO COBBLESTONE

O' LORD, MY SPIRITS NOW FINALLY BROKEN
    MY THROAT GETS TIGHT; IT'S HARD TO SWALLOW
ANTICIPATIONS OF OUR FUTURE UNSPOKEN
    ALL ENTHUSIASM FOR A LIFE TURNED SHALLOW.

O' LORD, I BESEECH THEE ASKING WHY?
    THE LOVE THAT I ONCE KNOWN FOR CERTAINTY
HAS BECOME MY EMPTINESS TO OCCUPY!
    AGAIN, I ASK THEE, O' LORD, WHERE IS SHE?

~

WINDMILL

WINDMILL

THERE STOOD THE OL' WINDMILL
    SHABBY SHINGLES ON ITS SIDE
SOUND OF A SHRIEKING' SHRILL
    AS THE WINDS HITCHED A RIDE.

TWIXT THE HOMESTEAD NEARBY,
    CROSSING A PATH OF LONG AGO
BIRDS WING FREELY THE SKY,
    SHARE TALES, TUNES THEY KNO'

A HOME FOR MANY NESTS,
    A LITTLE MOSS MIGHT APPEAR
THIS WINDMILL WAS THE BEST
    BACK A MANY FORGOTTEN YEAR.

TO ITSELF THE WINDMILL THOUGHT
    AS STANDING IN A GENTLE SUN
AS A BREEZE IT THEN CAUGHT
    I WAS AT ONCE THE FASTEST ONE.

I CAN REMEMBER MY PENNANT
    IT WAS A LONG TIME NOW PAST,
THEN TURNING IN A FLAT MINUTE
    SIXTEEN-HUNDRED TIMES FAST.

MY MAIN BEARINGS SINGING
    I DANCED UPON THE GROUND
AN' ROARED INTO BRINGING,
    A TUNE MANY MILES AROUND

THE JUDGES STOOD AWAY CLEAR
    AS THEY LOOKED AT MY BLADE
ASTONISHED WITH GREAT FEAR,
    AT THE SPEED THAT I HAD MADE.

HMMMMM' THE THRILL INSIDE
IN THOSE USEFUL YESTERDAYS
AND THEY PAINTED MY SIDE
ADJUSTED MY GEARS N' STAYS

I'M SURE I COULD ONCE AGAIN
IF I WERE GREASED ONCE MORE
TURN A NORTHEASTERN WIND
INTO A SPEED AS I DID BEFORE.

BUT AIR PASSES THRU' N' ROUN'
AS IF TO JUST TEASE ME TODAY,
BECAUSE I'M NOW RUN DOWN,
MY BENT RUDDER TURNS AWAY.

ONCE THERE WAS FAMILY I LOVED
DREW WATER FROM EARTH'S CORE
BUT THE WIND, I ONCE SHOVED
FOR THEM I'LL SHOVE NO MORE

NOW WITH RUST UPON MY GEARS
I CRANK ON BUT SLOWER STILL
NOW AGED WITH THE YEARS,
I'M THE OL' FORGOTTEN WINDMILL....

~

I DON'T CARE

MOST OF MY SOCKS HAVE HOLES,
SOME THE HEELS OR IN THE TOES,
      BUT I DON'T CARE.

SHIRTS HAVE THEIR BUTTONS GONE,
SOME PANTS ARE WAY TOO LONG,
      BUT I DON'T CARE.

MY JACKET HAS THE SAME HOLE,
WHICH IT HAD A LONG TIME AGO,
      BUT I DON'T CARE.

SO MY SHIRTS NEVER SEE STARCH,
SOMEONE LOST MY SHOES ARCH,
      BUT I DON'T CARE.

WORK TROUSERS SPOTS OF GREASE,
OR MY KHAKIS HAVE NO CREASE,
      BUT I DON'T CARE.

ZIPPER'S BROKEN, I DON'T GRIEVE,
MY UN-IRONED RED HANDKERCHIEF,
      BUT I DON'T CARE,
         I JUST DON'T CARE...

~

UNUSUAL SNO' IN BEND

UNUSUAL SNO' IN BEND

Outside where sno'
      Now so whitely glo'
An' silvery sung,
      Were cycles hung,
    Each flake floats roun' winding

An' down from flight
      Birds again recite,
To shelter they go,
      From a fallin' sno'
    To hide from the cold a finding.

The juniper berry,
      Has snow to carry,
An' sage is bound,
      Frozen to ground,
    Tumble weeds no longer tumble,

An' little Deschutes
      Tis walked by boots,
Or where its wide,
      Has iced its side,
    Quietly does its ripples rumble.

On surrounded hills,
      Of its white icy sills,
Then frozen terrains,
      Into silence remains,
    Until the wind of echoes drown.

And in the streets,
      A drifts now meets,
Around the stores,
      Settles its scores,
    Unusual sno, has come to town.

Rock tops now white,
        Snow holding tight.
Then hidden some,
        As sno' now come
      The road meets sand an' plow.

The flowers grace,
        Now hide their face,
An' moisture about,
        Frozen waterspout
      A cold blanket surrounds now.

O' people who meet,
        An' walk the street,
They talk to show
        They like the snow,
      Unusual sno' this year, so say.

An' I have to laugh,
        At the jokin' staff,
Who stays inside,
        An do so well hide,
      But love snow, when its away,

There under a tree,
        Some life may be
To hide for awhile,
        In a sheltered style,
      The umbrelled trees will defend

With waters freeze,
        Where sky's sneeze,
The winter's abide,
        It's so cold outside,
      This, an' unusual sno' in Bend....

~

LO! MY LORD

LO! my Lord, I'm coming home
Yea into a spiritual flight
A seer of strange visions
Of enlighted vibrating light.

Lo! my Lord, who I fall before
Hear my spiritual request
I'd walk Thy holy streets
From its east to its west.

Lo! my Lord, whom is my light
O' restrengthen my stand
Behold a sight of Thy face
To the touch of Thy hand.

Lo! My Lord, it so shatters me
Sins from the day of birth
Reflection of my life itself
Finding it of little worth.

Lo! My Lord, who I love much
Thou forgave yesterday
Made way for my escape
And find the passageway.

Lo! my Lord, Oh, King of Kings,
O' bind my spirit to Thine,
Leading into the Holy City,
Out of this physical time.

~

HOPE

HOPE IS THE GREAT LEVER
THAT LIGHTS UP THE WORLD
IN PROGRESS.
NOR MAN DOES NOT HOPE
FOR THINGS HE ALREADY
NOW POSSESS

FOR HE WHICH HAS HOPE
CLEANSETH HIMSELF THEN
WILL BE SAVED.
HOPES ARE THE JEWELS
THAT MAKES THE CROWN
WITH SINS WAVED

HE WITH A BREASTPLATE
WITH FAITH AND OF LOVE
SHALL NOT SLEEP
PUTTING ON, FOR HELMET,
THE HOPE OF SALVATION
A SOUL TO KEEP

MAN NOT SEEKING HOPE
HE CANNOT OBTAIN FAITH,
AN' IS CONFUSED.
BUT AS ANGELS MINISTER
WITH HOPE IN THE HEART,
ERROR IS EXCUSED.

AS FAITH PRESSES FORTH
AND LOOKING BACKWARD
FAITH ACCEPTS
BUT HOPE IS THE FUTURE
SO HOPE LOOKS ONWARD
HOPE EXPECTS

HOPE IS INSPIRED FAITH
LEADING INTO GLORIOUS
NEW POSSIBILITIES,
SUPPORTED SIDE BY SIDE
MAN'S FAITH AND HOPE
CHANGES REALITIES...

~

NEW YOUTH

NEW YOUTH

Ever since my youth,
    I never knew the truth
Of God and His power,
    No, not until this hour.

With pressure pressing,
    I found this confessing,
Unto my God all alone,
    Could reach His throne.

My quest then mended,
    I realized the intended,
Then His call I obeyed.
    An' I'm no more afraid.

So today I have forgot
    Any troubled thought,
As that old way ends,
    Even different friends.

A new interest arises,
    From my old sacrifices,
And now it's my goal,
    To inspire another soul.

So to Him I will abide,
    He alone is my guide,
Of promise and truth,
    I have a second youth.

~

A REASON TO REASON

Tonight my heart weeps in memories shadow,
       Echoing a voice in dreams of yesteryear.
       Those mirrored smiles will not disappear
From that city of souls calling out to me low,
In voices reflecting that of joy and of sorrow,
       Anyway, that's how it seemed to appear,
       Reclaiming a vision with someone dear,
Beyond any reasons, facts attempt to show,

Though reasoning alone I can't always find,
       So then I pause to see what time brings,
       For as time itself confirms other things,
Mysteries exposed when fading figures bind.
Until they fade, to then reappear in my mind,
       Tracing reason on experienced feelings,
       I'm a puppet of reason drawn by strings,
When reasons can appear reasonably kind.

Behold, the one, which was my strength died,
       Leaving a kind of ghost that never fades,
       In becoming my nightmare that invades,
Neither can a replacement ever be supplied,
Or reasonable reasons for this loss justified,
       Life continues rehearsed as it's played,
       Without manuscript a future portrayed,
Nevertheless I'll seek reasons to be satisfied.

For it's difficult facing death when that's that
    Burn vibrations inside like a final quake,
    From unseen illusions experiences wake,
I resist this ceaseless pain with silent combat,
To reason in perspective where my loss is at,
    Nor can I allow feelings alone to partake,
    To be unreasonable would be a mistake,
O' what good reason can I find to live thereat?

What direction might I turn to again restore?
    Shedding light upon path of the old way,
    Circumstance I thought was here to stay,
Neither could I by chance any longer ignore,
As I once thought things would be evermore,
    I wonder isn't there something I can say,
    To remove this void that grows each day,
Oh! How can I reason peace as once before?

For desire of life I'm much too weak to fight,
    I must somehow deal with this absentee
    From gray tomorrows O' how can I flee?
Although dreams turned to ashes one night,
The fact remains I must reason what is right.
    Bewildered and amazed yet I now agree,
    I'll press on for the living as they for me,
Then to reason together in memories delight.

~

UNDER JUDGMENT

YEA! WITHIN MY MIND
    DRIFTS A FOGGY CLOUD,
PURPOSE I CANNOT FIND,
    BUT I CAN HEAR IT LOUD,
    A JUDGMENT BEFORE ME IS REAL

NO! NONE OTHER KNOWS
    NEITHER DO THEY CARE,
OR CAN THEY I SUPPOSE
    FOR THEY'RE NOT AWARE
    OF THE CONDEMNING THAT I FEEL.

GAMES WE OFTEN PLAY
    BY WAYS AND DREAMS,
LEFT TO APPEAR A WAY,
    THAT IS RIGHT IT SEEMS
    REGARDLESS HOW IT SHOULD BE

THEN SPEAKS MY HEART
    SAYS, "CHANGE TODAY"
WHEN I BEGIN TO START
    ANOTHER VOICE WILL SAY
    "AH, ENJOY YOURSELF WITH ME"

THEN I'LL SEARCH INSIDE
    TO ANOTHER WAY I SEEK
A WAY THAT WILL DIVIDE
    THE STRONG, THE WEAK
    TO THE ONE WHO CAN FORGIVE

I MUST PIERCE THE FOE
    WHO CLOUDS MY DREAM
THE ONLY WAY I KNOW
    BY JUDGMENT EXTREME
    TO CONDEMN MYSELF AND LIVE

Fools judge foolishly
    Assume, point or stare
I've learned patiently
    To judge but beware
    And need only to judge but I

While some entertain
    Choosing my destiny
In seeking their gain,
    A people of mutiny
    Personal judgment for alibi.

Their heads turn away
    Friendships fall apart
They attempt to sway
    Feelings in my heart
    They but stumble in the night

A man's past retraced
    Cause to be hardened
By judgment placed
    Instead of pardoned
    In man's own eyes he's right.

O' fool who judges me
    They excuse their way
Deeming selves justly
    Even to this very day
    This became their own snare

In gossip they believe
    Sentencing me the less
Foolishness to achieve
    They felt better, I guess
    But frankly...what do I care?

I PAUSE ONLY TO RECALL
    OF MY DREAMS DENIED,
THINKING WON'T ILL FALL
    UPON THOSE UNTRIED?
    THEREFORE WILL TRIALS APPLY.

THEN IN TEARS OF REGRET
    OF FACTS I DO CONFRONT,
OF THINGS I CAN'T FORGET,
    MY SMILE'S JUST A FRONT.
    WHILE CONVICTIONS MULTIPLY.

MY JUDGMENT I SENSED
    FOR ME IT'S IN MY HEART
FOR CERTAIN CONVINCED
    TEMPTATION IS THE PART
    THAT TURN TRIALS TO TREASURE.

MY SAFETY IT MUST BE
    TO DESIRE THAT OF NONE
TO JUDGE ONLY BUT ME
    FOR I AM THE ONLY ONE
    I CAN JUDGE IN FAIR MEASURE.

~

VAPOR

In a moment of silence
    Between some blank space
Such a dwelling of spirit
    In burst of vapor emptiness
Shadow-less dimension
    Unrevealed in hollow trace.
Recording every detail
    For the Author's awareness

Spirit convicting flesh
    Back into its vapor it leads
Like wind chasing wind
    The Author knows its goal
The grave is a storehouse
    Where only a fool succeeds
Wide is the path prepared,
    For that lost, dormant soul.

In the silence of vapor
    Awaiting those final hours
And yet few are the wise
    Whom seek for its source
Mankind like unto spirit
    Drawn by its many powers
Yet one narrow pathway
    Trails the Author's course.

So man moves evermore
    Molding desire in pleasure
Flesh conforming vapor
    Mingling in foolish matters
Man's desires and wants
    In false images of treasure
His foundation crumbles
    His transforming, shatters

As vapor remains silent
    Un-noticed or un-revealed
Received by the Author
    In life's wave of existences
Recorded and is written
    Judged, sorted, then sealed
For the Author prepared
    Life with its interferences.

Foolish gleans of flesh
    Yields for liberties intended
Claiming other doctrines
    Believing in its own delight
But the Author swiftly
    In a justification, defended
By the dividing of truths
    Separating dark from light

Another chance whirls by
    So speedily, so unexpected
In its moment of silence
    Will come on judgment day
Where the trials of vapor
    Be condemned or perfected
Again the Author speaks
    Making a way for the stray.

In conversion of vapor
    The temptations are varied
As the trials of the flesh
    Hear the moans of the spirit
To who much been given
    Much required to be carried
But skills of allurement
    Draws forth sins to exhibit.

One day the deepest seas,
    And all the earth will shake
Vapor shall be judged
    Then all truth shall be clear
This judgment to expose
    Each vapors unworthy sake
At the great resurrection
    So the Author shall appear.

Man's soul is but vapor
    A body's shadowless mist,
Spirit restored to Author
    As hope and faith embrace
Flesh shall return to dust
    And souls' verdict that exist
Will on that judgment day
    Confront Author face to face.

~

THEIR WHEREABOUTS

MEMORIES CLOUDED WHERE THE PAST ABIDE
 AND IMAGES FORM THOUGHTS OF YESTERYEAR
ONCE AGAIN I SENSE THEM NEARBY MY SIDE
 PROJECTING THIS INVISIBLE SHADOW OF CHEER

AH! HOW I STILL LOVE TO HEAR THEIR NAMES
 OR RECALL FAMILIAR TONES THAT WHISPER STILL
THE EARLY ABSENCE FROM LIFE PLAYS GAMES
 MOCKING THE GOALS I CAN NO LONGER FULFILL

THESE THEY WERE MY VERY HEROES OF OLD
 FROM THE GOOD OLD DAYS AND THEREABOUTS
MY LOVE WAS MORE THAN A HEART CAN HOLD
 WHEN I LOST A VISION OF THEIR WHEREABOUTS

YEA, THEIR LIFE HERE WAS SUCH A SHORT SPAN
 THEN TO FADE FROM DUST TO THE OTHER SIDE
MY HEART CRIES OUT "I HAVE DONE ALL I CAN"
 BUT ANOTHER PART OF ME DISAGREES INSIDE

OH FOOLISH THINGS I ONCE STROVE TO CLAIM
 SPECTACULAR BLEND OF POSSESSIONS IN LIFE
BUT ALL PAST IS GONE AND REMAIN THE SAME,
 TIME BECAME VOID, HOURS WASTED IN STRIFE.

AS THOUGHTS STRAY IN THIS LAND OF DREAMS
 WITH SHATTERED TEARS AND OF SILENT SHOUTS
MY BLANK IMAGINATION SHIELD THE GLEAMS
 AND AGAIN I WONDER OF THEIR WHEREABOUTS

Oh! If only again those days I could re-do.
    I would fill the void and change the past
By finding the time and then fill the shoe
    Fitting the mold of the shoemaker's last

Repeated thoughts of visions I've seen,
    Bathed in a mist, where dreams seem true
Although the past is past I press between
    Toward their shadowy presence I pursue

Such little time a fulfillment they shared
    In the land of the living with ins and outs
My heart starts throbbing as I get scared.
    From just a wonder of their whereabouts

Those yonder, times which I seek after
    Become less greater, less plain, less clear,
That meeting place I entwined hereafter
    In hopes their whereabouts may re-appear

Life itself has attempted to block the trail
    By removing persons that once appeared
But their void in my life is of great detail,
    So silent are the echoes I've always feared

Unequalled in all this, you can be certain
    Life's not the same here in the hereabouts,
I pray for them on this side of the curtain,
    Lord, bless the souls, in their whereabouts.

~

KEEPSAKE MEMORIES

Now as timeless memories reveal,
    Emptiness from awkward pride,
Nor can I show how I should feel,
    For I am lonely, and not a guide.

Last time together, was frailest,
    I kissed you tender on the cheek,
The calling to you, was just a test,
    For you could not hear me speak,

Memories have become my light
    Since death has put us far apart,
Your soul wings a path of flight,
    Beholding keepsakes in my heart.

In whispering wisp silence is hid
    Such is what dreams are made of
Thereby recalling things so vivid
    Things difficult to forget thereof

Little things you did somewhere
    Still seems it's where you belong
I find keepsakes here and there
    Leaping out from wordless song.

Much about you I'll never know,
    Because the future's given away
Yet voices cry words to bestow
    In little games the past will play.

Memories space of images shone,
    Mysterious scene I cannot quote
A kind of ghost or a corner stone
    That puts a lump into my throat.

IN HOLLOW OF HEART YOUR ENGRAVEN
      SHADOW OF IMAGINATION COMPARE,
BENEATH STARS MIST RISE IN HEAVEN,
      I FIND YOUR LIKENESS EVERYWHERE.

MEMORIES RECALL, AS OFTEN BEFORE,
      ALTHOUGH YOUR IMAGE WILL APPEAR
NEITHER WHAT I LOST CAN I RESTORE,
      I CAN BUT REMINISCE OF YESTERYEAR.

THEN PART OF ME, SO STRONG I SEE
      SAYS "HERE'S WHAT IT IS ALL ABOUT"
BUT THEN COMES OUT ANOTHER ME,
      THAT IS WEAK, CONFUSED IN DOUBT.

BLURS TURN MY HEAD YOUR WAY,
      EXPRESSING FEELINGS FAR OVERDUE,
LIKE MID-AIR THAT SHIFTS ASTRAY,
      TIS' MY VOICE CALLING OUT TO YOU.

MEMORIES KEPT AS LITTLE TREASURES
      ASSORTED VALUES OF IMAGES INSIDE
DEVELOPING MY CHOSEN PLEASURES
      PUT INTO WORDS THAT CANNOT HIDE.

IF I COULD LIVE AGAIN OF OLDEN DAY,
      TO CHOOSE THE BEST LIKE FANTASIES
ONLY YOUR JOY WOULD LIFE PORTRAY
      FULFILLING MY KEEPSAKE MEMORIES

~

YEA, I REMEMBER

YEA, I REMEMBER

YEA, REMEMBER DAD
    WHERE ONCE WE ROAM
OF A PLEASANT PLACE
    WITH LOVE BACK HOME
I RECALL THE PEACE,
    AS WE ALL UNDERSTOOD
AND ALL CIRCUMSTANCES,
    COULD BE MADE GOOD.

ONE YEAR OVER HERE
    THEN ONE YEAR THERE
WE FOLLOWED THE WORK
    TO ALMOST ANYWHERE
FOLLOWING THE FRUIT
    FROM VINE TO A GROVE,
FROM FIELD TO FIELD
    TO OUR TREASURE TROVE.

WITH TENT FOR HOME
    AND LIGHTED BY LAMP
JOININ' AROUN' THE FIRE
    THAT LIT UP THE CAMP.
FOR SONG OR TUNE
    WITH A LAUGH OR JOKE,
OUR FAMILY GATHERED
    AROUND FIRE'S SMOKE.

YEA, REMEMBER MOM,
    THOSE HARD OLD DAYS,
THE WAY THINGS WERE,
    ON THE OLD PATHWAYS.
CREEK-WASHED CLOTHES.
    ATOP A WASHIN' STONE,
OR MAKE A POT OF SOUP
    FROM A BIG DOG BONE.

AND YOUR MOODS, MOM
    THE GOOD OR THE BAD,
THE ROUGH AND HARD
    HAPPY TIMES AN' SAD
YOUR COOKIN' FLAPJACKS
    OVER EARLY MORN FIRE,
OR COFFEE IN A SOCK
    THAT HUNG ON A WIRE.

I REMEMBER YA SWEEPIN'
    A BOARD FLOORED TENT,
IN NEARBY WILDERNESS
    O' COUNTRY SIDE SCENT.
BOXIN' UP OUR THINGS
    SO NEATLY YOU'D TUCK.
PREPARE ANOTHER MOVE
    TO LOAD IN OUR TRUCK.

YEA, I REMEMBER FOLKS
    I COULD NEVER FORGET,
OF TIMES WE'VE SHARED
    OF GREATER TIMES YET.
FROM UP AND DOWN,
    THROUGHOUT THE WEST
NOW A TIME LONG GONE
    WITH MEMORIES, I REST.

O' PACKIN' FRESH WATER
    TO FILL UP OUR SUPPLY,
DIGGIN' AN' OUTHOUSE
    OR TRASH PIT NEAR BY.
WOULDN'T TRADE TIMES
    FOR ANY DIFFERENT WAY
FOR THOSE MY MEMORIES
    THAT LIVE AGAIN TODAY.

Yea, I remember sis
    You in sweetest ways
Little notes you wrote
    To your doll displays
Your hobbies or crafts
    With smiles and tears
Then came between us
    Many miles and years

Yea, I remember brother
    The games we played
Of rules we changed
    Characters portrayed
Sought different ways
    Making old things new
Enjoyed life together
    In happiest ways knew.

For unforgotten times
    Of scenes living ever
Unusual experiences
    I'll again rediscover
Nor shall ever forget
    Doubt or dismember
When I do reminisce
    Yea, for I'll remember

~

GOING HOME

GOING HOME

OH' BURY MY BODY IN
            A PLEASANT SOIL,
WITHOUT HEARTACHE,
            AND WITHOUT TOIL,
WHERE I GO NEEDS NOT,
            CANDLES AT NIGHT,
FOR THE LORD HIMSELF,
            HE ALONE, IS LIGHT.

OH' TRIALS OF DESPAIR
            CAME TO ME OFTEN
SOME SINS I OVERCAME
            SOME I BEGOTTEN
NONE OF MY WORKS
            WILL COUNT AT ALL
WITHOUT HIS GRACE, I
            WOULD SURELY FALL.

OH, BELOVED, LET NOT,
            A FAITH FALL AWAY,
HOW GLAD I AM I WAS
            SAVED YESTERDAY,
THUS DEATH'S STING,
            CAME SO QUICKLY,
YEA, I'M GOING HOME
            TO BE WITH THEE...

~

THE HOLLOW

THE HOLLOW

A DAYDREAM BRINGS US CLOSER,
    TOGETHER IN A SHADOWED PAST,
ANOTHER WALK IN MEMORIES LANE
    WHERE YESTERDAYS CAST A CAST.

INTO THIS HOLLOW PLACE I VISION,
    IT IS YOUR SHADOW I SEE THERE,
THEN STARS MIST RISE TO HEAVEN,
    AND I TOUCH YOUR LOVELY HAIR

AS YOU TURN YOUR HEAD MY WAY,
    IN LOVELY EYES OF AZURE BLUE,
THE MID-AIR WAS SHIFTING SWEET,
    LIKE THATCH WITH A HEAVY DEW.

I WHISPER, "I'LL ALWAYS LOVE YOU",
    AND KISSED YOU ON THE CHEEK,
BUT WHEN I CALL OUT YOUR NAME,
    YOU COULDN'T HEAR ME SPEAK.

VISUAL MEMORIES ARE WITH ME,
    SINCE DEATH PLACED US APART,
MY SOUL WINGS A PATH OF FLIGHT,
    YOU'RE THE HOLLOW IN MY HEART.

SO NOW TOGETHER HERE N' THERE,
    IN THE HOLLOW WHERE I BELONG,
FOR IN THIS TRANCE I SHALL DWELL,
    THO' IT LEAPS AT WORDLESS SONG.

~

THE FANTASY

TONIGHT I LIE IN BED AND WATCH YOU SLEEP
     YOU HAVE BEEN ALL THAT I LOVE AND ADORE
THE QUENCHING OF HOPE MAKES ME WEEP
     WITH THE THOUGHT OF LOSING YOU EVERMORE.

I'M A SIMPLE MAN, OFTEN MISUNDERSTOOD
     BECAUSE I ATTEMPT TO HIDE WHAT'S INSIDE
WITH PERSONALITY YOU ONCE UNDERSTOOD
     BUT NOW PATIENCE WITH ME YOU SET ASIDE

NOW, FANTASY HAS SURFACED INVOLUNTARY
     AS BUNDLED SECRETS OF PART TRUTHS RECITE
ALTHOUGH TRUTH HURTS YET IT'S NECESSARY
     TO BREAK TO MEND, STRENGTHEN AND UNITE

IN KNOWING MY HEART MELTS AND IS TENDER
     YOU TAKE ADVANTAGE TEARING IT TO SHRED
BUT IN BOLDNESS, I AM ONLY A PRETENDER
     REACHING FOR LOVE, GETTING HURT INSTEAD

YOU KNOW MY FEELINGS, WHAT THEY RELAY
     THOUGH I HIDE IT FROM OTHERS IN DISGUISE
BUT YOUR COMPASSION TURNED INTO CLAY
     FANTASY HAS MADE YOU FOOLISH, UNWISE.

IS THERE SOMETHING WRONG WITH MY DESIRE
     THAT I SHOULD SO GREATLY LOVE SOMEONE
I AM GRATEFUL FOR YOU, WHOM I DID ADMIRE
     SOMEHOW, SOMETHING WAS LEFT UNDONE.

YOU LISTEN TO OTHER OPINIONS BY GLANCE
     FABRICATING THOUGHTS OF ILL CONCLUSION
FROM GIBBERISH TALK YOU TAKE A CHANCE
     BUILDING YOUR FANTASY UPON CONFUSION

The babble from friends bring you snare
　　Surface a hardness with darkness inside
It swallows up your reasonings unaware
　　Distorting truth causing your backslide

Now myself being very unsophisticated,
　　I feel so sorry indeed for those who are
They conceal a truth or truth fabricated
　　Without conscience they hide the scar

Therefore, hidden scars shall never heal
　　Till the shame of guilt and truth mends
By this the soul allows peace to reveal
　　So repentance and forgiveness blends

This complicated world waters it down
　　By diluting the moral standards of love
Your dedication to church, your crown
　　Is now allowing a raven to kill the dove

Your lovely faithfulness thru the years
　　Your consciousness, charm or inner joy
Your faith, future where image appears
　　To satisfy your lust, all this you destroy

The great price that you choose to pay
　　As a cloud of passion fantasies pass by
In this game chosen you shouldn't play
　　Surrendering a future of bright supply

Why hearken to the council of this fool?
　　Was our commitment the value of none?
Over this fantasy dear, you can get rule
　　And see what this foolishness has done

BEWARE OF THE STRANGER WHO MAKE TOUCH
    USING SMOOTH WORDS, MELTING YOUR HEART
I'LL ASK HOW CAN YOU BE SO BLIND TO SUCH
    WOE, THE ENEMY'S CHARM OF CUNNING ART

SO BEWARE NOW OF THE STRANGER YOU SEEK
    MOMENTS OF PLEASURE PUT IN HARMS WAY
FANTASY CAME WITH A KISS ON THE CHEEK
    FROM THERE CAUSED YOUR HEART TO SWAY

WHAT TYPE OF A PERSON REACHES THIS LOW
    DO THEY LOOK IN A MIRROR WITHOUT SHAME?
CONSIDER NOT THE HEARTBREAK AND SORROW
    THEY MAKE LIGHT OF IT, PASSING THE BLAME.

YOU BOTH HAVE MUCH IN COMMON YOU SAY
    OH, DEAR WOMAN, THAT CANNOT POSSIBLY BE.
FOR THIS, CLEVER MAN IS BUT ONLY A STRAY,
    AGAINST THE YEARS OF COMMON STOWED WE.

CAN'T YOU SEE HOW THIS PATTERN DESTROYS?
    FROM MISQUOTED WORDS YOU OFTEN REPEAT
THEREBY IMAGINATION BUILDS AND ANNOYS
    UNTIL THE STRONGEST OF LOVE FACES DEFEAT.

IF YOU DON'T LOVE ME ANYMORE, BE IT FAIR
    DON'T ACCUSE ME OF SOMETHING I AM NOT
BY IGNORING THE TRUTH YOU WON'T DECLARE
    OR TO CLAIM THOSE FACTS YOU JUST FORGOT.

I DO NOT DESERVE THE TREATMENT THIS WAY
    QUENCHING A SPIRIT, GRASPING MY BREATH
DILUTING MY HEALTH AND ALL HOPES AWAY
    SHADOW MY DREAMS, MY YEARS, MY DEATH.

Why invite such a foolish tainted affair
        Experience teaches truth without excuse
We shared too many years to be unfair
        Our tender hearts don't need this abuse.

You were my best friend who I did trust
        As together, we went up, together down,
Blending a friendship and love to adjust
        We struggled together to gain our crown.

In counting down, our final years of life
        You lost the focus, of your heart's intent
Two souls were swayed by an evil strife
        Professed Christians, full gospel advent

Before it's too late, open up your eyes,
        You became unstable, walking in a daze
Together in church became your alibis
        Two fools exposing their justified ways

The stranger can be known by his deed
        And then he preyed on you to misguide
A brother's scripture you wouldn't heed
        Behind the lust in your heart you hide.

Teach me how to let feelings intertwine
        When bruised from element of surprise
You gave no warning, no signal or sign
        Then suddenly changed your disguise

What is it standing between you and I?
        What caused change? What have I done?
Write out the list telling me what or why?
        What changed the love that made us one?

Oh, what is worse than a broken heart?
    A hurt from the deepest part of the soul
From your foolish words spoken in part
    Allows evil fantasy to take false control

What compares to a heart that's broken
    No greater sorrow could mankind face
To explain in words it cannot be spoken
    When the depth of true love takes place

I've always loved you, my only sweetheart
    Without hesitation and without remorse
Believed, somehow, 'till death do us part',
    Thinking we are one, for better or worse.

I can think of no reason to not embrace
    Those wonderful wonders to me you are
The past is past but whenever I retrace
    My delight was in you, my morning star

Your repentance seemed a familiar act
    Clutching the feeling you couldn't resist
A change without depth or matter of fact
    The serious repentance that didn't exist.

If I had to go back into time once again
    In choosing a love, it would still be you
In all our ups or downs you still remain
    The only lady to whom I would pursue

Knowing I can't make you love me more
    Or careth for me the way I care for you
I sense emptiness in your heart's core
    Whenever you reject me the way you do.

WHAT TYPE OF A SPIRIT CONTROLS THE HEART
WHAT EXPRESSIONS WILL BE UPON THE FACE
ISN'T IT BY THEIR FRUIT THAT SETS US APART?
INTENTIONS CAN CAUSE TO FALL FROM GRACE

LET IT BE FORGOTTEN, RECOGNIZE THE WRONG
THE CHOICE NOW, WHAT'S IN YOUR THOUGHT
DON'T JUSTIFY THE SIN, PUNISHMENT IS LONG
HOLD ME ONCE AGAIN AND FORGET-ME-NOT

CONSIDER ME LOVE, DON'T THROW ME ASIDE
I HAVE NOTHING ELSE IN THE WORLD BUT YOU
SINCERE IN MY HEART IS SO DEEP, SO WIDE
AND HE COULD NEVER EVER FULFILL MY SHOE

MY LIFE WITHOUT YOU WILL LOSE ALL INTEREST.
THESE THINGS HAVE REACHED INTO MY SOUL
MY HEART MORE FRAGILE AND AT ITS FRAILEST
WITHOUT VISION, BRITTLE, I JUST DON'T KNOW.

AND WHAT PURPOSE IS LIFE FOR HALF A MAN?
FOR SO FEW YEARS ARE LEFT WHICH REMAIN.
WILL NOT LIFE'S PATTERN END HOW IT BEGAN,
IF I LOSE MY OTHER HALF, AND NOT REGAIN?

SO IT IS, HERE AM I, BUT…WHAT DO I KNOW?
WITH THESE THINGS BEING SAID AND DONE
WERE YOUR CLAIMS OF LOVE THAT SHALLOW?
THEN I ASK MYSELF, WEREN'T YOU THE ONE?

POEMS ARE WRITTEN BY FOOLS JUST LIKE ME
TAKING FOR GRANTED WHAT IS IN THE HEART
YET THIS EXPERIENCE HELPED ME TO SEE
THAT I WAS NOT QUALIFIED FROM THE START.

∼

DESERT

DESERT

The desert sands shall now
REPEAT
Miraged scenes waves of
HEAT
Mid of noon the high sun's
FOUND
Upon a bleached an' open
GROUND

Tumble-weeds tumble from
BREEZE
Among thistles of cactus
TREES
Buzzards circle a mid-day
LUNCH
Peaceful gliding shadows
HUNCH.

Sandy city castle without
SOUN'
Ants swarmin' about their
MOUN'
With desert insects busy
STREETERS
Bees n' flies, centipedes n'
SKEETERS.

Rock and sage for shelter
MAKE
A cool shade for the rattle
SNAKE
Bounce around a desert
RABBIT
Long-ear creature nervous
HABIT.

FROM STONE TO STONE WITHOUT
WAIT
SCORPIONS MOVE SLATE TO
SLATE
A DESERT LIZARD PEACEFULLY
SUNS
A SUDDEN MOMENT TO SAFETY
RUNS

SAGE IS FULL AN' SMELLIN' SO
SWEET
BLOSSOMS BLOSSOM IN THE
HEAT
THE STRUGGLE FER LIFE IN THIS
LAND
CHALLENGES ALL BUT SUN AN'
SAND

ANTELOPES FEED ON DESERT
FLOWER
BADGERS DIG WITH MIGHTY
POWER
WITH THE EAGLE SEARCHING A
PREY
PORKY PINE AN' PRAIRIE DOG
PLAY.

SUNSHINE HOURS PASS DAYS
DISCRETION
TIS TURNED ITS EYE THE OTHER
DIRECTION
A MANY EYES AT NIGHT NOW
SEE.
ACROSS SANDS SO STILL AND
FREE

THE BATS FLY ABOUT INTO ITS
NIGHT
TRADE RATS, HAWKS OWLS OF
FLIGHT
LONELY SOUNDS IN DESERTS
SKY
A STILLNESS ECHOS COYOTES'
CRY.

OH DESERT WHERE SECRETS SO
HIDE
FROM STRANGE LANDS SPREAD
WIDE
WITH YOUR DAY N' NIGHTS OF
MYSTERY
YOU ARE DESERT, A LAND FOR
ME......

THE FOOL

THE FOOL GOSSIPS BEHIND THE BACK
      MURMURS SECRETS IN WHISPERING WAY
THEY CUSS OR CURSE, CAUSING GRIEF
      SHAMEFUL DISCOURSE UNSEEMLY STRAY
SPEAKS THEIR MIND AS ALL FOOLS DO
      BRINGING TO LIGHT WRONG EXPLANATIONS
THEY'RE JUDGE, CRITIC, OR EVALUATOR
      ILL MEANINGS, WASTED INTERPRETATIONS
THEY'LL SAY SAYINGS INCONSIDERATE
      EXCESSIVE IMITATIONS FOOLISH INSIGHT
IN TYPICAL ENTHUSIASM TO CRITICIZE
      IF YOU THINK THEY'RE FOOLS, YOU'RE RIGHT.

THE FOOL PLANS MALICIOUS PUT-ONS
      TACTFULLY INVOLVED IN SHADY DEALINGS
UNLAWFUL, DECEIVING, UNFAIR, CLEVER
      UNJUSTIFIABLE MEASURE OF CONCEALINGS
IF CHANCE IN ERROR, UNDERCHARGED
      THEY'RE SILENT CONCEALING THE MATTER
THEY WILL IMPOSE UPON TO SWINDLE
      TO ENCROACH UPON TO TRICK OR FLATTER
MISREPRESENTED IN FALSE PRETENSE
      WITH ALL INTENTS INACCURATE FORESIGHT
ALL THE TIME WELL KNOW THE ACTIVITY
      IF YOU THINK THEY'RE FOOLS, YOU'RE RIGHT

THE FOOL FORCE VISUAL IMPRESSIONS
     HAVING PASSION WITH FLESHLY DESIRES
INVENTS SENSUAL THOUGHTS AT TIMES
     CARNAL ATTRACTIONS THAT LUST INSPIRES
INTO SIN'S TRANSGRESSIONS OF ERROR
     IMAGINES WRONGFUL VIOLATIONS OF LUST
ARTIFICIALLY CONCEALS THE AFFECTION
     TEMPTING THOUGHTS SENSUALLY UNJUST
THIS IS THEIR ADULTERY IMMORAL ACT
     FULL OF RISK ROMANCING INTO THE NIGHT
COMMITTED IN MORE WAYS THAN ONE
     IF YOU THINK THEY'RE FOOLS, YOU'RE RIGHT.

THE FOOL PRETENDS TO BE INNOCENT
     UNAFRAID AND TAMPERS IN SPARE TIME
BOASTFUL OR BOLD IN FEARLESS WAYS
     BEWILDERED INEQUITIES PROVOKE CRIME
BREAKING RULES OF MORAL CONDUCT
     DARING IMAGINATIONS OF UNTRUE ALIBIS
ILLEGAL SHADOWS CLOSED ALL AROUND
     FANCY SENSELESS INVENTION JUSTIFIES
UNTOLD EXCESSIVE DRINKING DISCLOSE
     THE FOOL, A DUNCE CONFORMING TO FIGHT
AS IF THEY'RE HYPNOTIZED TO COMPLY
     IF YOU THINK THEY'RE FOOLS, YOU'RE RIGHT

THE FOOL BELIEVES MUCH IN HIMSELF
    THEIR FORCES REBEL AND RIGHTFULLY FALL
BEING DISHONEST WITHOUT REMORSE
    ALL TO A SELF ENJOYMENT AS THEY RECALL
ADMIT NOT THINGS DONE IN SECRET
    BEHIND CURTAINS THE FOOL DOES UNJUST
ALL ALONG WHILE GRASPING FOR FAITH
    IN HOLLOW PRAYER DO WHAT THEY MUST
SINFUL NATURE REPEATEDLY SURFACES
    DECLINING ENDLESS SOURCE OF DELIGHT
HIDING BAD BEHIND SECRET CLOUDS
    IF YOU THINK THEY'RE FOOLS, YOU'RE RIGHT.

THE FOOL WAS USUALLY TAUGHT BETTER
    BUT CHOSE GRASPING GRIEF IN DISGUISE
BY BENDING TRUTH AS IT APPEARED
    UNPRODUCTIVE WAYS TO COMPROMISE
ALL THIS UNWARRANTED DISHONESTY
    BEGET GUILEFUL REVEALINGS TO APPEAR
THEY CAN'T CONCEAL TRUTH FOREVER
    BY THE ILLUSTRATIONS IT BECOMES CLEAR
KNOWING THE BIBLE WARNS OF SIN
    THEY SIT IN JUDGMENT EVEN THIS NIGHT
ACKNOWLEDGING EXCUSABLE WRONG
    IF YOU THINK THEY'RE FOOLS, YOU'RE RIGHT.

I WAS THE FOOL WHO CHASED SHADOWS
    FORSAKING THE FONDNESS LEARNED, YET
I EMBRACED CHALLENGES TO SUCCEED.
    NO WONDER MY DREAMS, MANY I REGRET
I NEVER EMBRACED GLAMOUR OR GLITTER
    BUT ALL ELSE DESCRIBED I HAVE REMORSE
I AM BUT THE FOOL WHO MOLDED MYSELF
    TAMPERING LIFE'S SIN DRAWING SOURCE
I NO LONGER PRETEND TO FAKE PARDON
    I'LL SEEK REPENTANCE WHEREVER I MIGHT
I FLEECE MY FINAL HOURS IN DESPAIR
    IF YOU THINK I WAS A FOOL, YOU'RE RIGHT.

~

VIET NAM WAR
(1972)

THE WAR ENTERTAINED A CHANGED PHASE,
OPENED CURTAINS ON BLOODSHED PLAYS
OF BOMBINGS, KILLINGS AND ROTTEN POT
O' FROM THIS WAR THEY'VE LEARNED A LOT.

COMMUNIST PRESSURE OF HIDDEN TRUTH
INFLUENCED MINDS OF AMERICAN YOUTH
OUR PRISONERS OF WAR AND US TROOPS
FACED NAM'S UNKNOWN BATTLE GROUPS

THEN US BOMBINGS INCREASED AGAIN
AT HOME MORE PROTEST MEETS BEGAN
RAIDS, REBELLIONS, CONSPIRACIES, TRIALS
IN DEMONSTRATIONS, FIRES, ROWDY RILES

DRAFT CARDS BURNED, CASUALTIES HIGH
A WAVE OF DESCENT, POLLUTED THE SKY
PHYSICAL DISTRESS ON BATTLEFIELDS SIGHT
VETERANS FACE MUCH FEAR AND FRIGHT

BUT BACK HOME, THE WAR OPENED SIGNS
AND FOLKS NOW SPEAK OUT THEIR MINDS
FROM A DISRESPECT, MANY STOOD ALONE
TO DISHONOR WOUNDED COMING HOME.

RELIGIOUS GROUPS PROTEST BY WRITING
STUDENTS ARE SICK OF WAR AND FIGHTING
AMERICA'S MORALITY HAS DRIFTED AWAY
TO THE SEARCH FOR REVENGE SOME SAY

Veterans witnessed fellowmen dying
Mothers, widows back home crying
Armies from both sides suffered loss,
Death and casualties in jungle moss

It's hard to remember when or know
Oh' where did the days of peace go
Confused veterans return State's side
As crippled heroes and crushed pride

O' Viet Nam war, a battle unblessed
Troops desire to come home and rest
Our nation suffered its so-called gain
A war unended where clouds remain.

~

TONIGHT

TONIGHT

AMBER DARKNESS GATHERED
    THROUGH ITS SUNSET GATES,
WITH DIM SEPARATED STARS
    PRANCING UP HIGH ABOUT.

AND ABOVE THE THIN MIST
    UPON BLUR OF SILENT LAKES
CAME A UN-MENDED WIND
    GUSTING A SMOOTH SHOUT.

FLOWERLY WATERS TREMBLE
    ITS SOFT MUSIC OF PRAYER,
MOON OF DANCING FLAMES
    ENGULFING SHADOWS GRIP.

AN AMPLE CIRCLED HEAVEN
    DARK GLEAMY ATMOSPHERE
SURELY EVERYTHING TONIGHT
    WAS MOUNTED FOR THIS TRIP.

~

ZEST OF WHITE WINTER

The winter geese prouder,
Upon the white powder,
    As their wilderness call.
    Absorbed by the sno-fall,
Where stillness surrounded a terrain

Ah' the freshness of those,
Of whom it does expose,
    Thereby enjoy the center,
    Of this cold white winter,
Unpainted season difficult to explain.

Cuddled beneath a tree,
Where warmth might be,
    To rest or hide for a while,
    In a cozy sheltered style,
Some creature, dry needles did invite.

While stilled waters freeze,
And the cold skies sneeze,
    In a chill of seasonal joy,
    Whereas snow is the toy.
A sno' white winter of white on white.

~

IF ONLY SHE

IF ONLY SHE REMEMBERED WHAT LOVE WAS
     BUT SHE NOW HESITATES AND SOON FORGETS
OR COULD THE ANSWERS BE JUST BECAUSE
     SHE CHASES RAINBOWS OF DEEPEST REGRETS

IF ONLY SHE CALLED TO MIND THE OLD WAYS
     THERE STRIFES AND ENDEAVOR BUILT OUR TIE
IN TRIALS OF DISAPPOINTMENTS AND PRAISE,
     FROM BLENDINGS WHERE BACKGROUNDS LIE,

IF ONLY SHE RECALLED WHERE ECHOES RING
     WHICH EPISODES OF EXPERIENCES REMIND
HOW ONCE TOGETHER HELD HANDS IN SING
     WHEN WE WERE YOUNG AT HEART AND MIND

IF ONLY SHE KNEW WHAT BONDING MEANS
     A TEAM ENTHRALLED, EACH WITH THE OTHER
WITHOUT SURROUNDING SHADOWED BEAMS
     SWAYING THE CONFIDENCE IN ONE ANOTHER

IF ONLY SHE CAN FATHOM LOVE IS SHARING
     PASSIONATE FEELINGS BY A SIMPLE TOUCH
OR BECOME LIGHTHEARTED IN IDLE CARING
     LONG TO HEAR EACH THEIR WHISPERS MUCH.

IF ONLY SHE STOPPED AS PRIORITIES STRAY
     TO QUESTION COMMENTS OR CHOICES DONE
HER SYMBOL OF GENTLE INNOCENCE SWAY.
     WHEN DOUBTING HOW TWO BECOME AS ONE.

IF ONLY SHE WOULD RECONSIDER OUR LIVES
     THOSE CIRCUMSTANCES THAT MADE US "WE"
SETTING THE ISSUES ASIDE CAUSING STRIFES
     TO SHARE MORE WITH ME...OH, "IF ONLY SHE".

~

GLOOMY SKY

The Northern star,
  So great, so far,
    Yonder it be,
But tonight afar
  It's dark as tar,
    Hard to see.
May night's light
  Again be bright
    To show me.
A sight of delight
  Might tonight
    Yet spin free.
The high grayed,
  Clouds strayed
    Hung nearby
An overcast parade
  Invade and fade
    Grey supply
I wish this gloom
  I could broom
    And thereby
To light an' groom
  This dark room
    Of gloomy sky.

~

MOTHERS DAY

MOM,
TODAY, I STOP TO REMEMBER
    HOW SWEET AND PRECIOUS YOUR TOUCH,
WITH DAY TO DAY MEMORIES,
    HOW I LOVE YOU MOM, SO VERY MUCH
ALTHOUGH YOU DON'T LIVE FAR,
    ONLY I COULD KNOW WHAT I LEFT BEHIND,
NEITHER COULD I EVER REVEAL,
    ALL THE MEMORIES THAT COME TO MIND.

MOM,
MY VISIONS OF YOU OUTSIDE,
    AS IF THEY WERE ALIVE THIS VERY HOUR,
I FANCY YOU PULLING WEEDS,
    JUST TO FREE ANOTHER CROWDED FLOWER.
YEA, I CAN NEVER REMEMBER,
    ALL HAPPIEST TIMES TOGETHER WE KNEW
FOR EVEN TODAY, DEAR MOM
    SO PRECIOUS WERE ALL TIMES WITH YOU.

MOM,
YOU ARE THE FOND MEMORIES,
    THAT DREAMS, THOUGHTS ARE MADE ON,
AGAIN I WALK INTO SHADOWS,
    A PLACE WHERE REMINISCINGS BELONG.
I SEE IN A DAYDREAM PAUSE,
    DESIGN HOBBIES AND MAKING THINGS,
OF POTTERY, CONES, OR NESTS,
    ROCKS, NUTS, MOSS TO SEASHELL RINGS.

Mom,
You're a violet in a song,
    Whistling tunes where music flowed,
A flower of many smiles,
    As sweet petals into your life unfold.
Your rough, stained hands,
    From a weeding that you called play,
And vessels that protrude,
    From the many labors of yesterday.

Mom,
You've special hope within
    That's kept me strong thru the years,
Oft times when I have failed,
    Yes, you were there to wipe my tears.
My most measureless desire,
    To give you flowers, see you smile,
Oh, just to watch you beam,
    The surprise makes it all worthwhile.

Mom
Your jolly voice oft quotes,
    Silly, funny solutions to a problem
Yes, and I still smile inside,
    When I think of you I'll think of them.
You're my treasure in life,
    A sporting, innocent patterned way,
Yesterday's bright flowers,
    N' you're the crimson rose of today.

Mom,
You spoke without sound,
    Your inner feelings came into sight,
How you tried to hide hurt,
    O' mom you never could hide it right.
You're the songs of a bird,
    Peace of the flowering meadowland,
Your voice is in the waters
    Like the sea as it slaps against sand.

Mom,
You're the fields beyond,
    Into mountains where forest strayed,
You're the breeze in a tree,
    Where a music of winds have played.
Yes, my land of sunny skies,
    My light of one hope upon another,
So much love I'd have missed,
    If it weren't for you, my dear mother.

~

MY PATH

MY PATH

My thoughts stray
  They sway and stay away
Without delay, I say
  May I today yield to pray,

I found that my fight
  Would invite simple spite
Lest I might unite
  My sight on what is right

I fought my thought
  To besought what I ought
Put draught to naught
  Then forgot not, His plot

For confirmation of
  Relation in sanctification
A glorification to
  Justification of inspiration

On my knee, I can see
  The fee of destiny is free
A path to be, I agree
  For me is the key to Thee.

~

INSIDE SCARS

WHEN I SEARCH WITHIN THIS WORLD OF MINE.
A PLACE MEMORIES AN SORROWS COMBINE
    FOR THE PAST IS PAST AN I CAN'T RE-BRIDLE
    NOR REACH BACK TO CHANGE WHICH IS IDLE
I FEEL THEIR PRESENCE IN CELLS OF MY PRIDE
HEARD THE FOOLISH VOICE OF MYSELF INSIDE
    BETWEEN PAUSES THAT INTERRUPTS THOUGHT
    AN SAW AGAIN SELFISHNESS I ONCE FORGOT
FROM THEIR HUMBLE GRAVE I CANNOT RE-DO
NOR CAN THEY FORGIVE MY WAYS TO RENEW
    GONE ARE THE DAYS I CAN'T RELIVE OR SAVE
    WHAT IS DONE IS DONE, TAKEN TO THE GRAVE
OH' BUT IF ONLY THE PAST CAN BE REWRITTEN
MY PRIDE OF FOOLISHNESS CAN BE SMITTEN
    I CANNOT UNDO OR SMOOTH OUT THE ROUGH
    NOR HOLD THEM ONCE AGAIN CLOSE ENOUGH
SOME MEMORIES ARE BITTER TO MY TONGUE
JUDGMENTS RECORDED WHERE ANGELS SUNG
    O MANY WERE THE TIMES WISELY SCHEMED
    WHEN THEN THOUGHT I DID RIGHT IT SEEMED
THEREFORE WHO AM I NOW THAT WERE APART
OR WHO ARE THEY THAT CAN READ MY HEART
    OF THE UNSEEN HURT INSIDE WHO CAN KNOW
    WHEN EACH SCAR PAUSES IN EACH SHADOW.
I STILL FEEL TODAY THEIR TOUCH AN EMBRACE
AN SEE THE EXPRESSIONS UPON THEIR FACE
    THEY ARE AGAIN AS NEAR AS NEAR CAN BE
    I TREMBLE STILL FOR WHAT THEY WERE FOR ME
HERE I MUST REMAIN YET INSIDE, I DECLARE
THE DEEP FEELINGS OF JOY I CANNOT SHARE
    THE VOICE OF HIDDEN SCARS OF YESTERYEAR
    SCARCE SEEMS TO BE THE WAY MADE CLEAR.

~

THE STRANGE

Lo! Tonight I sit in wonder amazement
    Of matters misunderstood
Events grasping deeper discernment
    Beyond what I view could.

Fragments of a life's purpose in mind
    From corners of my heart
Cannot fight against that I would find
    Nor set the changes apart

At first I just shook my head in doubt
    To the strange and bizarre
But time has changed my heart about
    Where sweet to bitter are.

For treasures from the heart are free
    A mysterious this or that
What is not predictable, some degree
    Begets a critical chit-chat

Life's journey accepts things familiar
    But the strange is without
Cluttered foolishness to the peculiar
    For mind to soul thru-out

I saw his physical nature walk in pain
    A people murmured in jest
His desperate desires of hope remain
    Yearning to soon manifest

I FELT HIS DEEP SADNESS OVER ME INSIDE
    AND SENSED A HURTING CHILL
I PRAYED THAT HE WOULD SET IT ALL ASIDE
    AN' CONVERT HIS HEART'S WILL.

I YIELDED SOME, BUT WAS PARTLY AFRAID
    A WOUNDED UNDERSTANDING
THE HEALTH OF HIM I THOUGHT MAY FADE
    OF CHANGES TOO DEMANDING

NEITHER COULD I COUNT THE TIMES SPENT
    LONG NIGHTS, I LAID AWAKE
FOR MEMORIES HAVE ITS FRAGRANT SCENT.
    AND HIS I CAN NOT FORSAKE

BEHOLD! SO STRANGE, ODD AND UNUSUAL
    A VICTIM ASTRAY IN DESPAIR
SHROUDS MY HEART; SPECIAL INDIVIDUAL
    YET TRY TO FATHOM HIS AFFAIR.

IN SPITE OF REJECTIONS, HE INTERWEAVES
    THIS WARM RAY THAT'S SUNNY
NON-VIOLENT TO PEACEFUL THEN CLEAVES
    IN EMOTIONAL WIT AND FUNNY

A DELIGHTFUL DISPOSITION FOR ONE TRIED
    A BUOYANT, SPIRITED SMILE
CONTINENCE EXPRESSING CHARM INSIDE
    IN A PLEASANT HUMOR STYLE

Fragments of immense determination
A daydream of tomorrows
His persistence for new identification
From yesterday's sorrows

So from here his fresher life embarks
The old individual is dead
New confidence in his life now marks
Reveals inner one instead

Hear ye, hear ye, Oh ye curious eyes
Who criticizes differences
Await, ye Christians of poor disguise
Who justifies interferences

O mercy, why worry about little cares
Gossiping, the fool desires
Beware what a private belief declares
Or what a rebuke requires

Even still, my memory extends fonder
Awkward suddenly broken
It divides weeds from thistles yonder
A conduct once unspoken.

Now that transforming is finally made
His fulfillment of a dream
Go forth no more in that masquerade
Rebuild your self-esteem

IF YOU COME ACQUAINTED TO ONE ALONE
WHO SEEMS STRANGE TO YOU
RECALL AGAIN HOW YOUR NEW LIFE SHONE
GIVE THEM THE CHANCE DUE.

WHEN YOU'VE SEEN ALL AND ARE SKILLED
A TIME WILL COME WITH COST
YOUR DEBT, WHY DREAMS WERE FULFILLED
IS YOUR WITNESS TO THE LOST

WHAT MANNER OF MEN JUDGE STANDARDS
BE UNCOMMON OR UNIQUE
WOE TO FOOLS WHOSE SMILE DISREGARDS
WHAT ODD OR CURIOUS SEEK

MAN'S ENCOUNTERS AREN'T WITHOUT MERIT
LEST IF ONE JUDGES ANOTHER
SENTENCING THAT BEHAVIOR SHALL INHERIT
A BROTHER AGAINST BROTHER

WE KNOW THAT EVERYONE, EVEN STRANGE
LORD MAKES NO MOCKERY
BUT, EXPECTS US ALL TO BEAR THE CHANGE
FOR HIS GLORY, A MYSTERY

~

ALONG THE HIGHWAY

ALONG THE HIGHWAY OF FERN GREETINGS
       A BLANKET OF MAPLES CROWD THE BRUSH
ON THE EMBANKMENT NEW FIR SEEDLINGS
       BEYOND ITS SLOPE THE CEDARS ARE LUSH
NEW BUD GROWTH CHANGES COLOR HUE
       DEAD LIMBS SCATTER AMONG THE GREEN
LAUREL'S ORANGE SKIN AS PEELINGS DUE
       UPON TRUNK OF FIR HEAVY MOSS IS SEEN.

ALONG THE HIGHWAY UPON THE ROADSIDE
       TWIGGED BRANCHES LIE ON ITS SHOULDER
DRY GRASS COMPASS AN OLD RAIL DIVIDE
       ABOVE RIDGE OF RIVER ROCK OR BOULDER.
AND WHERE THE ROAD FOLLOWED A CREEK
       A TWO WAY JOURNEY TWISTING PATHWAY
REACHING BLACKBERRIES SAVAGELY SEEK
       AND BITTERBRUSH AMONG WEEDS SWAY.

ALONG THE HIGHWAY FOLLOWING A FENCE
       AROUND MEADOWS NEAR THE BIRCH TREE
AND HIGHWAYS LITTER MAKES ME TENSE
       FROM JUST THE LITTLE WHICH I COULD SEE.
ONE SIDE, A SHOULDER; REDDISH CLAY DIRT
       ROAD DROPS QUICKLY A CANYON BELOW
BETWEEN THE DOGWOODS SOFT WINDS FLIRT
       HERE RAW TIMBERS PUT ON THEIR SHOW.

ALONG THE HIGHWAY OF SOME PAST FIRE
       WITHERED CUT TIMBERS OF SINGED SLASH
DEPOSIT OLD LIMBS AMONG CHARRED BRIAR
       DEVOURING THE GREEN REDUCED TO ASH
WHERE A TREE FELL INTO THICKETS OF BRUSH
       A NEW BOUQUET OF FLOWERS WILL BLOOM
WILD ROSES CRAWL THE GROUND IN BLUSH
       ACROSS THE ROAD TREE'S SHADOW LOOM

ALONG THE HIGHWAY, A SUN WARMED HILL
      UPROOTED STUMP BY A PONDEROSA NEAR
DEAD AGED SPURS STAND STOUT AND STILL
      NEAR ROCKY CLIFFS WHERE DAISIES PEER.
WILD FLOWERS SMILE IN GRASSES BRIGHT
      WILD BERRIES TWISTED AND WILDLY TURNS
A BRISTLE OF PINE NEEDLES GLOW IN LIGHT
      NOW ITS SHADED SHADOW HID THE FERNS.

ALONG THE HIGHWAY THAT SMOOTHES OUT,
      GLANCE LEADS TO KNOLL OF PINES NEARBY
BIRTH OF A NEW LEAF; PEA-GREEN SPROUT
      ON UNSEASONED HERB RESTS A BUTTERFLY
ACROSS THE VALLEY SCRUB TREES ABOUND
      A CASCADE SPRAY OF WINTER WATER FALLS
SO MUCH BEAUTY THAT HERE SURROUND
      A DRIVE THRU PARK ATTRACTION ENTHRALLS

ALONG THE HIGHWAY OF SIGNS AND CURVE
      GUARDRAILS WRAP NEAR THE CLIFF'S LEDGE
BREATHTAKING VIEWS OF CANYONS RESERVE
      INCREDIBLE BEAUTY ON MOUNTAIN'S EDGE
SOME SCENERY FAMILIAR AND SOME NEW
      NATURE'S TERRAIN CHANGES DAY TO DAY
FROM SUNSET HOURS TO A MORNING DEW
      AS GLIMPSES ALTER ALONG THE HIGHWAY.

ALONG THE HIGHWAY, MUCH TO OBSERVE,
      WITH VIEWS ON BOTH SIDES OF THE ROAD
AND WHAT LIES BEYOND THE NEXT CURVE,
      A DEER, A SQUIRREL, A BIRD OR THE TOAD
UNTAMED PARADISE, ODD THINGS GROW
      FIND REDWOODS TO MYRTLEWOOD TREES
PUTTING TOGETHER THIS GREAT ROAD SHOW.
      AN ENTERTAINMENT IN LIFE'S CERTAINTIES.

~

A STEPPING STONE

O' YEARS HAVE PASSED, BUT I RECALL
    A SCENE FROM YESTERYEAR
WHEN I SAW A BROTHER'S JOY BEFALL
    IN BURDENS OF HEAVY TEAR

DEAR GOOD FRIEND OF MINE BEHOLD,
    THE MAN IN NEED WILL PRAY
HIS HEART DID WEEP OUT SEVENFOLD
    AS FATE TOOK HIS SON AWAY

THE CHILD HE GRASPED WAS LIFELESS
    MY BROTHER LOOKED AT ME
EMPTINESS WHICH HE DID EXPRESS
    A MOURNER'S HEART I SEE

EMBRACING CLOSER UPON HIS ARMS
    IN LOOKING DOWN HE WEPT
A BREATHLESS LIFE OF DEATH ALARMS
    THE LAD'S SOUL NOW SLEPT

HE TRIED KEEPING THE HURTS INSIDE
    SORROW WOUNDS THE HEART
IT'S HERE THE SOUL AND FLESH DIVIDE
    WHEN LIVES ARE TORN APART

I SHARED HIS GRIEF WITH MOURNING
    AND DESPAIR WITH A DAZE
THE CHILD DIED WITHOUT A WARNING
    ONE SUMMER DAY IN HAZE

TOGETHER WE WEPT OUR MANY TEARS
    FROM THE LOSS OF HIS SON
WHEN A MOURNER'S HEART APPEARS
    THE DOUBTFUL EYE BEGUN

O' STRANGE IT WAS THE FEARFUL SIGHT
   I LOOKED UPON HIS SORROW
I SAW HIS FACE SO WHITE WITH FRIGHT
   AND EYES BECAME HOLLOW

HIS DREAMS SUDDENLY UN-FULFILLED
   OF MEMORIES TO EMBRACE
THE CHILD'S SOUND BECAME STILLED
   GONE TO A HEAVENLY PLACE

OR WHAT COULD I POSSIBLY SUGGEST
   A SILENT QUIVER ON MY LIP
I SHARE HIS ANGUISH THAT MANIFEST
   I SAW HIS HOPE LOSE GRIP.

A SEARCH FOR THE LITTLE ONE ENDED
   AS HIS WIFE'S HEART RACED
LOOK OF DEATH HER FACE EXTENDED
   HER INTUITION'S UN-LACED

A MISSING SON, SHE SENSED FEARS
   THEN SAT DOWN IN DISMAY
HER HUSBAND WENT TO HER IN TEARS
   TELLS WHERE THEIR SON LAY

HER SOUL'S A RESTLESS VACANT SPOT
   WEARIED PAIN WOULD START
FOR PATCHES IN DARK SORROWS BLOT
   GREAT PAIN CAME TO HEART

DRAWN TO WHERE THE LIVING VANISH
   TO COMING BACK NO MORE
MOURNFUL PAIN, A HEART TO TARNISH
   SHE CRIED AS NEVER BEFORE.

TORMENTING MOANS INSIDE SWELLS
   VAST TENSION IN HER CHEST
THROAT TIGHTENS WHEN PAIN DWELLS
   THIS PAIN I KNOW THE BEST.

O' HAPPENINGS THAT WE REMEMBER
   NO MEASURE TO COMPARE
THAT SORROW FROM JOY DISMEMBER
   THE CHILD'S DEATH DECLARE

A FACT ANY SURVIVES THE WARNING
   APPEARS TO BE NO CHOICE
I CAN IMAGINE THEIR NEXT MORNING
   OF A SON'S UNHEARD VOICE

ALL STEPPING STONES HAVE CRACKS
   SO WE MUST LEARN TO BEAR
AND STEP ASIDE; WATCH OUR TRACKS
   IN TRIALS OF CHOICE BEWARE

THIS YOUNG CHILD FOREVER MISSED
   LIFE'S RIDDLE OF SURPRISE
HIS SPIRIT TODAY, GOD HAS KISSED
   SO WE MUST COMPROMISE

MY BROTHER'S SMILE THAT IS SHOWN
   SHALL NOT BE HID BY PAIN
NOR SHALL HIS WILL BE OVERTHROWN
   FOR FAITH IN GOD REMAIN.

STEPPING STONES THE MASTER MADE,
   TO DISTRACT VIEWS OF MAN
THAT MAN MAY FIND AND PERSUADE
   HIMSELF TO FIND GOD'S PLAN

STILL NOW AND THEN WHEN I'M ALONE
   I'LL THINK UPON THAT SCENE
HOW HE CROSSED A STEPPING STONE
   AN' FOUND GOD IN-BETWEEN.

~

NOW IT IS, WHAT GOOD AM I

MY UNDISTINGUISHED FAMILY'S CORE,
    FOR IT CAME, IT LEFT, AND DID NOT LAST
    BUT OH' HOW PRECIOUS WAS THAT PAST.
SUCH GREAT LOVE FROM A PEOPLE POOR,
FOR THOSE WERE HAPPY DAYS OF YORE,
    NEITHER COULD THE RICH EVER FORECAST
    THESE SIMPLE FOLK OF GREAT CONTRAST
YEA, THESE SIMPLE FOLK WHOM I ADORE.

RECALLING THE SHADOWS I VISION STILL
    INCLUDING THINGS MY DAD HAD TAUGHT
    THE GREAT EXAMPLE TO ME HE BROUGHT
THEN THE PEACE OF MY MOTHER'S SKILL
AND HOW HER SMILE DID BRING A THRILL
    SIMPLE THINGS ARE WHAT THEY SOUGHT,
    LIVING HOW THEY THOUGHT THEY OUGHT
SUCH FONDNESS IN LIFE THEY DID FULFILL.

    NOW IT IS, THEIR LIFE HAS VANISHED
    THEIR ABSENCE LEFT ME ASTONISHED
        FOR I WAS FOOLED IN LIFE'S CALCULATION
        THEIR LIFE DID NOT GO MY EXPECTATION
            NEITHER CAN I JUSTIFY THAT AS MY ALIBI
            BUT CAUSE TO ASK, "WHAT GOOD AM I?"

My wife I have loved from the start
       For she alone forever captured me
       Her presence brought me harmony
Thru years she became counterpart
And so it was when we would part
       Her lack of presence away from me
       Was lonely silence by her absentee
But being near she calmed my heart.

But over our many years by and by
       She found her path in life's scheme
       Finding ways to capture her dream
And what could be gained thereby
In ways only her heart would justify
       Once our life was a parallel it seem
       Together at one time we were a team
Whereas now she can singly apply.

    Now it is, as our youth faded away
    Come new visions, goals on display
       She stands up in an unfamiliar place
       Different expressions upon her face.
         Then I ask myself, and then so reply
         Without excuse, "What good am I?"

AND THEN, OH HOW MY HEART WAS GAY
  AS MY YOUNG KIDS WERE BY MY SIDE
  I WATCHED THEM, IN THEIR JOYFUL PRIDE
TO DIFFERENT CHARACTERS THEY PORTRAY
IN AN INQUISITIVE MIND IN EVERY WAY.
  THEN AS THEY GREW UP I STOOD ASIDE
  WATCHED THEM GROW, MATURING INSIDE
EACH FORMING THEIR LIFE'S PATHWAY.

AND IT WAS, WHEN THEY WERE YOUNG
  I HAD FOUND PURPOSE HERE AND THERE
  A JOYFUL PRESENCE IN THE ATMOSPHERE
FROM STORIES TOLD AND SONGS SUNG,
THOSE SCATTERED MEMORIES ARE HUNG
  TODAY I AM TOLD THAT I JUST INTERFERE
  MY SIMPLE SUGGESTIONS TOOK SINCERE
NOT KNOWING MY HEART OR MY TONGUE.

  NOW IT IS, BECAUSE OF TIMES OF OLD
  WITH MY OWN REASONS I GRASP HOLD
   I'LL TAKE A DEEP BREATH TO BE STRONG
   QUESTIONING JUST WHERE DO I BELONG
    THE FACT SURVIVES, BUT I WONDER WHY
    THEN ASK MYSELF, "WHAT GOOD AM I"?

I'VE BEEN FOOLISH AS I'VE BEEN WISE
  FROM SORTING OUT THE HEARTS OF MEN
  BY REACHING FOR FEELING DEEP THEREIN
MAKING ADJUSTMENTS TO COMPROMISE
BUT AH! I DISCOVERED TO MY SURPRISE
  THAT EXPRESSION IS CAREFULLY CHOSEN
  REVEALING ONLY WHAT IS SORTED WITHIN
SO WHAT WE SEE IS OFTEN OTHERWISE

AND ABOUT THOSE WHO WERE NEAR ME
  FROM WHAT MY INSTINCTS UNDERSTOOD
  WE ALL DID AS WE THOUGHT WE SHOULD
OUT OF THE HEARTS, I COULD CLEARLY SEE
NO MAN'S PURPOSE IS THE SAME AS ME
  WE EACH FOLLOWED A PATH WE WOULD
  EACH GRASPING TO GET WHAT WE COULD
NOT A GOOD CHOICE OF MAN, I AGREE

  NOW IT IS, FROM ALL THAT I HAVE WRIT
  THESE ARE THE THOUGHTS THAT I ADMIT
  THESE WERE REASONS FOR A LIFE AND YET
  SOME TO BE CHERISHED, SOME TO REGRET
   BUT THIS IS WHAT MY LIFE DID MULTIPLY
   MAKES ME WONDER, "WHAT GOOD AM I?"

Do scattered memories calm a soul?
   Is friendship a friendship it seemed?
   Or motive of a smile wisely schemed
Does bitterness in man have a goal?
Are not walls built to gain control?
   A selfishness dull judgment deemed?
   For justifying a man's ego esteemed
Such acts have become life's symbol.

Wear and tear by losses on my face
   Are from the paths my feet had trod
   Leading to reasons I find life so odd
Yes, I recall memories to embrace
And other times I'd wish to replace
   They came, then left, a dividing rod
   To wait in judgment before our God
In a life that none other could trace.

   So now it is, with all that being said
   Don't judge a walk you haven't tread
    If my life should end, a death declare,
    Knowing a few would but hardly care
     I realize in this life I'm but a passerby
     So what difference, "What good am I?"

~

1966

Mom and Dad
Vi and John (Red) Hastings

1974

Our Three Sons
Bend, Oregon (left to right)
Ray (Middle) ~ Jerry (Oldest) ~ Reggie (youngest)

1965
Swede and Linda Hastings